SEARCHING FOR BERTHA:

My Cane River Odyssey

By

Linda S. Manuel

Searching for Bertha: My Cane River Odyssey
Copyright©2014 by Linda S. Manuel

All rights reserved. No part of this book may be reproduced or transmitted in any form by any means, electronic, digital, or mechanical including photocopying, recording or by any information storage and retrieval system, without permission in writing from the copyright owner.

Cover Design / Typeset / Layout: Herbert R. Metoyer, Jr.
www.CaneRiverMedia.com

Foreword by Tammy Manuel

Includes bibliographical references.

Library of Congress Control Number: 2014911155

ISBN: 978-0-9905018-5-5

Published by Creole Publisher
4692 Winery Way, Gahanna, OH 43230
www.caneriverodyssey.com

Manufactured in the United States of America

DEDICATION

*This book is dedicated to my husband, Glenn, and my beautiful daughters, Tammy and Ashley.
Thanks for believing in me.*

Acknowledgements

To many, I owe a huge heartfelt "Thank you." Thanks to Kathleen Balthazar Heitzmann for giving me the first real lead that led to the discovery of my Cane River family. Thanks to CJ McGinty for being the first to acknowledge the worth of my story. Thanks to Dee Justice for editing my story in its infancy.

To my mother-in-law, Edith, thanks for editing and encouraging as my story grew. Beth Weinhardt, thanks for reviewing my manuscript in its final stages.

Thanks to my daughter, Tammy, for the numerous hours she spent reading and rereading my manuscript and encouraging me to move forward. To my daughter, Ashley, thanks for building a phenomenal website for my book.

Mimi Methvin, without your generosity I would never have discovered my French ancestry, thanks.

To Elizabeth Shown Mills, thanks for your tough love and the numerous hours you spent answering my questions, reviewing my manuscript, and sharing your infinite knowledge about my ancestors.

Thanks to Mary Linn Wernet and Janet Colson for their help with my research.

Renee Roque-White, thanks for giving me photographs of my second great aunt and my third great grandfather, they helped me to visualize the grandmother I never knew.

To Herb Metoyer, thanks for the countless hours you spent mentoring, encouraging, editing, designing, and helping me publish my book.

To my husband, Glenn, thanks for your love, patience, and understanding as I spent countless hours at the computer. For any I may have forgotten to mention, thanks from the bottom of my heart.

About The Author

Linda S. Manuel is a third grade teacher, wife, and mother of two daughters with two grandsons. She grew up in Shreveport, Louisiana and received her bachelor's degree from Louisiana State University in Shreveport. After moving to Ohio, she furthered her education and received a master's degree from Ashland University. A love for solving the unknown led her to research her family history which led to the writing of *Searching for Bertha: My Cane River Odyssey*. Among her interests are home design, traveling, gardening, and reading.

Foreword....

When my mother first told me she was researching our genealogy, I suppose I considered the idea with mild interest and continued on with my day. Little did I know, that her decision and the journey she would take would eventually fill enough pages to become a book. *Searching for Bertha* represents years of deep breaths and long exhalations. I am so inspired by her; so in awe of her tenacity, and so very proud.

As a child, I was never good at hide and seek. As an adult, I am even worse. I have neither the patience nor the emotional fortitude to look for things. In fact, I find looking for lost things the bane of my existence. To think that my mother spent years of her life repeating this maddening episode of hide and seek humbles me. I know that she found things and people on her journey that had not been a part of her original search. She held those discoveries lovingly in her arms and resolved that they should not be lost as well. She paid edifying tribute to each one in turn, rebirthing souls long lost in our family history.

I do not think I will every truly know why my mother took such a journey when the terrain was so uncertain or how she must feel now that it has come to an end. I am profoundly grateful to have this gift that is a written testament to our heritage and that my sons will know, unequivocally, that they are descendants of strong men and mighty women. I know that if our greatest of grandparents, aunts, uncles, and cousins could speak one last time, they would say, "Thank you," for so many things.

At this moment, I know one thing for sure: If I am ever lost, my Mama will find me.

....Tammy Manuel

TABLE OF CONTENTS

Searching for Bertha: My Cane River Odyssey

Introduction	1
Chapter 1 Out of Africa	3
Chapter 2 Our African American Beginnings	7
Chapter 3 Our French Beginnings	13
Chapter 4 The Natchitoches Post and Louis Juchereau de St. Denis	25
Chapter 5 Two Lovers Meet	31
Chapter 6 Two Lives Converge	39
Chapter 7 Two Lives Diverge	53
Chapter 8 The Children Make Their Marks	73
Chapter 9 Nicolas Augustin Metoyer and Marie Agnes Conant: *Partners for Life*	77
Chapter 10 Marie Susanne Metoyer and Dr. Joseph Conant: *Ships Passing in the Night*	95
Chapter 11 Marie Louise Metoyer and Florentin Conant: *A Family Affair*	107
Chapter 12 Louis Metoyer and Françoise Lecomte: *Young and Tenacious*	115
Chapter 13 Marie Rose Metoyer: *A Life Laced with Tragedy*	129
Chapter 14 Jean Baptiste Louis Balthazar and Marie Antoinette Coton-Maïs: *Stability at Last*	143
Chapter 15 Pierre Félicien Balthazar: *Civil War Soldier*	149
Chapter 16 Marie Resida Balthazar: *Gone too Soon*	161
Chapter 17 Bertha: *The Grandmother I Never Knew*	173
Appendices	189
Bibliography	205

ILLUSTRATIONS

Map of the African Coast	5
François and Marie Françoise's Family Genealogy Chart	11
Portrait of Port LaRochelle	20
Claude Pierre Metoyer's Ancestors' and Siblings' Genealogy Chart	21
Madame de St. Denis Slaves Partitioned to Heirs	35
Marie Thérèse and Children Genealogy Chart	36
Contract to Buy Nicolas Augustin, Marie Susanne, Pierre, and Louis Metoyer	48
Contract to Buy Dominique and Eulalie	49
Claude Pierre and Marie Thérèse's Family Genealogy Chart	50
Contract to Buy and Manumit Marie Louise	59
Emancipation Document for Nicolas Augustin Metoyer	62
Emancipation Document for Louis Metoyer	63
Emancipation Document for Pierre Metoyer	64
Emancipation Document for Susanne Metoyer	65
Surveyor's Map of Marie Thérèse's First Property	68
Marie Thérèse's Homestead Claim	69
Augustin Metoyer and Marie Agnes Poissot's Family Genealogy Chart	87
Portrait of Augustin Metoyer	88
Portrait of Marie Agnes Poissot Metoyer	89
Portrait of Auguste Augustin Metoyer	90
Photograph of Plate Commissioned in Honor of Augustin and Louis Metoyer	91
Marie Susanne Metoyer's Family Genealogy Chart	103
Portrait of Marie Thérèse Carmelite Metoyer	104
Portrait of Marie Agnes Conant Christophe	112
Florentin Conant and Marie Louise Metoyer's Family Genealogy Chart	113
Louis Metoyer's Family Genealogy Chart	124
Louis Metoyer's Main House at Melrose Plantation	125

ILLUSTRATIONS (continued)

African House at Melrose Plantation	126
Yucca House at Melrose Plantation	126
Marie Rose Metoyer's Baptism, Purchase, and Manumission Records	137
Marie Rose Metoyer's Family Genealogy Chart	138
Portrait of Thérèsine Carles	139
J. B. Louis Balthazar and Marie Antoinette Coton-Maïs' Family Genealogy Chart	146
Corps d'Afriques at Port Hudson	153
Pierre Félicien Balthazar and Marie Laura Christophe's Family Genealogy Chart	156
Portrait of Félicien Balthazar	157
Marie Resida Balthazar's Family Genealogy Chart	168
Portrait of Marie Odalie Balthazar Roque	169
Bertha Metoyer's Genealogy Chart	181
Photograph - Willie V. Pikes-Smith and Fred Taylor	182
Photograph - Addie Mae Green-Jackson and Linda Manuel	182
Photograph - Lillian Green and Melvin Randall	183
Photograph - Marie Agnes LaCour	183

Searching for Bertha: My Cane River Odyssey

"Until the lion writes his own story, the tale of the hunt will always glorify the hunter." ~ *African proverb.*

Introduction

Where one begins and one ends is sometimes lost in history, but one must not stop trying to find those elusive ones that seemed to have vanished into the unknown like puffs of smoke never to be seen again. They did exist and do exist in the footprints of our lives no matter how minute their lives may have appeared to some. We know they were here because we see them in the reflection of our mirrors, the dance or drag of our steps, and the wide sometimes-crooked grin we expose to the world. All are worthy of remembrance because they planted the seeds that became us as we will plant or have planted the seeds that will become you.

As a young child, I never wondered about my past. My grandmother died when my mother was ten, and I knew nothing about my grandfather. What my mother held in her memories about her mother was never discussed. Perhaps, the past was too painful, or maybe the passage of time had erased the brief time they had spent together. I will never know. Our modest family consisted of my mother, two brothers, an aunt, an uncle, and five cousins. This was the nucleus of my small world where no one ever spoke of the past. We lived one day at a time working toward the future.

In 1980, my mother passed away, leaving a hole in my heart that I could not heal and a connection to my past that I would never know. It wasn't until I was in college that I developed a burning curiosity about my roots. My curiosity was peaked with a biology class discussion on blood analysis and DNA. For reasons long forgotten, I wanted to know more about my past. My father was never a part of my life, so all I had was one detail in my mother's history to guide me. From my mother, I knew that her mother was Bertha Metoyer. From where she had come and where she had gone, I never asked. It just didn't seem very important. Now, with only my grandmother's name and no direction, I am determined to unravel my past.

Searching For Bertha

With high hopes and endless curiosity, I begin this journey to uncover my ancestors lost in history hoping to discover not only who I am but why. As with all journeys there will be surprises along the way. I welcome those surprises, both good and bad, because they make up the essence of my soul. With an open mind and an open heart I welcome my past to the present with hopes it will enhance the future of my descendants.

Chapter 1

Out of Africa

To truly understand who we are, we must know from where we came. Scientists have determined that our beginnings, like all human beginnings, started in Africa. Exact times, places, and faces (unrecorded) have faded with time and may never be recaptured. It is only with DNA that we are able to identify our place on the human family tree and trace our migration through Africa. In 2006, with a swab of the cheek, a journey began that would take me back to the place where my grandmother's earliest maternal ancestors originated over 80,000 years ago.

In the study of human genetics, scientists use the term "Mitochondrial Eve" in reference to the most recent common matrilineal ancestor from whom all humans are said to have descended. To understand our journey, one must go back to the deepest branches, or haplogroup, of "Eve's" tree. They are what scientists refer to as the L haplogroup.[1]

Our branch, the L3 haplogroup, is unique because it created the first modern humans to leave Africa, and it represents the deepest branches outside of Africa. Analysis of my DNA showed that I, and consequently my grandmother, Bertha, belong to one of the L3 groups (L3b).[2] Further analysis of my mitochondrial DNA showed a 99.7% match with the Masa people who live in Cameroon today.[3] It is from these people that our story of trials, triumphs, and tribulations began.

Scientists were able to trace our migration throughout Africa, but coming out of Africa numerous branches were broken and tossed aside like meaningless pieces of debris in a tumultuous storm. Unfortunately, some may never know their ancestors' ports of exit from Africa. But, with the help of genetics, Bertha's matrilineal ancestors' port of exit is traceable. Belonging to the Masa tribe, the port of exit from Cameroon for her ancestors would have been the Port of Bimbia. At one time, this port was one of the busiest departure points on the West Coast of Africa. Thousands of captured men and women were transported from the Port of Bimbia to the Americas to be sold. When slave trade ceased, the Bimbia port was overtaken by a tropical rainforest and the heartache and devastation it had caused was hidden from view. The people of the village felt that the port was cursed and would not visit or talk about it.[4]

Although the point of exit for Bertha's Masa ancestors was, in all probability, the Port of Bimbia, the exact time they were enslaved will forever be lost in history. Sometimes, a tide turns when it is least expected. It may have been during a time of feast and celebration that her ancestors were snatched from their familial security. Perhaps it was during the rainy season, under the cloak of darkness, that they were chained and dragged through a familiar muddy lagoon. Or maybe, it was a sweltering summer's day, while they were admiring a magnificent gazelle in flight, that they were forced to walk through the savannah from the only life they had ever known. With such circumstances so unknown, the exact date and time that Bertha's African ancestors were taken from their homeland and brought to the unfamiliar terrain they would come to know as Louisiana may never be uncovered for eyes to see. But somewhere, at some time, her first traceable African ancestors were torn from Africa and brought across the Atlantic to begin lives of degradation.

For most African-Americans, none of their African progenitors are ever identified. They are but distant memories that creep into one's deepest sleep, only to slip away at the first light of dawn. But, one branch of Bertha's African ancestors clung to memories of the familial ties that were deeply entrenched in their hearts and minds as they reluctantly adjusted to their new homeland. Their unwillingness to completely forsake their motherland is evident in the nicknaming of their children. By bestowing African nicknames on some of their children, Bertha's fifth great-grandparents, François and Marie Françoise, retained memories of their African heritage and left clues that would be beneficial to their descendants who chose to uncover their African roots.

The Slave Coast

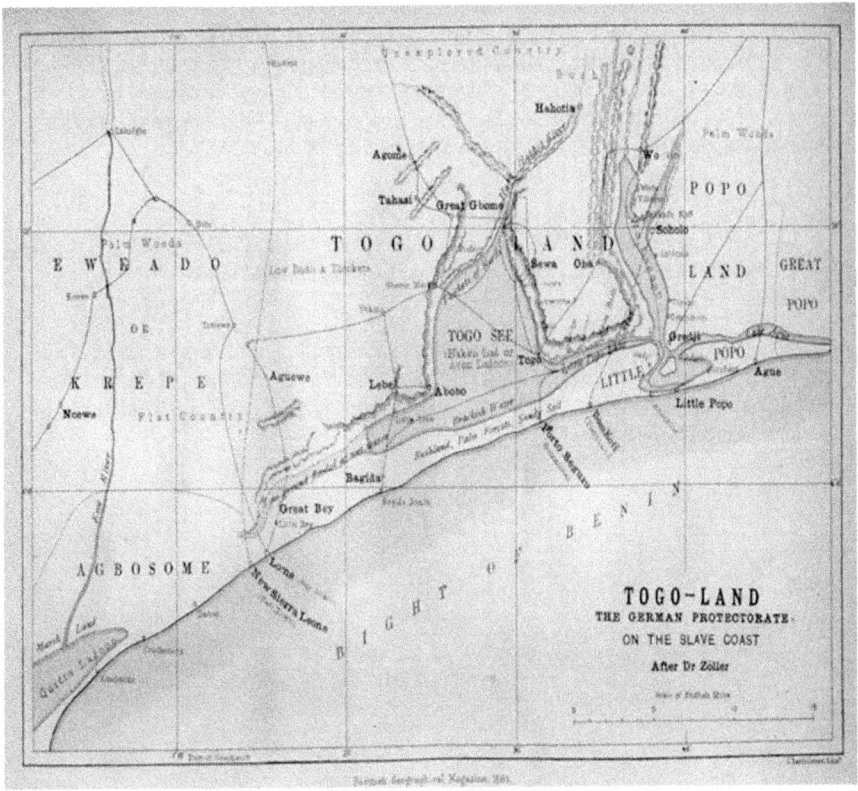

Map courtesy of the University of Texas Libraries,
the University of Texas at Austin

Endnotes

1. "Atlas of Human Journey," National Geographic, *The Genographic Project*, (2006), https://genographic.nationalgeographic.com/genographic/lan/en/atlas.html. Choose Genetic Markers > L3 for discussion of my mitochondrial haplogroup; FamilyTreeDNA (Houston, TX), "Mitochondrial DNA Sequence Report, Kit N81988," prepared for Linda Manuel, Gahanna, OH , 25 May 2010; privately held by Manuel, 2013.

2. Ibid.

3. African Ancestry (Washington, D.C.), "Mitochondrial DNA (mtDNA) sequence Report, Kit 1022762," prepared for Linda Manuel, Gahanna, OH, 3 May 2011; privately held by Manuel.

4. Frederick H. Lowe, "Cameroon Plans Restoration of Notorious Slave Trade Port," *The NorthStar News and Analysis*, 19 July 2012, *the northstarnews.com*, accessed April 13, 2013, http://www.thenorthstarnews.com/Story/Cameroon-Plans-Restoration-of-Notorious-Slave-Trade-Port.

Chapter 2

Our African-American Beginnings

Unlike Bertha's matrilineal ancestors, whose roots trace back to the Masa tribe in Cameroon, her fifth-great-grandparents, François and Marie Françoise's roots have yet to be identified. But it is these two ancestors who were very significant in establishing the roots of Bertha's African beginnings in America.

François and Marie Françoise began their new lives as the property of Louis Juchereau de St. Denis in a remote part of central Louisiana known as the post of St. Jean Baptiste des Natchitoches.[1] Like so many stripped from their homelands, only a small ripple is left in the streams of their lives to expose the seeds from which they sprang. Not even their names were their own. François was an adult when he was transported to his new home.[2] Whether he was new to America or from another post has never been ascertained. François was baptized on December 26, 1735 in the Catholic Church of St. François and given the name François after his godfather, surgeon François Goudeau.[3] Louis Juchereau de St. Denis selected one of his slaves, Marie Françoise, to be François' wife. On January 8, 1736 they became man and wife in a Christian ceremony. Recorded for future generations to discern in Register 1 of the Catholic Church of the French and Spanish Post of St. Jean Baptiste des Natchitoches were the words, "François and Marie Françoise, January 8, 1736, marriage of Francois, *nègre*, and Marie Francoise, *négresse*, both slaves of Mr. de St. Denys, commandant."[4] With their sacred vows completed, the couple's journey of love and heartache began.

Were François and Marie Françoise initially in love, or did their circumstances force love to develop? Only they know, and their secrets have long departed. But the couple's marital journey would produce eleven children, who, like them, would be subjugated to the hard and often cruel life of slavery.

François and Marie Françoise became parents within nine months of their marriage. Thanks to the Natchitoches Catholic church registers some records can be found documenting the evolution of this family. Inconsistencies in the recording of their vital information may have been due to the fact that there was no permanent priest allocated to the Natchitoches settlement or to the attitudes of each priest towards the slaves on his watch. Nevertheless, information gleaned has proven to be invaluable.

The first-born of Marie Françoise and François was Marie Gertrude. She was baptized on November 18, 1736. According to the Natchitoches Catholic Church records, she was the "legitimate daughter of François, *nègre*, and Marie Françoise, *négresse*." Her godparents were none other than the commandant of the Natchitoches post, Louis de Juchereau St. Denis, and his daughter, Marie Gertrude.[5] From these records, one can surmise that baby Gertrude was named by and for her godmother. From the African nickname, or dite, Dgimby, bestowed upon her by her parents, one may one day be able to surmise her precise roots.

No baptismal records have been found for the next two children born to the couple. It is believed that a brother, François, Jr., was born around 1738. He, like his sister Marie Gertrude was also given an African dit. He would be known as Choera. About two years later, around 1740, another boy-child was born and was named Jean Baptiste.[6]

Following Jean was the fourth great-grandmother of Bertha, Marie Thérèse dite Coincoin—another indication of an African heritage. She was baptized on August 24, 1742. Unlike the baptismal record of her older sister, Gertrude, Marie Thérèse's record did not specify her parents' names. It simply indicated that she was a "*négritte* belonging to Mr. de St. Denys." Her godparents were St. Denis' son-in-law, Jacques de la Chaise and Marie de St. Denis, daughter of St. Denis.[7]

Another boy child, Barnabé, was born on September 9, 1744 and baptized two days later on the 11th. He was registered as the son of Marie Françoise and François and the slave of Madame Sánchez de Navarre. Records indicate that his life was short-lived. At the age of 4, on September 20, 1748, Barnabé was buried.[8]

A girl child, Jeanne, was born about 1746. There is one baptismal record in the church registers that simply stated, "…baptism of Jeanne, *négritte*, born of a *négresse* belonging to Mde. St. Denis."[9] Definitively, I cannot say that this is the daughter of Marie Françoise and François because St. Denis owned three slave children with similar names. It is highly plausible because Jeanne's age does correspond to the age of Marie Jeanne who was integrated in the distribution of the family of Marie Françoise and François on April 28, 1758.[10] The family expanded again in 1748 or 1749 with the arrival of Marie Louise.[11]

Child number eight, Marguerite, dite Yancdose, was born around 1750. Bonaventure made his cries heard in 1751. He was baptized April

8, 1751, and it was indicated that he was born to a *"négresse* belonging to Madame de St. Denis." A sister was to follow, Anne Hyacinthe, baptized September 13, 1753. The priest at the post in 1753 recorded the mother of Hyacinthe as Marie Françoise. There was no reference to her father.[12]

Finally in 1758, the family was completed with the appearance of François (later records revealed this was a female despite the masculine spelling)[13] baptized April 21, 1758. Her parents were recorded as François and Marie Françoise. Unfortunately, eight days later this youngest daughter died. She was buried on May 4, 1758.[14]

The daily lives of the family of François and Marie Françoise was probably typical of most slave families. From the faintest hint of daylight until darkness replaced its glow, the obligations of the slaves were to satisfy the desires of their masters. Fortunately for this family, they resided in the French possessed territory of Louisiana. Unlike slaves in most American territories, this family was permitted to stay together because of the *Code Noir* of 1724, enforced by Governor Jean-Baptiste Le Moyne Bienville of Louisiana.[15] *Code Noir* (i. e. Black Code) was a set of laws originally decreed by France's King Charles XIV in 1685 and revised in 1724. The document, in essence, dictated how slaves were to be treated. Among numerous other stipulations in Louisiana's *Code Noir*, Article XLIII did not allow husbands, wives, and children under the age of 14, belonging to the same master, to be separated. The law stated, "Husbands and wives shall not be seized and sold separately belonging to the same master: and their children, when under fourteen years of age, shall not be separated from their parents, and such seizures and sales shall be null and void… in case such sales should take place in violation of the law, the seller shall be deprived of the slave he has illegally retained."[16]

This law must have allowed for some sense of comfort and security for the family as they toiled from day-to-day snatching happiness and joy whenever and wherever they could discover it in the corners of their fragile existence. For twenty-one years, from 1735, when François was baptized, until 1756, when the estate of their deceased owner, St. Denis, was settled, Marie Françoise and François knew the stability of being owned by one master. After the death of their original owner and for the next two years, the couple and their children were the property of St. Denis' widow.[17] In April of 1758, the widow died.[18] As fate would have it, François and Marie Françoise followed their owner three days later. Not to be separated by death, the couple was buried on April 19, 1758. Church records simply stated "April 19, 1758, burial of François and Françoise, a Negro slave couple of Mde. St. Denis."[19] Although smallpox and yellow fever were prevalent in some colonies during this period, the cause of their deaths was not recorded. It is plausible that Marie Françoise died of complications caused by childbirth. Her final child François was baptized on April 21, 1758, which meant she was undoubtedly born a short period before the death of her mother; though not a certainty, her birth could have been the catalyst for the mother's death. What is on record is that there was a cluster of deaths from April to May at the Natchitoches post. Several deaths were in the St. Denis household within a matter of days. This would be indicative of some type of epidemic.[20] With the death of St. Denis and his widow, there was no choice but to distribute the children among the heirs of the deceased.

The subsequent lives of the majority of the children of François and Marie Françoise, who lived and loved, hoped and dreamed, have faded with the passage of time. Their parents, in their infinite wisdom, chose African names for some of their children as a legacy to their past. We may not have encountered them, but we know they were here, and are here. We see them daily in the reflections of our mirrors, the dance or drag of our steps, and the wide sometimes-crooked grin we expose to the world.

One exception is the third child, Marie Thérèse "Coincoin" (Bertha's fourth great-grandmother), who would assure her humble parents a place on a worldwide stage. In the 18th century, the period that defined their existence, this worldwide stage was a place that neither they nor she could have envisioned.

Linda S. Manuel

Francois and Marie Francoise's Familly

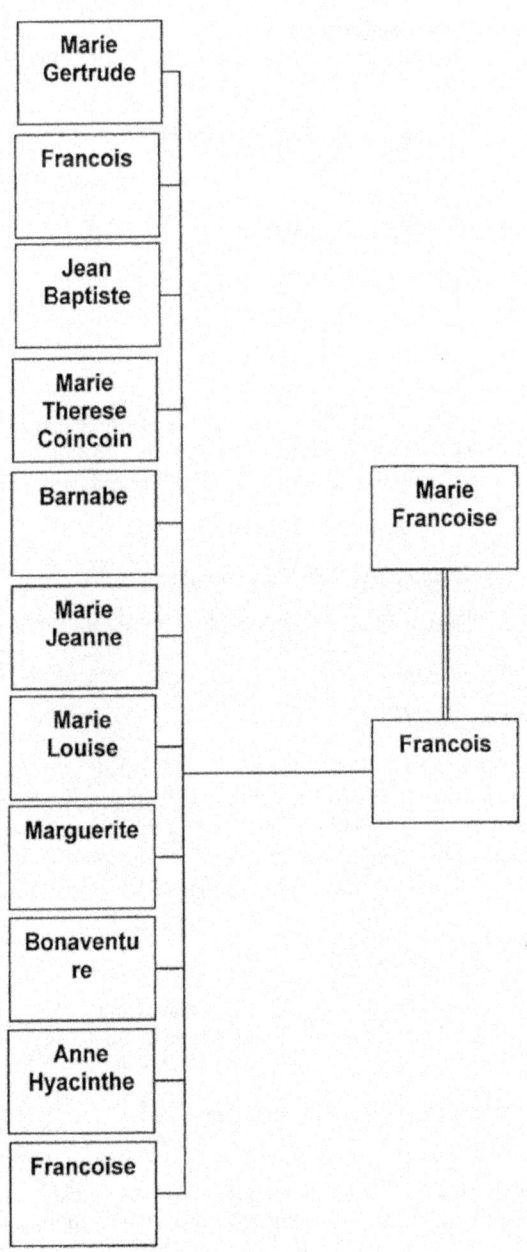

11

Endnotes:

1. Gary B. Mills, *The Forgotten People: Cane River's Creoles of Color* (Baton Rouge: Louisiana State University Press, 1977), 2.

2. Ibid.

3. Elizabeth Shown Mills, *Natchitoches, 1729-1803: Abstracts of the Catholic Church Registers of the French and Spanish Post of St. Jean Baptiste des Natchitoches in Louisiana* (New Orleans: Polyanthos, 1977), entry 33.

4. Mills, E. S., *Natchitoches, 1729-1803*, entry 11.

5. Ibid., entry 48.

6. Mills, G., *Forgotten People*, 3, footnote 7.

7. Mills, E. S., *Natchitoches 1729-1803*, entry 225.

8. Ibid., entries 253, 392.

9. Ibid., entry 269.

10. Elizabeth Shown Mills, "Documenting a Slave's Birth, Parentage, and Origins (Marie Thérèse Coincoin, 1742- 1816): A Test of 'Oral History'," *National Genealogical Society Quarterly* 96 *(*December 2008*)*: 245–66, specifically p. 258, footnote 55.

11. Mills, G., *Forgotten People*, 3, footnote 7.

12. .Mills, E. S., *Natchitoches 1729-1803*, entry 565.

13. Mills, E. S., "Documenting a Slave's Birth," 259, specifically footnote 60.

14. Mills, E. S., *Natchitoches 1729-1803*, entries, 677, 824.

15. Mills G., *Forgotten People, 5*.

16. "Louisiana's Code Noir (1724)," Quintard Taylor, et al., *BlackPast. org: Remembered & Reclaimed:* accessed February 2, 2010, http://www.blackpast.com/?q=primary/louisianas-code-noir-1724, extracted from B. F. French, *Historical Collections of Louisiana: Embracing Translations of Many Rare and Valuable Documents Relating to the Natural, Civil, and Political History of that State* (New York: D. Appleton, 1851).

17. Mills, G., *Forgotten People*, 2, 6.

18. Elizabeth Shown Mills and Gary B. Mills, "Slaves and Masters: The Louisiana Metoyers," *National Genealogical Society Quarterly* 70 (September 1982): 163–89, specifically p.166.

19. Mills, E. S., *Natchitoches, 1729-1803*, entry 820.

20. Elizabeth Shown Mills, "Marie Thérèse Coincoin (1742-1816): Cane River Slave, Slave Owner, and Paradox," *Louisiana Women: Their Lives and Times*, ed. Janet Allured and Judith F. Gentry. (Athens: University of Georgia Press, 2009), 14.

Chapter 3

Our French Beginnings

Records that would have helped me determine the parents of Bertha's African ancestors, François and Marie Françoise, were never written. But the lineage of her French ancestors has been documented. Originally documented in the local parish churches, the records were later copied and deposited in the French *Archives Départementales*. The *Archives Départementales of Charente-Maritime and de la Marne* unlocked the doors to Bertha's French past and beckoned me to enter. Because of these records, the roots of Bertha's French ancestors, Jean Metoyer, Nicolas François Metoyer, and Marie Anne Drapron, are fairly intact.

Shifting through documents that had withstood the tests of time, glimpses of Bertha's sixth-great grandfather's life began to unfold. With the unfurling of his life, I was in a sense uncovering Bertha's life too. For it was her sixth great-grandfather, Jean Metoyer, who had contributed the French blood that was an essential part of Bertha's heritage. To understand her legacy, I needed to understand her French ancestors. If I was ever truly going to know her, I had to pull back the layers of those who came before her and try to get to their core. It was with this objective in mind that I began to uncover Jean Metoyer.

Jean Metoyer was born in 1655 during the reign of the Sun King, King Louis XIV. Records suggest that Jean belonged to a "good social background." He was a lumber merchant and *"coutre"* in France. Though the term *"coutre"* has several meanings, a *"coutre"* may have been a beadle (minor parish official) or cleric in the parish.[1] As a lumber merchant, Jean would have bought wood and resold it for heating, construction, and manufacturing. His trade would have been a compulsory one because the need for wood was paramount during the seventeenth and eighteenth century. Wood was the foremost source of fuel needed for cooking and heating the home, and products from furniture to weaving looms are all made from wood.[2] The primary modes of transportation, carts, carriages, boats, and ships, essential for travel during the seventeenth and eighteenth century, were also made from wood. Lumber, always a necessity, was crucial during Jean Metoyer's lifetime. When Jean died in 1729, at the age of 74, his death certificate stated that he was a *marchand de bois* (wood merchant).[3] Of that I am proud. The contribution that Jean made to society cannot be undervalued. Lumber, as one writer penned, "…accompanied humans through life from the wooden cradle, to the stretcher, to the coffin."[4]

Jean's trade may or may not have been a constant, but his marital status was ever altering. Although he experienced the joys of marriage many times over, tragedy was never far behind. He was married at least four times. No record could be found for the name of his first wife or date of their marriage, but when he married his second wife he listed his marital status as widower. His second wife was Catherine Oudin from Reims. On May 15, 1691, Jean married for a third time to Suzanne Delaitre.[5] During his marriage, to Suzanne, he fathered two sons.[6] Two months after the birth of their second son, Suzanne died. Her death, on March 4, 1695, made Jean a widower once again.[7] With very young children to care for, and a trade that undoubtedly kept him away from home, less than five months later, on August 29, 1695, Jean married Françoise Galloteau, the daughter of Nicolas Galloteau and Marguerite Jobart.[8] It was Françoise who gave birth to Bertha's fifth great-grandfather, Nicolas François Metoyer, in the parish of St. Denis de Reims on May 16, 1715.[9]

In Reims, a place profuse with history, Nicolas may have literally walked in the footsteps of kings. The province where his life began is home to the Notre-Dame de Reims (the cathedral where the kings of France were crowned). The Palace of Tau, also in Reims, is where the kings resided during their coronations. As a boy, walking through streets rich with such history, Nicolas may have touched landmarks that had been graced by royalty.

Perhaps, while Nicolas experienced the royal history of Reims, Bertha's fifth great-grandmother, Marie Anne Drapron from Chagnollet, parish of Dompierre strolled along the Atlantic Coast bordering Aunis, France with her father, François, and her mother, Anne Naudin.[10] Anne may have fantasized of one day meeting a young man from Reims and being swept away from the small commune of Dompierre. Only she knew if this dream was tucked away in her heart, but we do know that she was destined to meet Nicolas. The couple lived, and perhaps first met, in La Rochelle, France.

La Rochelle, on the Atlantic Coast, is not only beautiful in face, but it is also abundant with history. In the tenth century it was little more than a swamp that had become a fishing village. With the passage of time and persistence, the village flourished. For a while it was the largest French harbor along the Atlantic coast. The port of La Rochelle sent sailors near and far to participate in triangular trade (trading slaves, fur, and sugar), colonize new lands, and visit ports in the new world, including Louisiana and Canada. Also, from the port of La Rochelle sailed the ship, *La Belle*, on its voyage to colonize Texas and the coastal cities around Mexico's gulf only to be tragically sunk in 1686.[11] It was against this historical and dramatic backdrop that Nicolas came to know Anne.

I have often fantasized about how Nicolas first met Anne. During the mid to late eighteenth century elaborate wigs were in vogue for women in the French court of Versailles. Following fashion's trend, Anne's intentions may have been to buy a wig from a business establishment. Nicolas had friends who were master wigmakers (Nicolas would later achieve the rank of master wigmaker).[12] A meeting that started as a casual business transaction may have led to a love affair. Although I long to romanticize their first meeting, reality speaks and I must concede what is probably truth. As was with many eighteenth century families in France, the meeting of Anne and Nicolas, in all probability, was an arrangement. After all, it was the father, not the daughter, who often controlled her destiny. In Anne's case, it may have been her brothers or uncles because her parents were deceased. The true account of their first meeting or their arrangement (not important enough to be recorded in French history) is a memory that only couples fondly recall. But history does record that in La Rochelle the two became man and wife.

Before the couple could become one, a marriage contract had to be drawn. Marriage contracts were important in eighteenth century France. They usually included the material contributions that were being brought to the marriage by the two parties. They also included what would happen to property held by the couple in the event of death. The bride-to-be would often bring a dowry to the marriage which her family had provided. All interested parties would appear before a notary, and the contract would be witnessed and signed. The amount of the dowry was often dependent upon the wealth of the family. In an article by Madame Adam written in 1891 for the *North American Review* entitled "The Dowries of Women in France," Adams writes, perhaps, tongue-in-cheek, "A DOWRY? The one important word which fills the imaginations of young French girls from the earliest childhood!" With a dowry, the father felt his daughter would not have to marry a poor man. With a dowry, a girl could find a suitable match.[13]

Anne was not without her dowry when she signed her marriage contract with Nicolas. The contract for Nicolas and Anne, filed February 14, 1743, four days before the marriage, stated that Anne's dowry consisted of one thousand livres in cash, some furniture, and other household goods. The contract also stated that if Nicolas were to die before Anne, she had the choice of either keeping the community property or renouncing it. If she renounced the property, she would be able to reclaim her dowry and would also gain some of the community property.[14] With the signing of the contract, by numerous attendants on the side of the bride and groom-to-be, the business of the contract was complete. Six days later, On February 20, 1743, after one bann (published church announcement) and two dispensations,[15] the fifth great-grandparents of Bertha, 28-year-old Nicolas François Metoyer and 29-year-old Marie Anne Drapron, became one.[16]

Young lives usually begin with much promise for the future. The hopes and dreams of Nicolas and Anne were probably no different from many others who had taken their vows of love and devotion. Their lives began quite fruitful. Less than one year and one month after the couple pledged their lives to one another, on March 12, 1744, in La Rochelle, they brought into the world their first child, a boy child, Bertha's fourth-great grandfather, Claude Thomas Pierre Metoyer. Two days later, in the presence of his parents and his godparents, Pierre was baptized.[17] His brother, Jacques Gerard, made his appearance a year later. He was followed by sisters Marie Jeanne Renée and Catherine Elisabeth. It was soon after the birth of Catherine Elisabeth, that tragedy came to visit the family. Sixteen days after the birth of Catherine Elisabeth, on April 27, 1748, their mother, Anne, only 34 years old, died. Like his father before him, Nicolas was left to care for a newborn and three other children under the age of five. After only five years of married life, Anne's life was over leaving Nicolas and her children to remind us of her existence. Despite the grief he may have felt, the need for someone to help with the care of his young children prompted Nicolas to remarry. Seven months later, on November 12, 1748, Nicolas married again.[18]

Nicolas second wife of choice, almost ten years his senior, was forty-two year old Marie Suzanne Vinault, the daughter of a post office controller.[19] This may well have been a marriage of convenience, but it provided the children with some sense of stability. But their stability was not without additional heartache. As if Nicolas and his young children had not suffered enough tragedy in their lives, it was less than a year later when tragedy surfaced again. On April 4, 1749, Nicolas' second born son, Jacques Gerard, died at the age of four. The life of Bertha's fourth great-grandfather, Pierre, began with enormous tragedy. Losing a mother and brother at such an early age must have had an impact on his future life decisions. And, as you will learn, as his life moved forward, there would be more tough decisions for Pierre to shoulder. But for now, because life only pauses for tragedy and does not stop, one must move on. And so the life of Nicolas, his new wife Marie Suzanne, and the children continued to advance. As they moved forward, Marie Suzanne and Nicolas welcomed two more children to their family.[20]

During their lives together Nicolas, Suzanne, and the children would live in several homes. For a period of time they lived in the home that the children had inherited from their mother.[21] In 1753, after several years of renting, Nicolas and Suzanne purchased their first home, "*Le Beaux Pines*" (The Beautiful Pines). Their new home was at the edge of La Rochelle. It included a room on the ground floor with a kitchen and storeroom, along with a room for housing the "*bordier*" (house and land caretaker) and a stable.[22] They also purchased a city home. Inventories of the city home, "*Rue des Dames*," and the country home, "*Le Beaux Pines*," of Nicolas and Suzanne tend to indicate that Nicolas was a wine merchant. There was a letter included in the estate, written by Nicolas to a ship captain, commanding him to pick up two baskets of Champagne wine. There were three sales contracts for vineyards "to the profit of the said Metoyer." Small barrels of wine" valued at two hundred and eight livres were inventoried in the home. Two wine barrels and a table for "grape pickers" were also found in the cellar. During the inventory, Suzanne reminded the notaries that they had not included a "barrel of red wine and a barrel of white wine in the large cellar." The notaries went back and their records indicated that they tasted the wine. Upon doing so, one wrote, "...we saw and tasted some Balzac wine, which was very good, and another barrel filled with white whine (*sic*), which totally went bad."[23]

The possibility that Nicolas was a wine merchant came as no surprise because Nicolas was born and reared in Reims – a city that was known for its vineyards and wines as early as the 17th century. Wine growing was an important part of agriculture in La Rochelle. In the fourteenth century, vineyards were so prolific that they were taking over horse pastures. Oftentimes vineyards would be bought by merchants in the city and rented to sharecroppers. This buying of vineyards was considered a safe and secure investment because the vineyard owners could make a profit in the European wine trade.[24] Surely Nicolas benefited from his venture.

Nicolas' ownership of vineyards, the homes, and the articles included in the inventory of the homes are indicative of someone who had some degree of wealth and were in all likelihood a part of the French bourgeoisie. A bourgeoisie, according to the early charters of the town counselors of La Rochelle, had to live in the city for at least a year and a day, have a residence there, swear an oath to fidelity to the ordinances of the city, contribute to the cities costs, and commit personal services and gifts to defend the communal security.[25] As a wigmaker and a merchant, Nicolas would have been able to fulfill all of those requirements.

A partial inventory of the Metoyers three-story home in La Rochelle, the *"Rue des Dames"* included a marble table with oak legs, nine chairs, and "a big cabinet with two doors, bottom drawers and side drawers, made of walnut." There was also a walnut table with turned legs. In one of the bedrooms was a cabinet made from "cashew-tree" with two openings and a drawer that locked. Of the linens (in one room of the house) "seven dozens of towels (or napkins), six table-cloths… sixteen dish-towels, and thirteen bed sheets" were inventoried. From a two hundred and seventy-two page diary, the notaries made a record of the initial words found on the first and last pages of the diary. The first page began, "my wife gave birth to a boy…" On the final page, dated May 5th 1758, were written the words, "The merchant Mr. Cascabel owes..." The sentiments from the commencement of the diary to the conclusion had definitely altered.[26]

The country home, *"Le Beaux Pines,"* housed several cabinets and tables made of fir-wood and several armoires and tables made from walnut. Most of the wine paraphernalia was at the country home. When one armoire was revealed there was a bottle of Dame Jeanne (wine) two thirds full. A grey mare was in the shed with an array of riding gear and in the stable there were two cows.[27] Bertha's fifth great-grandparents appeared to have some degree of prosperity.

For several years this bourgeoisie environment would have been home to the young and impressionable Pierre. It was in this class, with the guidance of Nicolas, Suzanne, and the charming city of La Rochelle, that Pierre would be molded into manhood.

Early in manhood, Pierre would have conceivably experienced more anguish, if not humiliation. On April 4, 1766, his father was arrested and imprisoned because of debts he had allegedly not paid to another merchant. Nicolas protested his guilt, but decided to pay the money (3,153 livres and 8 sols) and was released from jail.[28] A month later, on May 14, 1766, Nicolas died. Evidence tends to suggest that Pierre may have already been in Louisiana during his father's death, but bad news traveled thousands of miles across the Atlantic.[29]

Upon his death, Nicolas succession included the two homes, the "*Rue des Dames*" and "*Les Beaux Pines,*" both filled with furnishings, household goods, books, and private letters.[30] His wife, Suzanne, renounced the succession. With this renunciation, Suzanne's property would be separated from Nicolas', and she would not have to incur his debts. Two of the children, Pierre and Catherine, also renounced the succession. The system of "simple equality" could have applied to the children. According to this system, if Pierre and Catherine wished to share in the succession they would have to return to the estate any lands received by them from Nicolas so that it could be divided by the estate. Property had been given to the children by their mother, and there may have been land given to the children by their father. Their land or property may have been worth more than the estate. The system of "simple equality" did not preclude the child's renunciation of property if the property was valued as more than the estate.[31]

Despite the ties that could have bonded Pierre to his homeland, he, like many of his countrymen, selected not to stay. Thousands left France to come to the new world, or New France as they called the French territories of America. Varied were their reasons. Many left to seek new lands. Frenchmen, such as the Huguenots, left to avoid persecution. France sent soldiers to help colonize their new territories in America. But what was Pierre's motivation? Was it a business trip that sent Pierre to the new world, but the demise of his father the catalyst that caused him to stay? Or, could it have been the adventurous spirit inherited as part of La Rochelle's mariner history that beckoned Pierre to leave his home and cross the Atlantic into the arms of a woman and a land he would forever cherish? What I do know is that to the new world he did come, he did stay, and (based on his subsequent actions) he did love.

The port of La Rochelle, situated directly on a stormy seaboard, represented a treacherous departure for Pierre. When surveyed by royal surveyors, the port was usually considered the most treacherous in the area. The primary reasons that last wills and testaments were prepared were because of fear of death due to La Rochelle's close proximity to the sea or voyages on the sea. This fear caused the citizens of La Rochelle to hire others to conduct their business that involved traveling on the rocky Atlantic.[32] Pierre's father had commanded a captain to deliver goods for him.[33] The date of Pierre's departure from La Rochelle is indeterminate, but if he departed between September and June the westerly winds would have been fierce.[34] The fact that Pierre sailed on the rough seas of the Atlantic proved the tenacity of the man. This tenacious character would be called upon as he navigated the politics of his new homeland.

Pierre's first sight of Louisiana would have been in the Port of New Orleans. A letter addressed to his father from the port confirms that he was there.[35] For a period of time, it's conceivable he stayed in the port city. Being an adventurous spirit, he may have set out from New Orleans and along the way came to Natchitoches a thriving post and the oldest permanent French settlement in Louisiana. Exactly when and how he arrived in Natchitoches are but trivial details in my story. The fact is that he arrived, around 1767,[36] bringing with him Bertha's French ancestry. And as you will soon see, the post of St. Jean Baptiste des Natchitoches would never be the same.

Port of La Rochelle in 1762

1762 painting by Vernet, Musee de la Marine

Ancestors and Siblings of Claude Thomas Pierre Metoyer

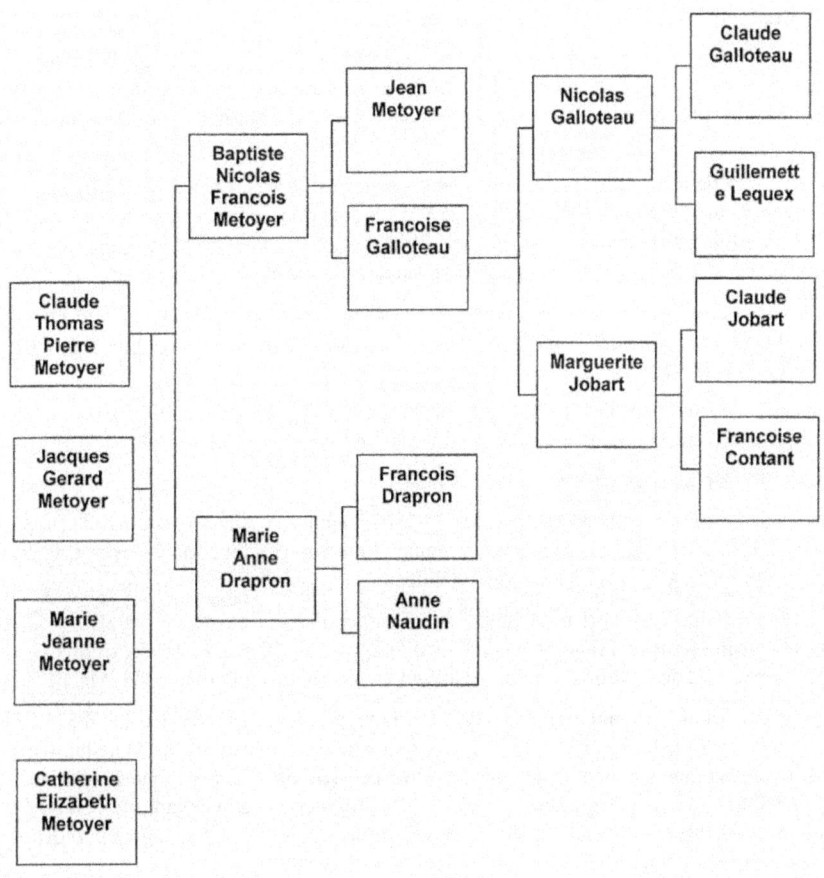

Endnotes

1. Saint-Symphorien Parish (Reims, France), Parish Registers, Cote 2 E 534 / 13, Nicole Metoyer baptismal entry, 14 September 1703; Archives Départementales de la Marne, Châlon-en-Champagne; entry refers to Jean Mettoyer as a *marchand coutre de cette paroisse*; photocopy provided by Ms. Mildred Methvin.

Saint Denis Parish (Reims, France), Parish Registers, Cote 2E 534/16, Jean Metoyer death entry, 26 December 1729; Archives Départementales de la Marne, Châlon-en-Champagne; entry refers to Jean Metoyer as a *marchand de bois;* photocopy provided by Ms. Methvin.

Eric Bourgoin, professional genealogist, Les Bordes, France, to Mildred E. Methvin, letter, 4 October 2002, translating French document explaining Jean Metoyer's French job titles; Personal Correspondence, 2002; Metoyer Family in France; photocopy provided by Ms. Methvin, Lafayette, Louisiana, a descendant of Jean Metoyer.

2. Bernd-Stefan Grewe, "Woodlands*,"* *European History Online (EGO)* (December 5, 2011), http:// www.ieg-ego.eu/en/threads/backgrounds/nature-and-environment/bernd-stefan-grewe-woodlands.

3. Saint Denis Parish (Reims, France), Parish Registers, Cote 2E 534/16, Jean Metoyer death entry; photocopy provided by Ms. Methvin.

4. Bernd-Stefan Grewe, "Woodlands."

5. "Marne, France Marriages, 1529-1907," database, Ancestry.com, 2008 (http://search.ancestry.com/search: accessed December 2009), entries for Jean Metoyer, Catherine Oudin, Suzanne Delaitre, and Françoise Galoteau.

Saint-Symphorien Parish (Reims, France), Parish Registers, Cote 2E 534/140, Jean Metoyer -Françoise Galoteau marriage entry, 29 August 1695; Archives Départementales de la Marne, Châlon-en-Champagne; photocopy provided by Ms. Methvin.

6. Saint-Symphorien Parish (Reims, France), Parish Registers, Cote 2 E 534 / 139, Jean Metayer baptismal entry, 28 December 1693; Archives Départementales de la Marne, Châlon-en-Champagne; photocopy provided by Ms. Methvin; Saint-Symphorien Parish (Reims, France), Parish Registers, Cote 2 E 534 / 140, Pierre Metoyer baptismal entry, 6 January 1695; Archives Départementales de la Marne, Châlon-en-Champagne; photocopy provided by Ms. Methvin.

7. Saint-Symphorien Parish (Reims, France), Parish Registers, Cote 2 E 534/140, Suzanne Delaitre death entry, 4 March 1695; Archives Départementales de la Marne, Châlon-en-Champagne; photocopy provided by Ms. Methvin.

8. "Marne, France Marriages, 1529-1907," accessed December 2009, entries for Jean Metoyer, Catherine Oudin, Suzanne Delaitre, and Françoise Galoteau.

Saint-Symphorien Parish (Reims, France), Parish Registers, Cote 2E 534/140, Jean Metoyer -Françoise Galoteau marriage entry.

9. Saint Denis Parish (Reims, France), Parish Registers, Cote 2E 534/15, Nicolas François Metoyer baptismal entry, 16 May 1715; Archives Départementales de la Marne, Châlon-en-Champagne; photocopy provided by Ms. Methvin.

10. Saint-Sauveur Parish (La Rochelle, France), Parish Registers, Cote 5 mi 1104, Nicolas François Metoyer -Marie Anne Drapron marriage entry, 20 February 1743; Archives Départementales de Charente-Maritime, La Rochelle; photocopy provided by Ms. Methvin.

11. Dial, Susan, ed., "La Belle Shipwreck," *Texasbeyondhistory.net*, accessed November 22, 2009, http://www.texasbeyondhistory.net/belle/index.html.

12. La Rochelle, Charente-Maritime, Acts of Me David, Royal Notary; 16 February 1743, Nicolas François Metoyer-Marie Anne Drapron, marriage contract; Cote 3E 2260. La Rochelle, Charente-Maritime, Acts of Me David, Royal Notary; 1 March 1745, Sale by Pierre Surget of his title of master barber and wigmaker to Nicolas François Métoyer; Cote 3E 2262; Archives Départementales de Charente-Maritime, La Rochelle; photocopy of translated document provided by Ms. Methvin.

13. Madame Adam, "The Dowries of Women in France," *The North American Review*, 152 (Jan., 1891): 37, accessed October 21, 2012, http://www.jstor.org/stable/25102113.

14. La Rochelle, Charente-Maritime, Acts of Me David, Royal Notary; 16 February 1743, Nicolas François Metoyer-Marie Anne Drapron, marriage contract.

15. Ibid.

A matrimonial dispensation is the relaxation in a particular case of an impediment prohibiting or annulling a marriage, or the relaxation from three banns being announced before a wedding. This dispensation appears to be the latter because two other banns had been announced in the parish of Notre Dame and granted by Menou, vicar-general and Monseigneur Francois.

16. Saint-Sauveur Parish (La Rochelle, France), Parish Registers, Cote 5 mi 1104, Nicolas François Metoyer -Marie Anne Drapron marriage entry, 20 February 1743; Saint-Sauveur Parish (La Rochelle, France), Parish Registers, Cote 5 Mi 1104 Claude Thomas Pierre Metoyer baptism entry, 14 March 1744; photocopies provided by Ms. Methvin.

17. Ibid.

18. Saint-Sauveur Parish (La Rochelle, France), Parish Registers, Cote 5 Mi 1104, Jacques Gérard, Marie Jeanne, and Catherine Elisabeth Metoyer baptismal entries, 7 May 1745, 2 May 1746, 13 April 1748; Jacques Gérard Metoyer death entry, 5 April 1749; Marie Anne Drapron death entry, 28 April 1748; Nicolas Metoyer-Marie Suzanne Vinault marriage entry, 11 December 1748; photocopies provided by Ms. Methvin.

19. Ibid.

20. La Rochelle, Charente-Maritime, Acts of Me Tardy, Royal Notary; 11 February 1767, AndrÉ Vincent Hippolyte Micou-Catherine Elisabeth MÉtoyer, marriage contract, Cote 5 Mi 1105; Archives Départementales de Charente-Maritime, La Rochelle; electronic disc with information provided by Ms. Methvin.

Saint-Sauveur Parish (La Rochelle, France), Parish Registers, Cote 5 Mi 1104, Louise Thomas Metoyer Baptismal entry, 31 July 1750;Archives Départementales de Charente-Maritime, La Rochelle; electronic disc with information provided by Ms. Methvin.

21. La Rochelle, Charente-Maritime, Acts of Me David, Royal Notary; 7 August 1750, Lease of house in Grand Rue and parish of Saint-Sauveur by Nicolas François Metoyer; Cote 3 E 861; Archives de la Départementales de Charente-Maritime, La Rochelle; photocopy provided by Ms. Methvin; photocopy of translated and untranslated document provided by Ms. Methvin.

22. La Rochelle, Charente-Maritime, Acts of Me Goizon, Royal Notary; 10 July 1753, Sell of home, "The Beautiful Pines," to Nicolas Metoyer and Suzanne Vinnault;Cote 3E/1921; Archives de la Départementales de Charente-Maritime, La Rochelle; photocopy provided by Ms. Methvin.

23. La Rochelle, Charente-Maritime, Acts of Me Tardy, Royal Notary; 7,8,17, 22 July 1766, Inventory of property of decease, Nicolas François Metoyer; Cote 3 E 1935; Archives de la Départementales de Charente-Maritime, La Rochelle; photocopies provided Ms. Methvin.

24. Kevin C. Robbins, *City on the Ocean Sea: La Rochelle, 1530-1650: Urban Society, Religion, and Politics on the French Atlantic Frontier* (Leiden, The Netherlands: E. J. Brille, 1997), 38-40.

25. Ibid., 31.

26. La Rochelle, Charente-Maritime, Acts of Me Tardy, Royal Notary; Inventor of property of deceased, Nicolas François Metoyer; photocopy provided by Ms. Methvin.

27. Ibid.

28. La Rochelle, Charente-Maritime, Acts of Me Tardy, Royal Notary; 4 April 1766, Security of 3, 153 livres by Nicolas Metoyer to prison warder for release from La Rochelle prison; Cote 3 E 1935; Archives de la Départementales de Charente-Maritime, La Rochelle; photocopies provided by Ms. Methvin.

29. La Rochelle, Charente-Maritime, Acts of Me Tardy, Royal Notary; Letter in inventory of deceased, Nicolas François Metoyer, property addressed to him from his son in New Orleans; photocopy provided by Ms. Methvin.

30. La Rochelle, Charente-Maritime, Acts of Me Tardy, Royal Notary; Inventory of property of deceased, Nicolas François Metoyer; photocopy provided by Ms. Methvin.

31. James F. Traer, *Marriage and the family in Eighteenth-Century France* (London: Cornell University Press, 1980), 44.

32. Robbins, *City on the Sea*, 10, 23.

33. La Rochelle, Charente-Maritime, Acts of Me Tardy, Royal Notary; Inventory of property of deceased, Nicolas François Metoyer; photocopy provided by Ms. Methvin.

34. Robbins, *City on the Sea,* 10.

35. La Rochelle, Charente-Maritime, Acts of Me Tardy, Royal Notary; Letter in inventory of deceased, Nicolas François Metoyer, property addressed to him from his son in New Orleans; photocopy provided by Ms. Methvin.

36. Mills, G., *Forgotten People*, 10

Chapter 4

The Natchitoches Post and Louis Juchereau de St. Denis

The Natchitoches post, home of Bertha's ancestors, was Louis Juchereau de St. Denis, and Louis Juchereau de St. Denis was the Natchitoches post. But, who exactly was this man who helped to generate a settlement in the middle of the wilderness and played a significant role in the lives of Bertha's ancestors? Did anyone *actually* know the true character of St. Denis? It is extremely unlikely, but what we can ascertain is this.

It was 1676, in Beauport, New France, known today as Quebec, Canada, when Louis Antoine Juchereau de St. Denis was born to Nicolas Juchereau and Marie Thérèse Giffard.[1] As a young man he traveled to France. It was from the port of La Rochelle, France, in October of 1698, that St. Denis sailed to New France with the French explorer Pierre Le Moyne, Sieur d'Iberville. Sieur d'Iberville was experiencing his second expedition to Louisiana.[2] Young and probably itching for adventure, St. Denis, a Canadian born volunteer French officer, was about to embark on a journey that would catapult him into history books around the world.

As their ship made its way to the fort at old Biloxi, the young St. Denis positioned his eyes on his new home.[3] Gazing at the new world, no one knows what may have been churning in the mind of the novice explorer. But if it was an adventure he was imagining, it was an adventure he would soon experience. With little over a year to settle in, St. Denis was underway on his first excursion. This expedition would take him along the Red River. He would be introduced to Native Americans whose cultures were as varied as the old world from which he departed and the new world to which he had come. Along the way he encountered the Natchez people. Those in the exploration party found admiration for the impressive Natchez men and the beautiful women. This admiration would one day turn to dread. As the journey continued, the explorers smoked the peace pipe with the Natchitoches Native

Americans.[4] It would be these Native Americans who would earn the confidence and mutual respect of St. Denis. On other missions, in search of gold and silver mines, St. Denis continued to be receptive to the varied Native American cultures. He listened and learned their language. He observed and learned their customs. He showed respect and thus was respected. By doing so, he forged friendships which would last him a lifetime.[5] It would be some of these friendships that would be of service as St. Denis established and protected Natchitoches.

Trade between the Native Americans and the French colonists was crucial if the new Frenchmen were to subsist in the wilderness. In 1700, to help facilitate trade, a Mississippi fort, later named Fort Boulaye de la Mississippi, was placed under St. Denis' command. During his tenure, St. Denis continued his mission of exploring the Red River, establishing trade alliances, searching for gold and silver, and maintaining peace with the Native Americans.[6] Unfortunately, one Native American group would prove anything but peaceful for St. Denis. It would be this group that would experience the wrath of the foreigner.

In 1703, the Chitamache Native Americans slaughtered a French priest and three other Frenchmen. To avenge these deaths, in 1706, St. Denis and soldiers under his command executed fifteen of the tribesmen and seized forty prisoners that included men, women, and children.[7] The prisoners, from the Chitamache campaign, were sold at Mobile and Biloxi. One of the men who participated in the campaign against the Chitamaches was Lieutenant François Derbanne. Derbanne would later take a Chitamache slave, Jeanne de la Grande Terre, for his wife.[8] François Derbanne and St. Denis had held the fate of the Chitamache slaves in their hands. One day, the son of François Derbanne and Jeanne de la Grande Terre, Pierre Derbanne, would hold the fate of Bertha's third great-grandmother in his hands.

With the Chitamache no longer an imminent threat, St. Denis pursued his agenda of extending French trade. In 1712, St. Denis was sent on an excursion to attain trade with the Spanish in Mexico. Trade between the Spanish and French was prohibited. Requesting trade between the two countries was provocation enough to place St. Denis in custody.[9] Despite his unfortunate detainment, not all went downward for the adventurous explorer. While he was sequestered, he encountered the woman who would become the mother of his children and his lifelong partner, Manuela Sánchez y Navarro.[10]

Manuela was a relative of Diego Ramón, commandant of the Spanish post, Los Adaes.[11] Because the Ramón family was politically and militarily connected to New Spain, this close association proved beneficial for Manuela and St. Denis for years to come. Between 1715 and 1716, the eighteen year old Manuela married the forty year old St. Denis in Tejas. The couple started their family soon after.[12] Years later, it would be Manuela, St. Denis, and the children of this union who would hold Bertha's ancestors in bondage. It would also be the spirited daughter of Manuela and St. Denis, Marie des Nieges de St. Denis, (aka Mme. de Soto) who would vehemently defend the rights of Bertha's fourth great-grandmother to love and live with whomever she chose.

"An island that a river forms by dividing into two branches," would be the commencement of the Natchitoches establishment, created by St. Denis, along with Native Americans. With the help of the Doustioni and the Natchitoches Native Americans, a rudimentary way station was fashioned. It consisted of two structures. One was utilized to house the Frenchmen's merchandise and the other was used for their shelter.[13] In 1720, St. Denis began his reign as commandant of the fort that had developed into an outpost. The jurisdiction of the entire Red River Valley would eventually be under his control.[14]

Situated in northwest Louisiana, on the west bank of the Red River which produced an abundance of fertile soil, breathtaking vegetation, and a paradise for a diverse population of animals native to the area, the post was theoretically ideal. As one year transitioned into another, the outpost grew with its population of French, Spanish, Native American and African slaves. In 1722, the outpost housed fourteen free men, ten free women, and ten free children. Twenty Black slaves and eight Indian slaves also resided there.[15] A fourth of the Black slaves and half of the Indian slaves were the property of St. Denis. As the post expanded, so did the stature of St. Denis. He was revered by the Native Americans and seen as an asset to France. But in the fall of 1731, life as St. Denis knew it would experience an unwelcomed transformation.

The Natchez, who St. Denis had so admired during his earlier expeditions, had become disgruntled with the French settlers. They were losing their land to tobacco plantations, and their people were dying due to disease introduced by the settlers. In 1729, the Natchez attacked Fort Rosalie slaughtering over two hundred white men and enslaving the women and children. For the next two years the Natchez were a force to be reckoned with. Their next target was the home of St. Denis, the Natchitoches post. On October 5, 1731, they attacked the post. The assaults went on until October 14th. With the help of several Native Americans, and some French and Spaniards, the

Natchez finally retreated.[16] Although the battle was over, the loss would be felt long after the Natchez had departed.

Along with the loss of men, crops had been lost. Foods that would have been shared with the settlers had to be used to compensate the allies who had come to rescue them.[17] With the settlers, under his watch, constantly in fear of more attacks, this must have been a low time for St. Denis. This may very well have been why St. Denis contemplated leaving the post. Despite the setback, he remained, and the Natchitoches post, under his vigilant eye, continued to expand. By 1737, the population had increased to 233. Included in the census were French settlers, along with Native American and Black slaves.[18] Two of those Black slaves counted, François and Marie Françoise, were Bertha's fifth great-grandparents.

In spite of the post's continuous expansion, in his final days St. Denis wanted to be relieved of his duties. His aspiration was to go to New Spain with his beloved Manuela to live out the remainder of his life. At the age of 68, he composed a letter to his niece. In the letter, dated April, 3, 1741, he relayed this about the wilderness that he had devoted his life to: "I do not advise any of them [relatives] to come, for I can assure you that it is a very worthless country; happy he who can get out of it and infinitely happier is he who never come to it, and no matter how old I should be I would wish with all my heart to be out of it…" St. Denis did get out of it, but not to live in New Spain as he had desired. On June 11, 1744, Denis died in that "worthless country" he wanted to depart.[19]

After the death of St. Denis, his slaves became the property of his widow who continued to reside at the post. By 1765, the miniscule population of 1722 had burgeoned to three hundred twenty-three free people, two hundred thirty-nine Black slaves, and thirty Native American slaves.[20] A percentage of the Black slaves belonging to St. Denis' widow were Bertha's ancestors. Counted among them were François, Marie Françoise, and their offspring.[21] The intermingling of these diverse groups gave the French outpost a distinct flavor. It was a flavor that was as unique and spicy as the gumbo, meat pies, and tamales for which the region would be acclaimed. In this flavorful atmosphere, Marie Thérèse Coincoin, Bertha's fourth great-grandmother, had been born, and Claude Thomas Pierre Metoyer, her fourth great-grandfather would make his home. It would be this intermingling that would create the heritage for which my grandmother, Bertha Metoyer, would be known.

Endnotes

1. Donald E. Chipman, and Harriett Denise Joseph, *Notable Men and Women of Spanish Texas* (Austin, Texas: University of Texas Press, 1999), 50.

   Ross Phares, *Cavalier in the Wilderness* (Baton Rouge: Louisiana State University, 1952), 59.

2. Richebourg Gaillard McWilliams, trans. and ed., *Fleur de Lys and Calumet: Being the Pénicaut Narrative of French Adventure in Louisiana* (Tuscaloosa, Alabama: The University of Alabama Press, 1988), 1.

   Phares, *Cavalier,* 2.

3. Phares, *Cavalier,* 2.

4. Ibid., 15-20.

   McWilliams, *Fleur de Lys and Calumet,* 28-29.

5. Phares, *Cavalier,* 27.

6. Ibid., 27, 33, 34.

   McWilliams, *Fleur de Lys and Calumet,* 54.

7. McWilliams, *Fleur de Lys and Calumet,* 70-72.

8. H. Sophie Burton and F. Todd Smith, *Colonial Natchitoches: A Creole Community on the Louisiana-Texas Frontier (*College Station, Texas: Texas A & M University Press, 2008), 55.

9. Phares, *Cavalier,* 51, 52.

   McWilliams, *Fleur de Lys and Calumet,* 151-52.

10. Ibid., 153.

11. Chipman and Joseph, *Notable Men and Women,* 259-60.

12. Ibid., 260.

13. McWilliams, *Fleur de Lys and Calumet,* 148-49.

14. Burton and Smith, *Colonial Natchitoches,* 7, 8.

15. Charles R. Maduell, *The Census Tables for the French Colony of Louisiana from 1699 through 1732* (Baltimore: Genealogical Publishing Company, 1972), 35.

16. Burton and Smith, *Colonial Natchitoches,* 11; Marcel Giraud, *A History of French Louisiana, Volume Five, The Company of the Indies, 1723-1731,* trans. Brian Pearce (Baton Rouge: Louisiana State University Press, 1991), 397-98; Phares, *Cavalier,* 201-02.

17. Giraud, *History of French Louisiana,* 386.

18. Burton and Smith, *Colonial Natchitoches,* 13, citing General Census of 1737, C13, C4.

19. Phares, *Cavalier*, 260-63.

20. Burton and Smith, *Colonial Natchitoches*, 21, 56, 62, citing French Census of Natchitoches, January 27, 1766; Elizabeth Shown Mills, ed., *Natchitoches Colonials: Censuses, Military Rolls, and Tax Lists, 1722-1803* (Chicago: Adams Press, 1981,) 9-14.

21. Mills, E. S., "Marie Thérèse Coincoin (1742-1816)," 14, citing partition of St. Denis slaves, document no. 176, 203-5, NCA, and Louisiana State Archives microfilm Natchitoches F. T. 565, Miscellaneous Archives Records 1733-1820, particularly 232-50.

Chapter 5

Two Lovers Meet

While living at the Natchitoches post from 1735 until 1758, Bertha's earliest known African ancestors, François and Marie Françoise, were owned by Louis Juchereau de St. Denis and his wife, Manuela Sánchez y Navarro. François, Bertha's fifth great-grandfather, was one of her first African ancestors to belong to the St. Denis family. About four years after St. Denis had withstood the assault by the Natchez Native Americans at the Natchitoches' fort, François became part of the St. Denis household. He was a slave of the family when they experienced some degree of prosperity. And he remained their slave, after the death of St. Denis, when leaner days may have been the norm.

Prior to 1737, France, the motherland of the French colony, was experiencing an economic downturn, but in 1737 France was financially more stable. Subsequently, Natchitoches benefited from the effects of that boom. It was a period when fine clothes, china, and other imports made their way to the post.[1] For a frontier home, the St. Denis home was not lacking in finery. An inventory of the home, after St. Denis' death in 1744, included, among other belongings, "twelve silver forks and spoons, two silver goblets, a kind of silver pitcher, nine decorated platters, three iron cooking pots, a cauldron, two dozen napkins, six tablecloths, five mattresses, a feather bed, three beds, two of printed calico and one white, three fine coverlets." Inside the residence there was evidence of prosperity, and outside the home the hundred cattle and fifty horses spoke volumes about the family's financial standing.[2] St. Denis' wardrobe was also impressive. The clothes of St. Denis would have been worn by the bourgeoisie in France. His wardrobe comprised damask, taffeta, and velvet surtouts (coats) of assorted colors with silver and gold braids at the bottom. Included were dress items with gold buttons, taffeta hats, and a red cape with red breeches.[3] For a frontier family, the St. Denis family did not lack the finer things in life.

The St. Denis family was also a family that wielded much influence. This family was militarily and politically well positioned. Early during the development of the Natchitoches post, St. Denis was the commandant from 1720 until 1744. In 1733, his oldest daughter, Marie Rose, married a French officer, Jacques de la Chaise. La Chaise's father was an official in New Orleans. In 1750, St. Denis' daughter, Marie des Douleurs, married Cesaire de Blanc, the new commandant who had taken over the post after her father's tenure. In 1746, another daughter, Petronnella Feliciana, married Athanase de Mézière, a nobleman; he later became the commandant of the post replacing de Blanc.[4] Despite the demise of St. Denis, these marriages kept the family militarily and politically connected.

This was the St. Denis family into which François had come, and his daughter, Marie Thérèse was born. When St. Denis died, his widow inherited the couple and their children. The inventory of his estate revealed that he owned "twelve [adult] Negroes as many male as female, twelve little Negroes male and female, three adult Indian women, one adult male Indian, [and] five little Indians, as many male as female."[5] Bertha's ancestors were among these slaves. They would have included her fifth great-grandparents, François and Marie Françoise, her fourth great-grandmother, Marie Thérèse, and her great-grand uncles and aunts.

It would be Marie Thérèse who would assure her parents a place in history as she carried on their legacy and became the matriarch of our family. From 1744 until 1758, while in the possession of the widow of St. Denis, Marie Thérèse's life appeared uninterrupted. Unfortunately, at the age of sixteen, tragedy struck. Within the span of three days, Marie Thérèse (frequently called Coincoin) experienced the death of her parents, François and Marie Françoise, and her owner, Mde. de St. Denis. As laws would dictate, Marie Thérèse now became the property of the heirs of St. Denis. For the first time, the family would be separated. Each of the St. Denis children would inherit slaves from their parents' estate. By lot, St Denis' eldest son, Louis Juchereau, Jr., became Marie Thérèse's new owner.[6] Soon after being inherited by Louis, Jr., the teenaged Marie Thérèse gave birth to her first child, Marie Louise. Two years later, a second daughter, Thérèse, was born.[7]

Marie Thérèse's tenancy with Louis, Jr. was brief. With the exception of Marie Thérèse, the sons of St. Denis sold their inherited slaves outside of their family.[8] Marie Thérèse became the property of Louis, Jr.'s sister (who was also Marie Thérèse's godmother) Marie des Nieges de Soto. In 1763, while in her household, a third daughter, Françoise was born to Marie Thérèse.[9] In 1764 or 1765 her first boy-child,

Nicolas Chiquito, was born.[10] Another son, Jean Joseph, was born and baptized on March 29, 1766.[11] Official records indicate that the fathers of all five children were Black, but according to oral family history their father was Native American.

Unmarried, orphaned, the property of Madame de Soto, with five young children to rear, life could not have been easy for young Marie Thérèse. Fate had not shown favor to the young slave. But a year after the birth of Jean Joseph, her life slowly began to slide in a different direction. It took a turn that even the wisest seers could not have foretold.

After having arrived in his new homeland, young Claude Thomas Pierre Metoyer (like most adventurous spirits who had navigated the vast Atlantic to get to the new world) undoubtedly had thoughts of love, family, and a chance to experience the dream that could only be extracted from America. Unlike Marie Thérèse, Pierre's life was his own, and his lot in life could only be hampered by a lack of ambition. For a period of time, Pierre lingered in New Orleans. A letter to his father written on December 1, 1765 from New Orleans substantiates this.[12]

Arriving at the Natchitoches Post, around 1767, Pierre soon set up his establishment. Like his father, he became a merchant. Having grown up around vineyards and wines, it is little wonder what type of business he would establish. Pierre's knowledge of the wine industry from his father, and his stint in New Orleans (where the selling of alcoholic beverages was flourishing) would have afforded him ample opportunity to contemplate his occupation of choice.[13] His establishment was said to be "in competition with at least fifteen other sellers of alcoholic beverages and owners of cabarets."[14] This venture would be the springboard for a consequent life of wealth and privilege.

As Marie Thérèse, mother of five, toiled in the home of Madame de Soto, accommodating the needs of her mistress, Pierre established himself as a merchant, perhaps, envisioning the wealth he could accumulate in this untamed frontier of New France. Marie Thérèse and Pierre, sharing bipolar lives, probably never fathomed, as they went about their lives in the miniscule Natchitoches post, that the mysterious laws of chance would thrust them together and seal their destinies forever.

No one knows precisely when the couple's first encounter occurred. It may have been a frigid December or a mosquito infested July when the paths of Marie Thérèse and Pierre converged. On that day, despite the weather, the older and conceivably wiser twenty-five year old Marie Thérèse caught the eye of twenty-three year old Pierre. His subsequent actions seem to indicate that whatever garnered Pierre's attention eventually captured his heart. How or why is insignificant, but it is often said that forbidden fruit is often the fruit most desired. In this Natchitoches outpost, fate had introduced a couple who, despite their diverse stations in life, would forge a friendship and a family that would endure a lifetime.

When love is fresh and new, one imagines all things are possible, and no matter how vast love's mountain, it will be surmountable. What may have been in the minds of Marie Thérèse and Pierre is not known. It may have been Pierre's intention to experience the exotic Marie Thérèse and move on to someone who better fitted society's mores. Maybe it was an opportunity for Marie Thérèse to advance her station in life. Was it finances, love, or lust that brought the two together? Their motives have long since parted with their spirits, but despite their objectives, a force stronger than the both of them kept them together.

Marie Thérèse and Pierre would produce a family that would be uniquely their own; a family that would be remembered for many generations to come. No one could have gambled on the odds that Marie Thérèse and Pierre would develop a bond that neither church, nor society, nor time would be able to splinter no matter how hard they tried. And they did try.

Linda S. Manuel

Madame de St. Denis' Slaves Partitioned to Heirs

Document 213[16]
Natchitoches Clerk of Court

Today the twenty-fifth of the month of April one thousand seven hundred fifty eight has been brought about the partition of the slaves of the deceased Madame de St. Denis, between the heirs of the said Madame who are Monsieur Deblanc, commander of this post, to whom there falls the said slaves named Jinby, and her son and Pierre; to Monsieur Mesierre [Mezieres] there falls the named Gregoire, Bonnaventure, and Marie Jeanne; to Monsieur de la Chaise there has fallen Mathianne, Andre, Michel, Hyacinthe; to Monsieur de St Denis the named Coin Coin and Jean Baptiste; to my lord the Chevalier de St Denis those named Guerin, Maman, La Bouillie, and Quioquira; to Monsieur Don Manuel has fallen those named Isabella, Bambara, Jacob, and the little one the orphan negress of eight days; all the said partitions made in [the] presence of witnesses, under-signed, [on] the days and years as above; witnesses: Monsieur Decour, Monsieur Demongist, both of them officers of the troops, and Sieur Trichel and Sieur Jobar and Sieur Poissot, living at the post.

De Blanc	Marie St. Denis
	St. Denis
Manuel Desoto	Chevalier de St Denis
Monginot, witness	Demeziere
Le court, witness	(mark of)
Dominique Monteche	Sieur Trichel
(officer of the militia)	Poissot(witness
(mark) of Jobar	

35

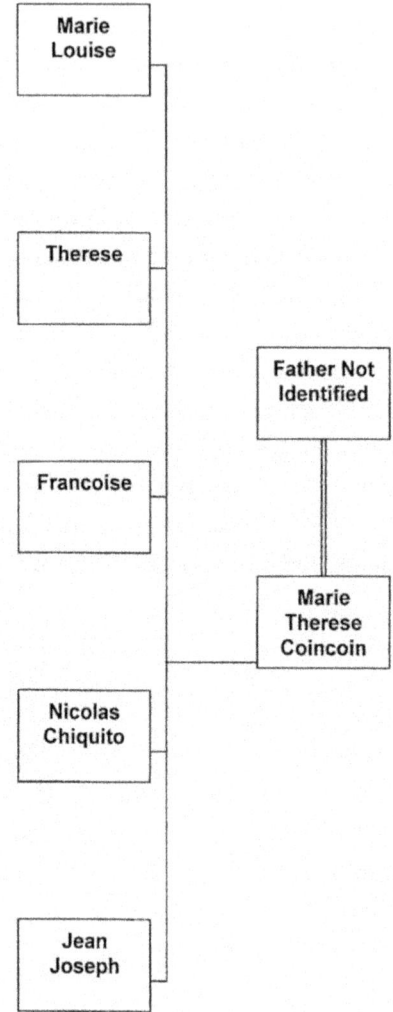

Endnotes

1. Phares, *Cavalier,* 249.

2. "Estate Holdings of Monsieur de St. Denis (June 27, 1744)," document no. 151, Natchitoches Colonial Archives, Clerk of Court Office, Natchitoches, LA.

3. Phares, *Cavalier,* 254-55.

4. Mills, E. S., *Natchitoches, 1729-1803,* entries 144, 347, 355.

5. "Estate Holdings of Monsieur de St. Denis."

6. Mills, E. S., *Natchitoches, 1729-1803,* entries 817, 820; "Mde. de St. Denis' Slaves Partitioned to Heirs," document no. 213, Natchitoches Colonial Archives, trans. Translations Services, Ltd.

7. Mills, E. S., *Natchitoches, 1729-1803,* entries 713, 462.

8. Mr. de St. Denis and Chevalier de St. Denis sell inherited land and slaves, doc. 345, Miscellaneous Series, Archive Conveyance Records, Natchitoches.

9. Mills, E. S., *Natchitoches, 1729-1803,* entry 484.

10. Mills, E. S., and Mills, G., "Slaves and Masters," 171.

11. Mills, E. S., *Natchitoches, 1729-1803,* entry 862.

12. La Rochelle, Charente-Maritime. Acts of Me Tardy, Royal Notary; Letter in inventory of deceased, Nicolas François Metoyer, property addressed to him from his son in New Orleans; photocopy provided by Ms. Methvin.

13. Giraud, *History of French Louisiana,* 269.

14. Gary B. Mills, "Claude Thomas Pierre Metoyer, "*A Dictionary of Louisiana Biography; Ten-Year Supplement 1988-1998,* ed. Carl A. Brasseaux and James D. Wilson, Jr., (Lafayette: Louisiana Historical Association, 1999); pp. 154–56.

15. Giraud, *History of French Louisiana,* 326.

16. "Madame de St. Denis' Slaves Partitioned to Heirs," document no. 213, Natchitoches Colonial Archives, trans. Translations Services, Ltd.

Searching For Bertha

Chapter 6

Two Lives Converge

In a frontier environment, like the Natchitoches post, some relationships are created out of necessity. Because males normally arrive before females to settle the untamed wilderness, lack of female companionship prompt men to select mates or lovers they may not have chosen in their motherland. Natchitoches was no different from other settlements. Before European women populated the post, a few men chose to make alliances with Native American slaves while others waited for the arrival of their French counterparts.[1]

During the period that Marie Thérèse was in her mid-twenties, and about the time when Pierre arrived at the post, the population of white males and females were comparable. The post had seen an influx of and native born Europeans and Black slaves. There were 170 white males and 138 white females; 55 adult males and 54 adult females. There were adequate numbers of French female immigrants arriving, or being born, in Natchitoches, to provide partners for the male population. The majority of the French men did form marriages with their female counterparts. The population of female and male Black slaves was also about evenly dispersed; respectively 128 to 141; 94 adult males and 67 adult females. Unlike the male/ female population in New Orleans, the sexes, though not equal, were not entirely out of balance.[2] Both Pierre and Marie Thérèse could have found mates within their own racial and social status. So what could have possibly prompted Pierre and Marie Thérèse to begin an affair and form an alliance outside their races that would essentially endure their lifetime?

When Pierre encountered Marie Thérèse, she was 25 years old with five children, and he was 23 years old without wife or children. He would have probably been considered desirable to the females in the colony. If the male tendency was to marry younger women, Marie Thérèse (although he could not marry her) was not a typical fit for a French colonial bachelor.

Historical accounts, written about long-term black/white sexual relationships, or concubines in the eighteenth and nineteenth century, tended to consist of women who were not primarily African, but were of mixed racial heritage. When one reads about the Quadroon Balls in New Orleans that were formed to spur alliances between free women of color and white men, the women were described as free people of color - mostly mulattoes or quadroons, but not slaves. Their skin color varied from brown to almost white. During the colonial era, records reveal that the term négritte or négresse was used to describe Marie Thérèse, a term that was equated with "unmixed" African heritage[3]. The fact that Marie Therese was likely of pure African heritage and not a free person of color makes her long term relationship with Pierre exceptional for the period. Though several men in Natchitoches had slaves for mistresses, few relationships were as open, endured as long, and were as severely scrutinized as that of Pierre and Marie Thérèse. So one begs to ask, what was the bond that held the two together?

There are occasions in life when we do things not because of necessity but because of desire. We know what feels right. It takes courage and tenacity to break away from society's imposed morality to develop one's own sense of self. This is precisely what Pierre appeared to do, but why? The odds of acceptance were against him. He could have, like many before and beside him, come to Marie Thérèse under the cloak of darkness, but he did not. She was there exposed for the world to witness. In his youth, Pierre appears not to have been a person who let others define who he was. It was he who determined the path that he would travel. Could this have been the rationale for Marie Thérèse's seemingly unwavering devotion? Or perhaps, he saw not what others perceived, he saw her the way I envision.

For me, the true essence of Marie Thérèse cannot be fully appreciated without visualizing her in the mind's eye. Though no likeness seems to exist of her, I only have to look to images of her descendants to envision her beauty and indomitable spirit. When I close my eyes, I see an ebony face that displays serenity in a storm. I see a tantalizing and somewhat teasing smile on an otherwise tranquil face. When she is extremely pleased, she tosses back her head and flashes a smile that reveals the whiteness of her teeth against her perfectly balanced lips. When she is annoyed, she speaks softly but with command. Her body is feminine, yet sturdy and strong. Her hair's natural curls, often restrained by a tignon (kerchief), frame a perfectly oval face. She is beautiful, she is confident, and she is charismatic. She is the perfect woman to overcome the circumstances into which she was born. It was this exotic ebony beauty that enchanted the young Frenchman from abroad.

After Pierre arrived at the Natchitoches post, around 1767, it did not take him long to become captivated by Marie Thérèse. It could not have been less than love at first sight, because Pierre was soon at the household of Madame de Soto arranging to lease her.[4] Shortly after the contract had been negotiated, the two lovers began to populate the colony with a generation of

Franco-African children. These children would forever alter the landscape of the wild untamed post.

A Family Affair

As the lovers did what all young lovers do, it should have been no surprise when twenty-four year old Pierre and twenty-six year old Marie Thérèse became parents. On January 22, 1768, the couple presented twins to the world. (Due to unusual circumstances to be discussed later, both of these children would become Bertha's third maternal great-grandparents). If Marie Thérèse's parents, François and Marie Françoise, had still been alive, they would have been extremely proud of their second born daughter. Marie Thérèse had been blessed with not one but two children. On February 22, 1768, they were baptized at the post of St. Jean Baptiste des Natchitoches and became a part of the Christian faith.[5]

Pierre must have been ecstatic about his new offspring because it is believed that he named them after his French ancestors. Pierre's first born son, Nicolas Augustin, bore the first name of Pierre's father, Nicolas François Metoyer. Pierre's first born daughter was given the name Marie Susanne. The name may have been in honor of his grandfather's second wife, Suzanne Delaitre, or his stepmother, Suzanne Vinault.[6] Although, Pierre and Marie Thérèse were not cognizant of it at the time, they were creating a Metoyer family that would be remembered for generations to come.

For two years, the couple lived in harmony with the twins. Like all new parents with twins, they, undoubtedly, shared each new milestone with double the joy and laughter. As Marie Thérèse cared for the house and children, Pierre worked to provide for his new family. In 1770, the twins were joined by a new brother, Louis. (He, too, would be Bertha's third maternal great-grandparent). Like clockwork, every two years the family expanded. In 1772, Pierre arrived, and in 1774 along came Dominique.[7] Although the priest, Father Stanislaus, was at the post during the birth of the boys,[8] and they would have been baptized, no records have been discovered to validate the precise time of the baptism of Louis, Pierre, and Dominique. In January of 1776, with four boys and one girl, it was only fitting for Marie Eulalie to make her appearance. The priest, Father Luis de Quintanilla, baptized Eulalie within thirteen days of her arrival.[9]

For more than eight years Pierre had worked hard, provided for his family, and was becoming a man of reasonable means. He had the love and devotion of Marie Thérèse and a rapidly growing family. Absolute happiness may have been theirs if they had been born in a different place or time. Unfortunately such circumstances are beyond ones control. And so it was for Marie Thérèse and Pierre. Because of the place and time when love thrust them together, neither Marie Thérèse nor his six children belonged to Pierre. They were all slaves who belonged to Madame de Soto, Marie Thérèse's owner.

The laws of Louisiana, and other territories that prospered from the labor of slavery, clearly specified that a child born to a slave was not the property of the slave but the property of the slave's master.[10] This being the circumstance of their existence, if Marie Thérèse and Pierre wanted complete control of their children, Pierre would have to purchase them from their owner. This was the position in which the two soul mates found themselves. A situation that might be too much for the faint of heart, but not one that would deter these strong willed lovers.

In 1776, the four oldest children, now eight, six, and four, were at the ages when they could have been working for their mistress. Dominique, two-years old, a toddler, and Eulalie, still a suckling baby, would have still been under the care of Marie Thérèse. For Pierre, the two youngest were not an immediate concern. But what did it do to the heart and mind of Pierre to see his older children, Augustin, Susanne, Louis, and Pierre, working at such tender ages for their mistress? It was Madame de Soto, not Pierre, who controlled the fate of his children. They were in her charge, not his. As the years passed, did he detect the unhappiness in the eyes of Marie Thérèse as child after child was taken away to attend to the whims of someone else? Was it the compassion for the children or his love for their mother that persuaded Pierre to claim what was naturally his? Or, did seeing Eulalie, sweet and innocent in the arms of her mother trigger the reality of the children's destiny and initiate fear in his heart and mind? No one knows Pierre's motives; but two months after the birth of Eulalie, Pierre determined it was time to take control of his children's future.

When Pierre finally made the decision to claim his oldest offspring, I imagine a day when the clouds opened their puffy eyes and cried torrential tears of joy. Historical records during the time did not record such mundane acts of nature, so only Pierre knows for certain the temperament of the weather. But it is written, on May 31, 1776, Claude Thomas Pierre Metoyer stood before Lieutenant Governor Athanase Christophe Mauguet de Mézières and bought the twins, Nicolas Augustin and Marie Susanne, along with Louis and Pierre; the price—two thousand silver livres (French currency) and a ten or twelve-year-old male slave he owned.[11] The irony of a life exchanged for a life, surely, could not have been lost on those who witnessed the transactions. But, little did the couple know that this happiness would be fleeting. As they were trying to build a strong family, an unsuspecting force was trying to tear it apart.

It is unimaginable the happiness the couple must have experienced knowing they were now a family. The tears, the laughter, and the joy in the Metoyer household the first night the family was united must have been pure bliss. A feast, surely, was in order as the family celebrated together. In all probability, there was a long night discussing and recapturing the day's event. Afterwards, there was possibly passionate lovemaking between Marie Thérèse and Pierre after they tucked the children away. Marie Thérése and Pierre were together, and four of Pierre's children were now naturally and legally his. The two youngest, Dominique and Eulalie were probably living in his home, as well. Pierre had reclaimed his manhood, and Marie Thérèse was in high spirits again. In the little post of Natchitoches, 1776 was proving to be a very good year for the family. Were there any signs that their year of tranquility would soon become a raging storm?

In 1777, while Marie Thérèse was pregnant with their seventh child, Father Quintanilla, the priest who had baptized Eulalie, felt it was his [Christian] duty to end the unsanctioned [scandalous] relationship of the couple. In a letter to the commandant of the Natchitoches post, he complained that he had previously attempted to stop their illicit relationship, but he was unable to do so. Since they would not end their cohabitation, which had produced several children, he wanted them either married or punished.[12]

The letter, in part, reads as follows:

23 Oct 1777
Formal Charge, Luis de Quintanilla against Mme. De Soto and Mr. Metoyer

"Fr. Luis de Quintanilla...compelled by virtue of his ministry to eradicate vices and relate scandals as these occur [reports that] he has failed, after much diligent effort, to put an end to the scandalous concubinage of a Negress named Cuencuen [Marie Thérèse dite Coincoin], a slave of Dn. Manuel de Soto, who has been hired for many years to the cited Metoyer and in whose house and company the said unmarried Negress has produced five or six mulatto children, not counting the one with whom she is now pregnant. This cannot happen in the house of an unmarried man and unmarried women

without the public thinking and judging there to be illicit intercourse between the two partners in concubinage, from this there has ensued a great scandal and damage to souls. According to the mandate sent to your petitioner by this superior, the Most Illustrious Senor, Bishop of Cuba, if these concubines do not desist after my apostolic counsel, they must deliver themselves to the Royal Court of Justice so that they can be coerced and punished - - the text of the decree actually reads: 'These concubines must make use ... of the sacraments supplied by the Church, they must be persuaded to sanctify their bad concubinage by marriage, and- -if they persist- -you must, Your Reverence, denounce them to the Royal Court of Justice so that they can be forced to do so and the scandal can be removed.'"[13]

Marriage, between Marie Thérèse and Pierre, was not plausible because it was illegal for a white person to marry a slave; therefore, in accordance with the priest's other wishes, the commandant ordered Pierre to banish Marie Thérèse from his home. Pierre, having no legal alternative, petitioned to have his lease terminated[14] and gave Marie Thérèse, pregnant with their seventh child, along with Dominique and Eulalie, back to Madame de Soto.

For the couple, undoubtedly devoted to each other and expecting a new child, this must have been a painful and gut wrenching ordeal. What were they to do? How could they overcome such a devastating fate? Could they weather this unforeseen storm? For some, this may have been the ultimate blow, but this obstacle would test the strength of their commitment and ultimately fortify their love.

If caught, their devotion would have to be stronger than the consequences they were sure to face. According to Code Noir, article VI, "Should there be any issue [child] from this kind of intercourse, it is our will that the person so offending, and the master of the slave, should pay each a fine of three hundred livres."[15] Unable or unwilling to sacrifice each other, they went on doing what lovers do. So when the watchful eyes of the Natchitoches' commander and the parish priest were not interfering into their private lives, Marie Thérèse and Pierre continued to find solace in each other. It appeared that what love or lust had brought together, neither church nor laws were able to cast asunder.

Father Quintanilla, in his quest to gain support to "morally reform" the religious wayward post, traveled to New Orleans to present his case to the governor and church officials. He was absent for several months.[16] While he was away, Marie Thérèse and Pierre were blessed with the expected arrival of child number seven, Joseph Antoine, on January 26, 1778.[17] When the priest returned, it did not go without notice that Marie Thérèse, still the property of Madame de Soto, was again residing in the household with Pierre and their newborn, Antoine. This family once again united, but not yet completed, was about to witness their devotion put to another of love's unrelenting tests.

In a second letter to the commandant, Father Quintanilla insinuated that instead of chastising Marie Thérèse, Madame de Soto was ignoring the behavior of the couple.[18] Father Quintanilla underestimated the wrath that he would incur by involving Madame de Soto. Not one to bend under pressure, Madame de Soto quickly responded to his accusation. She composed a letter of her own that was not short on attacks against the priest.[19] For a period of time, the priest appeared stifled, but he would once again raise his fist in protest.

Pierre was also determined to end the priest's interference. Unwilling to be separated from his lover and children again, in July 1778, he bought Marie Thérèse and their new son for one thousand five hundred livres.[20] He now controlled the destiny of Marie Thérèse and Joseph Antoine, along with their four oldest children, Augustin, Susanne, Louis, and Pierre.

After overcoming part of society's induced tribulations, one would think the couple's life would have some sense of calm. But, in a time when a person's color determined his status in life, this family would have its portion of obstacles and considerable heartbreak to overcome. To understand the extent of these problems, one must understand the society in which this couple coexisted.

As a part of Code Noir, Article VI, now that Marie Thérèse belonged to Pierre it was against the law for him to father her children. The law clearly specified "Free men who shall have one or more children during concubinage with their slaves…will be fined. If they are the masters of the slave who produced said children … the children will be removed and… she and they… shall be adjudged to the hospital of the locality never to gain their freedom."[21] The consequences were dire if this law was broken. Both mother and children could be sold and never freed. Pierre was determined to keep his family together and was not going to let this occur. With the stroke of his pen, Pierre secretly freed Marie Thérèse and his youngest son, Joseph Antoine.[22]

These newfound circumstances could not have pleased them more. After spending thirty-eight years of her existence as a slave, Marie Thérèse was free. Except for the legitimacy of marriage, they were a family. Little did they know that it would not be long before their commitment to each other would again be tested; this time it would not be by Father Quintanilla but by the American Revolution.

Together since 1767, Marie Thérèse and Pierre were never far apart. That would all change because Pierre was a member of the Natchitoches militia. In 1779, during the American Revolution, Spain declared war on Great Britain. The men in the militia were ordered by Colonel Bernardo de Gálvez to fight against the British. Pierre, a marechal de logis (quartermaster), was dispatched with Gálvez's troops as part of the cavalry. Pierre, along with other men in the Natchitoches militia, was ordered to participate in strikes against Fort Charlotte, Natchez, Mobile, Baton Rouge, and Manchac.[23]

Absence occasionally changes things between couples. They have time to revisit the decisions they have made. Marie Thérèse may have thought Pierre would be different when he returned from war. Would he still love and need her? Pierre may have pondered if Marie Thérèse would remain faithful during his absence. The images their minds conjured were not written for us to read. But, we do know that Pierre returned to his Marie Thérèse, and they continued their journey as a couple.

Having served his country, it was now time for Pierre to continue serving his family. With the exception of Dominique, six, and Eulalie, four, Pierre was in possession of his entire family. These two children, now, almost the age to begin working, may have prompted Pierre to take further action. It may have been a miserably wet day, as Aprils usually are, when Pierre appeared before Jean Louis Borme, Captain of the Militia and Commandant at the Natchitoches post. Despite the weather, on April 7, 1780, Pierre did come and did leave possessing six-year-old Dominique and four-year-old Eulalie after paying a sum of four hundred piastres (Spanish currency).[24]

With family now intact, this seemingly unstoppable relationship, which had weathered thirteen years of highs and lows, was not through contributing to the census of the tiny post. On December 9, 1780, the steadfast couple presented to the world, Marie Françoise Rosalie. Being of a free mother and father, she was the first of their children to be born free. Two years later, on October 31, 1782, with the business of buying complete, Pierre and Marie Thérèse brought into the world, child number nine, Pierre Toussaint.[25]

One year after the birth of Pierre Toussaint, Pierre discreetly composed a will in New Orleans providing for Marie Thérèse and their children. In this will, he acknowledged that Marie Thérèse was free, and indicated that no one was to take that freedom away. He also provided land for Marie Thérèse's children. Upon his death, his debts were to be paid and all remaining money was to be divided between his family in France and Marie Thérèse's Franco-African children. Two thirds of his estate was to go to his family in France and one third to the children. He also declared that as long as Marie Thérèse was alive she would have the use of any estate her children inherited from him.[26] Yet, in that same document, Pierre asserted that he was a bachelor and professed that he had no children. For years I have wondered why such an assertion was made when at the Natchitoches post it was no secret that Pierre had fathered the children and surely he cared for their mother. His will was such a paradox. Only recently did I understand that Code Noir forbade whites "to make paternal bequests to children of color." So in essence, Pierre was not denying the children; he was protecting and securing their future.[27]

Leaving or Staying

Now that she was free, some might conclude that Marie Thérèse and her free children, Marie Françoise, Joseph, and Pierre Toussaint would long for a space of their own. This was not the situation. In spite of the fact that Marie Thérèse was free to go anywhere her heart desired, she chose to continue her journey with her former owner, lover, and the father of her children.

Did she not leave because by doing so she would have to abandon her other children? Though she was their mother, they were the property of their father. In order to take them with her, she would have to buy them, and she was not a woman of means. Or was it devotion inspired by fourteen years of ordeals and struggles that forced her to stay with Pierre? Marie Thérèse knew, and so did Pierre, but some secrets are kept between lovers. For reason only they shared, Marie Thérèse remained with Pierre. And on September 26, 1784, at the age of forty-two, she presented Pierre with the tenth and final gift from their union, a boy-child, François.[28]

Unfortunately, love, devotion, shared hardships and condemnation are not always enough to keep a family together, and so it was with Marie Thérèse and Pierre. For sixteen years, the two had fought as one and had been virtually inseparable. In the worst of times, and in the best of times, they had supported one another. But two years after the birth of François, with motives only shared by the couple, they went their separate ways; he to a wife, Marie Thérèse Buard, who better suited society's mores, and she to a life that would almost certainly shock even the most liberal thinkers of today.

Searching For Bertha

Contract of sale of four young mulatto slaves by Madame Marie de Saint Denis, wife of Don Manuel Desoto to Pierre Metoyer, 31 May 1776[29]
Translated by Linda S. Manuel

Natchitoches Colonial Archives, Courthouse Book of Conveyance Number 10, Document Number 1161

At the post of Saint Jean Baptiste des Natchitoches today the thirty-first day of the month of May of the year one thousands seven hundred seventy-six, before me Athanase de Mezieres Lieutenant Governor of this said post, were present the ones named Nicolas Fournier and François Doucet, my undersigned witnesses of assistance, appeared in person Madame Marie de Saint Denys, wife of Don Manuel de Soto, absent, who recognizes and declares to have sold, ceded, quitted, transported, and left from now and forever, to Sieur Pierre Metoyer, inhabitant of this said place, here present and accepting, to enjoy, himself, his heirs, and assigns, and promises to guarantee to him four head of young mulatto slaves, here named, Marie Susanne, Nicolas Augustin, Louis and Pierre: for the price and sum of two thousand livres in silver, and a young negro boy of ten or twelve years; which two thousand livres the said Dame Marie de Saint Denis recognizes to have received in good currency from the said Mr. Pierre Metoyer and with regard to the above said young negro that he had to furnish said to the above-said mentioned lady that the above –said place? [very faint] had counted him in various supplies that he had made to her, as well as in some notes and silver money, the sum of thirteen hundred livres, of which she agrees and satisfies and discharges the above-said acquiring sir towards and against all. By means of which agreement and of the certificate of the annotator of mortgages, which the above-said lady, seller will cause to become evident for the most brief review possible, by which the above-said four mulatto slaves will verified to be free and clear of all charge and mortgage in order for the said certificate be annexed to the present sale and to validate it, making the above-said free and acquitted, one towards the other. So it was agreed between the parties, in testimony of which they have signed with me the above said Lieutenant Governor and the two above-said witnesses, of which I have evidence.1

/s/ Metoyer /s/ Marie de St. Denis
/s/ De Mézières /s/ Nicolas Fournier
/s/ F. Doucet

Metoyer Purchases Dominique & Sister from Marie de St. Denis Desoto [30]

Today, the seventh day of the month of April, one thousand seven hundred eighty, before me, Jean Louis Borme, Captain of the Militia, Commandant at the Post of Natchitoches, and in the presence of the witnesses here-after named, in default of notary and of public writer in this place, in performing the functions is appeared in person, Dame Marie de Saint Denis Desoto, an inhabitant residing in this place; the which has voluntarily recognized and confessed to have this day here sold and delivered from now and forever, to the Sir Pierre Metoyer, also (an) inhabitant residing in this place at this present time, and accepting for himself, his heirs and legal successors, two small slaves, Dominique, mulatto, aged six years, and one small mulatress his sister, aged about four years, whom the said lady endorsed guaranty from all reclamation claims, debts, and mortgages whatsoever, and recognizes to have had and received from the said sir, the buyer, in cash, the sum of four hundred piastres as the price of the above-said two small slaves, presently rendered, of which it was acquitted sir, the buyer; the which is also pleased and satisfied, having received the said two small slaves, this was thus done and passed at Natchitoches, the day and year above-said, in the presence of Messieurs Miguel Metch [? Name indistinct & cut off at margin] and Louis DeBlanc, witnesses, who have signed with the said parties and me, the above-said commandant, of which I do have faith.

    Metoyer   Marie de St.Denis
    Mr. Miguel Menechaca
    Serg.?

                                            Louis De Blanc
                                               Witness
                                                Borme

Claude Thomas Pierre Metoyer, Marie Therese CoinCoin, and Family

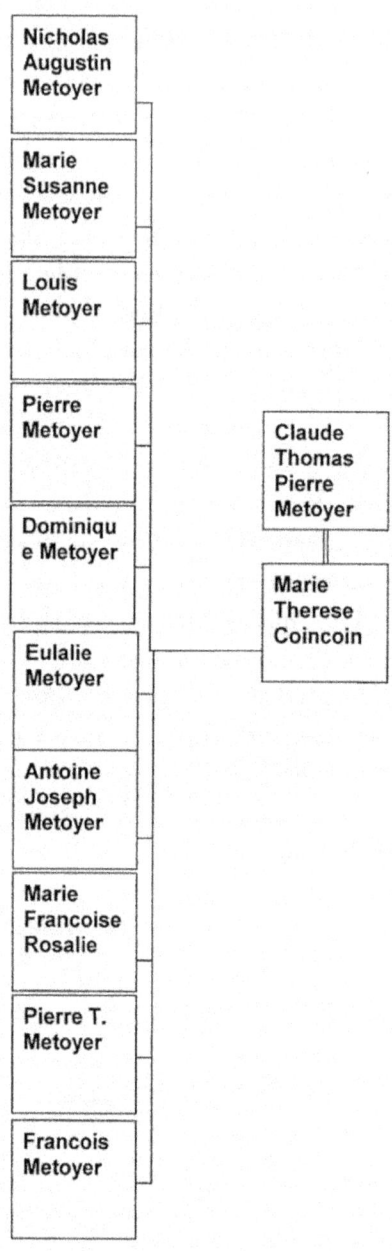

Endnotes

1. Burton and Smith, *Colonial Natchitoches,* 21, 29.

2. Mills, E. S., *Natchitoches Colonials,* 9-14; Burton and Smith, *Colonial Natchitoches,* 65, 93.

3. Mills, E. S., "Documenting a Slave's Birth," 260-61.

4. Pierre Metoyer to Athanase De Mézières, 1777, *Rex v. de Soto,* Natchitoches Colonial Archives, document no. 1227; Clerk of Court Office; Natchitoches, La.

5. Mills, E. S., *Natchitoches, 1729-1803,* entry 921.

6. "Marne, France Marriages, 1529-1907," accessed December 2009, entries for Jean Metoyer, Catherine Oudin, Suzanne Delaitre, and Françoise Galoteau; Saint-Sauveur Parish (La Rochelle, France), Parish Registers, Cote 5 Mi 1104, Nicolas Metoyer-Marie Suzanne Vinault marriage entry, 11 December 1748; photocopies provided by Ms. Methvin.

7. Mills, G., *Forgotten People,* 12.

8. Elizabeth Shown Mills, "Quintanilla's Crusade, 1775-1783: 'Moral Reform' and Its Consequences on the Natchitoches Frontier," *Louisiana History 42* (Summer 2001): 277-302, specifically p.281 for Stanislaus era.

9. Mills, E. S., *Natchitoches, 1729-1803,* entry 2283.

10. "Louisiana's Code Noir (1724)," Quintard Taylor, et al., *BlackPast.org: Remembered & Reclaimed,* accessed February 2, 2010, http://www.blackpast.com/?q=primary/louisianas-code-noir-1724.

11. Contract of sale of four young mulatto slaves by Madame Marie de Saint Denis [Marie Susanne, Nicolas Augustin, Louis, and Pierre], 1776 Natchitoches Colonial Archives, book 10, document No. 1161, Natchitoches Clerk of Court, trans. Linda S. Manuel.

12. Father Luis Quintanilla to Athanase. De Mézières, 1777, *Rex v. de Soto.*

13. Gary Mills, "The Ancestry of Sieur Nicolas Augustin Metoyer, fmc, Patriarch of Isle Brevelle," The Natchitoches Genealogist, 8 (October 1984) 28, citing Father Quintanilla to A. De Mèziéres, *Rex v. de Soto.*

14. De Mézières to Pierre Metoyer and Pierre Metoyer to De Mézière, 1777, *Rex v. de Soto.*

15. "Louisiana's Code Noir (1724)," Taylor, et al., *BlackPast.org.*

16. Mills, "Quintanilla's Crusade," 282-83.

17. Mills, E. S., *Natchitoches, 1729-1803,* entry 2324.

18. Father Quintanilla to De Mézières, 1778, *Rex v. de Soto.*

19. Marie de St. Denis de Soto to De Mézières, 1778, *Rex v. de Soto.*

20. Marie de St. Denis to Pierre Metoyer, doc. no. 1312; Mills, E. S., *Natchitoches, 1729-1803,* entry 2324.

21. "Louisiana's Code Noir (1724)," Taylor, et al., *BlackPast.org.*

22. Claude Thomas Pierre Metoyer Last Will and Testament, February 26, 1783, Acts of Leonardo Mazange, vol. 7, New Orleans Notarial Archives; Civil Courts Building, New Orleans, 188-91.

23. John Walton Caughey, *Bernardo de Galvez in Louisiana: 1776-1783* (Berkely, California: University of California Press, 1934) 152-154, 172-182.

24. Purchase of Dominique and Eulalie Metoyer, 1780, Natchitoches Colonial Archives, document no. 1473.

25. Mills, E. S., *Natchitoches, 1729-1803,* entries 2383, 2426.

26. Metoyer's will, 1783, Acts of Leonardo Mazange, vol. no. 7, 188-91.

27. Mills, E. S., "Marie Therese Coincoin (1742-1816)," citing Hans W. Baade, "The Law of Slavery in Spanish Luisiana, 1769-1803," in Louisiana Legal Heritage, ed. Edward F. Haas (Pensacola, Fla.: Perdido Bay Press, 1983), 43-86; Louis Moreau-Lislet and Henry Carleton, trans., *The Laws of Las Siete Partidas Which Are Still in Force in the State of Louisiana,* 2 vols. (New Orleans: James M'Karaher, 1820), esp. 210, articles 10, 12, and 14.

28. Mills, E. S., *Natchitoches, 1729-1803,* entry 2489.

29. Contract of sale of four young mulatto slaves by Madame Marie de Saint Denis.

30. "Metoyer Purchases Dominique & Sister from Marie de St. Denis," document no. 1473, Natchitoches Colonial Archives, trans. Transcription Services, Ltd.

Chapter 7

Two Lives Diverge

The reasons couples separate are varied, and sometimes falling in or out of love has no bearing on their decision. Some choose to stay when there is no love, and some choose to leave in spite of an undying love. Some love and never marry, while others marry and never love. Which was the case with Pierre and Marie Thérèse? Pierre's actions spoke volumes when his words could not.

Before Pierre severed intimate ties with Marie Thérèse, he initiated some life altering plans. In 1786, two years after the birth of their son, François, Pierre assisted Marie Thérèse in obtaining a concession in her own name for a tract of sixty-eight acres. This was a replacement for the property he had willed to his children in his unprobated 1783 will.[1] This land was adjacent to Pierre's property. In 1787, Pierre's longtime friend, Étienne Pavie, with whom Pierre was engaged in business, was assassinated. Marie Thérèse and Pierre had once shared a home with Étienne. Étienne, like Pierre, was initially a merchant, and he, along with his wife, had become landowners and slaveholders. A year after Étienne's demise, Pierre married Étienne's thirty-six year old widow, Marie Thérèse Buard.[2] In Pierre's marriage contract to the Widow Pavie, he specifically detailed that the Franco-African children he held in slavery, born of the previous Marie Thérèse, would *not* be part of the couple's community property. In the contract, Pierre also declared that it would be his privilege *alone* to free the children as he chose.[3] Surely, his new wife was privy to the fact that the children were not only her fiancée's slaves but his offspring. Pierre and the first Marie Thérèse had once lived openly in the home of her deceased husband, Étienne. *Five* days before his October 13th marriage to Marie Thérèse Buard, on October 8, 1788, Pierre, *privately*, instituted a lifetime annuity to Marie Thérèse, his ex-lover and the mother of his ten children, in the amount of one hundred twenty piasters.[4] This annuity was later annulled, but Marie Thérèse had enjoyed the fruits of the endowment for an extensive period of time, because the renouncement of the 1788 annuity did not take place until fourteen years later in 1802. At this time Marie Thérèse was a slave owner. In the written renouncement of the

53

annuity Marie Thérèse indicated, "Sieur [Pierre] Metoyer is well and duly relieved of the obligation to pay me each year the said annuity, which from this moment is paid off, just as though God had at this moment taken me from this world."[5] The actions taken by Pierre prior to his marriage to his wife are indicative of a man whose heart and soul remained with his lover and the mother of his children, Marie Thérèse. Was this a marriage generated out of love, convenience, or a promise kept that had been given to a dying friend?

Marie Thérèse (the mother of Pierre's ten children), now in her forties, had a tract of land on which to build a future, her children secure with their father, and money that Pierre pledged to pay her throughout her lifetime. It was up to her to determine her destiny. And determine her destiny she definitely would.

As for Pierre, he began a life with a French wife who better suited society's mores. Less than a year after his marriage, on September 5, 1789, he had a new son, Pierre Victorin. A year later, on November 14, 1790, his only daughter by the new Marie Thérèse, Marie Thérèse Elisabeth, was born. Less than four years later, on July 11, 1794, François Benjamin was born.[6] As Pierre's family expanded, so did his prosperity. He eventually became the largest slaveholder in Natchitoches parish (owning over 100 slaves).[7]

With fortitude and determination, the previous Marie Thérèse, once a slave, set out to make her mark in life, and at times, lingering by her side, was Pierre. As mentioned earlier, with Pierre's assistance, she petitioned the commandant for a concession and her petition was approved for 80 arpents (68 acres) as a replacement for the property that Pierre had willed the children in his unprobated 1783 will. With Pierre's support, Marie Thérèse resolved a dispute over the title and received an order of survey and settlement from the colonial land office. However, the absence of a surveyor at the post would postpone her receipt of the final title until 1795.[8] With title in hand, she endeavored to make the most of her life. She did what others did at the Natchitoches post—she cultivated her land.

Marie Thérèse's initial crop of choice was tobacco, a crop that was said to be challenging for even the most proficient farmer. For a period of time, this was a savvy choice that several planters in the area had made. With the fertile bottom lands and access to the rivers, tobacco production was an ideal crop for the Natchitoches area. It was one of the prime crops from the 1720s until 1731. Unfortunately, when the French government first took over, in 1731, it failed to support tobacco production. But, in the 1760s, the price of tobacco rose to an all-time high and over half the households in Natchitoches produced the crop. Strong interest in the tobacco began to deteriorate in the late 1770s, but it peaked again in the 1780s when the production of the crop was once again encouraged by the Spanish Crown. In 1789, Natchitoches produced 400,000 pounds of tobacco, and in 1790 production almost doubled.[9] With her children and her steely determination, Marie Thérèse's tobacco farm became a success, and she was able to send barges of her tobacco crop to New Orleans.[10]

Another crop that may have been cultivated by Marie Thérèse was indigo.[11] Indigo is a plant that is utilized to dye cotton and wool. It was originally cultivated in Louisiana in the early 1720s. Seeds were brought into Louisiana from Saint Domingue along with a Black worker who was knowledgeable about the plant. Unfortunately indigo did not yield much profit.[12] In the late 1770s it gained favor again by those who had the sufficient slaves to cultivate the crop. It was a plant that required an enormous deal of labor and consumed a significant amount of time. It would not be until the 1790s when it would bring profit to a number of the wealthier planters in Natchitoches.[13]

Marie Thérèse, an astute businesswoman, was not one to miss lucrative business ventures. She seemed cognizant of profitable enterprises. When interest peaked in the livestock industry, she invested in a *vacherie* (cattle ranch). In 1769, when Spain was in control of Louisiana, the commercial livestock industry advanced. Land concessions were granted to residences in order to encourage development of ranches. During the late 1700s and the early 1800s, ranch ownership tripled in the Natchitoches area. Forty-one residents owned vacheries along the Red River. These concessions were seen by some as an opportunity for family investments.[14] In 1794, Marie Thérèse sighted an opportunity, applied to the commandant for 800 arpents of land, and established her *vacherie*. Leaving the fertile bottomlands for raising crops, vacheries were commonly in the forested area of the town. Marie Thérèse's *vacherie* was situated among the pine trees west of the Old River. Like her fellow businessmen, she did not reside on her *vacherie*. Owning at least a hundred head of cattle, Marie Thérèse employed a Spaniard, José Maré, to tend her enormous herd. Maré not only managed her ranch, but he also cultivated corn and other vegetables for her.[15]

Although it is evident that Marie Thérèse owned this land, there has been speculation about her land title. Her original concession was issued under the name of Marie Thérèse, free *négresse*. The surname Metoyer was later generated on the paperwork by the American land officials. Her son, Pierre Metoyer, had created the paperwork. Assuming Pierre and his mother used the same surname, the American land office officials assigned the Metoyer surname to her land document.[16]

In addition to the farm and vacherie, in 1807 Marie Thérèse bought more farmland from Jean Baptiste LaLande. It was this land that she sold to her son, Pierre Toussaint, in 1814. Like the white planters and landowners in Natchitoches, Marie Thérèse understood the significance of land ownership. With three tracts of land, she was well positioned as a landowner.[17]

Although land ownership was important, Marie Thérèse and her sons did not shy away from other less desirable ways of making a profit. They killed bears and sold the furs and grease made from the bear fat. Bear fat was utilized for cooking oil and lard. It was also used as a substitute for butter and olive oil.[18] Familiar with the medicinal properties of plants, she may also have manufactured medicines.[19] All these endeavors, she did in preparation for her ultimate goal – buying and emancipating her Black enslaved children who were conceived prior to her liaison with Pierre. Her Franco-African children, who were in their father's care, were only slaves in technicality. They were given liberties that any father would grant his offspring. The children were just not free in accordance with Louisiana laws. These children, Marie Thérèse may have concluded, were not an imminent concern.

Marie Thérèse first purchase was her oldest daughter, twenty-seven year old Marie Louise, from slave owner Pierre Dolet.[20] Historians write that Louise was first bought and emancipated in 1786, but because of certain technicalities her mother had to proclaim her freedom again in 1795.[21] The manumission document revealed that "Marie Thérèse Coinquin," "renounces once for all time the slavery of the said Louise, her slave and daughter, who thanks her mother and promises to conduct herself as an honest woman and in obedience to our laws."[22]

In 1790, four years after buying Louise, Marie Thérèse bought her second oldest child and namesake, Thérèse, and Thérèse's son, Joseph, from Madame de Soto. A price of seven hundred dollars was agreed upon for mother and son, with some stipulations. The provisions were that Thérèse and her son had to serve Madame de Soto until her death. Marie Thérèse gave Madame de Soto a down payment of fifty dollars and vowed to pay the remaining six hundred fifty dollars over time. It would be seven years later, in 1797, when Madame de Soto would die. At that time, Marie Thérèse emancipated Thérèse and her son. After buying Thérèse and her son and while waiting to emancipate them, Marie Thérèse bought and freed another grandchild, five-year-old Catiche. Catiche was the daughter of her son, Louis. She paid one hundred and fifty dollars for her freedom.[23]

The same year Thérèse was finally freed, Marie Thérèse made plans to obtain and free her oldest son, Nicolas Chiquito. In 1772, Madame de Soto, Marie Thérèse's owner and godmother, heavily in debt, had sold Nicolas in order to buy some property along with housing at Los Adaes, the nearby Spanish post. It would be twenty-five years later when Marie Thérèse would send her second-oldest son, Augustin, to Nacogdoches with three hundred pesos to obtain the freedom of his brother. From September 23-25, 1797, there were proceedings in Nacogdoches regarding Augustin's petition to redeem Nicolas Chiquito from slave owner Antonio Gil Ibarvo.[24] With Augustin's assistance, Marie Thérèse finally procured and freed her first born son.

Marie Thérèse labored hard to buy and free her two oldest daughters, her oldest son, and two grandchildren, but she would never fully realize her dreams of freedom for all her children. She was unable to buy her fourth child, her third daughter, Françoise. Despite Code Noir, Marie Thérèse's owner and godmother, Madame de Soto, had sold Françoise, as she had sold Nicolas Chiquito. Money from the purchase of Françoise was to help pay debts left by Madame de Soto's husband, Manuel Bermudes y de Soto who had been sent to prison. Françoise was later resold to a planter in the region. Upon his death, she was sold again by his widow to her new husband. Françoise and her children remained with this family. Although her daughter lived only a short distance away in Opelousas, Louisiana, as a mother, I believe Marie Thérèse longed for her daughter's freedom throughout her lifetime.[25]

As for Marie Thérèse's fifth born child, Jean Joseph, destiny is an enigma. There are no records that indicate whether he survived past childhood, was freed, or left the vicinity. If he did not survive, or was not freed, Marie Thérèse had not one enslaved child to long for, but two.

While Marie Thérèse worked to make her mark in the world, Pierre, now married, was reluctant, or incapable of completely abandoning his ex-lover and was occasionally involved with her transactions. In 1792 when Pierre shipped a barge of goods to New Orleans, Marie Thérèse goods were shipped along with his. The passport for shipping the merchandise authorized two mulattoes to man the vessel. These two mulattoes, in all probability, were their enslaved sons, Augustin and Louis.[26]

In 1794, Marie Thérèse had acquired a concession for 800 more arpents (677 acres) of land in a grant from the Spanish government to be used for a cattle business.[27] Coincidentally, this petition for land was prepared at the same time that Pierre filed a similar petition.[28] Despite Pierre's marriage to the Widow Pavie, it appears as if Pierre had not completely severed ties to his mate of sixteen years.

Marie Thérèse had established herself as a landowner and an asset to her community. Unlike many in her community, she paid her taxes in a judicious manner.[29] Having been a slave, she understood the privileges and responsibilities associated with freedom. In Natchitoches, between 1774 and 1803, eighty-four slaves were freed. Nine were freed by white females and sixty-nine by white males. Marie Thérèse was the only free woman of color in Natchitoches to free at least five slaves.[30] As a slave her worth had been appraised by her owner at $1000; at the time of her death, her wealth surpassed the wealth of the majority of the residents in Natchitoches.[31] Bertha's fourth great-grandmother, Marie Thérèse Coincoin, was someone whom she could be immensely proud.

Marie Therese, Coinquin, Purchases and Frees Marie Louise
Natchitoches Colonial Archives, Book 26-A, Doc. 2596

Today, [the] Twenty-ninth Day of the Month of January of The year one thousand, Seven Hundred Ninety-five Before Me Don Louis Charles DeBlanc, Captain of Infantry of the Armies of the King, Commander, Civil and Military, of the Post of the Natchitoches and dependency, in default of [a] Notary and Public Writer in this place, in performing the functions: was present Marie Thereze Coinquin, free Negress, Residing in this Post, who declares and Confesses to have by these presents, of her Pure, and Entire Will, without any Constraint, but Well of her own volition, Given and granted Liberty to the Named Marie Louise, Her slave and her daughter, the which she has purchased from Sr. Pierre Dolet, By [a] Sale Taken place in this Office, so that from this day and in the Future, she Should Peacefully enjoy of the said Liberty, with all the Privileges accorded to the freed, without Experiencing the least Obstacle, nor opposition on her Part, nor on that of her heirs, or legal Successor, Being thus her Will, Wishes and Intends [it] should be accomplished without any restriction, and to this effect it declares, As firm, Stable and forever irrevocable, and in the Contrary Case Gives Power to Justices of His Majesty to Be Aware of her affairs and to compel to the execution of these Presents, As having the substance of a legal Action Judged, And Renounces Once and for All The Slavery of the said Marie Louise, her Slave and her daughter, who Gives Thanks her Mother and Promises to Conduct Herself as an honest woman and under Obedience to our Laws; For This was thus done and Passed at the said Place of the Natchitoches, the Same day and year as at the Head, in the said Presence of the Sieurs François Rouquier and Paul Marcollay, witnesses, who have signed with the said Marie Thereze Coinquin, who, not knowing how to write, has made her ordinary mark of a cross, whereof I bear witness,

Rouquier,
Ordinary mark of
   X
Marie Thereze Coinquin
Paul Marcollay Witness
Louis De Blanc[32]

Freedom Realized

As Marie Thérèse was procuring and emancipating the children she had given birth to before her liaison with Pierre, Pierre began freeing their Franco-African children. Conceivably, the catalyst that set the wheels in motion may have been witnessing Marie Thérèse emancipating her Black children. These children were enjoying liberties while their half sisters and brothers, Pierre's own offspring, were still enslaved.

Between 1774 and 1803, eighty-four slaves were emancipated in Natchitoches. Of those, whose ages were revealed and who were of the same racial identity as the Metoyer children, the majority, twenty-three, were between the ages of one and thirteen. Only fourteen were between the ages of fourteen and forty-nine.[1] Of the children Pierre freed, only one, Antoine Joseph, was a small child. The other children, Augustin, Susanne, Louis, Pierre, and Dominique were all adults ranging in age from nineteen to forty-seven. Did Pierre justify that keeping his children enslaved was in essence protecting them? Though not typical in Louisiana, freed slaves could be captured and enslaved never to be seen again. Did he free them because it was the only way they could marry? His sons married within days after they were emancipated. Or, had the immorality of keeping his children as slaves come to haunt him as he faced his own mortality? And why, I question, did he enslave his children for so long? These questions will forever be in my mind; but, realistically, I know the answers to these inquiries have long since been interred with Pierre.

Despite his intentions, on August 1, 1792, sixteen years after he purchased his oldest son, Augustin, Pierre decided to free his then twenty-five-year-old son. By this time, his son was almost the same age his mother was when she first encountered Pierre. Coincidentally, or not, according to laws in Pierre's homeland, preceding 1789, a father had authority over his son until he reached twenty-five; it was at this time, the law specified, that the son would be able to create wills, contracts, and acquire other forms of legal responsibility.[3] Pierre may have been so entrenched in the laws of his homeland that he felt this was the proper age at which to release Augustin. Within a few weeks after Augustin received his freedom, he married Marie Agnes Poissot.[4] Three years later, in 1795, Pierre freed Dominique.[5] He was much younger than Augustin when he was emancipated. At the age of nineteen, a free man, he immediately married fourteen-year-old Marguerite Lecomte.[6]

It would be seven years later before fifty-eight year old Pierre would grant the rights and privileges that freedom brought to Augustin and Dominique to three of his other children, Pierre, Louis, and Augustin's twin, Marie Susanne.

But finally, on May 28, 1802, with the swipe of a pen and the blessing of their father, the three were declared free. Louis was now thirty-two, Pierre thirty, and Susanne thirty-four. Regrettably, for Susanne, her freedom came with specifications (perhaps because she was the girl-child). Susanne had to pledge to care for her father and his wife for as long as they survived. She would not truly experience freedom until 1815, two years after the death of Pierre's wife.[7] When her father died, Susanne was a middle-aged forty-seven year old woman.

Pierre had finally freed all of his enslaved children with the exception of Eulalie. Of all the children, for me she is a mystery that has yet to be unraveled. I am at a lost as to why there are no records indicating her emancipation. It was Pierre's intention to free six of his enslaved children, and records clearly indicate that he freed five of them. Could Eulalie have died before she could be granted freedom? Did she die at an early age? No records have been disclosed indicating the time of, or reason for, her demise. It is known that in 1780, when Pierre purchased Eulalie, she was about four years old.[8] Three years later, in 1783, at age seven, Eulalie was alive because her name was contained within the will that Pierre had quietly filed in New Orleans.[9] On October 8, 1788, at the age of twelve she was also alive. This is known because in Pierre's marriage contract to Marie Thérèse Buard, transcribed on that date, he reiterated that he reserved the right to free his six *mulatto* slaves. Eulalie was identified as one of those six slaves. It was not until 1801 when Pierre composed his final will that the death of Eulalie was revealed.[10] The earliest she could have died would be after October 8, 1788 about age twelve, and the latest would be May 1801 about age twenty-five. Possibly, one day, the missing portion of this enigma will be uncovered. For this, I eagerly wait.

To the outside observer, it had taken Pierre a long time and undoubtedly a great amount of soul searching before he freed his Franco-African children. But, finally, he no longer controlled their destinies. His six oldest children (by his former slave, lover, and soul mate) had finally realized freedom; a freedom their half sisters and brothers, by Marie Thérèse Buard (his French-European wife), recognized as their God given privilege.

With the exception of Françoise, all of Marie Thérèse's children now realized their visions of freedom. It was time for the former slave to convert to a slave owner.

Emancipation of Augustin Metoyer[43]

At the Post of Natchitoches, the first of August of the year one thousand seven hundred ninety two, before me, D[o]n Louis Charles DeBlanc, Lieutenant of the Armies, Captain of the Calvary of Militias, Commandant, Civil and Military, of the said Post and Dependency, in default of Notary and Public Writer in this said place, in performing the functions [i.e. those duties]; is appeared Monsieur Claude Thomas Pierre Metoyer, Agent of this Post, the which by these presents, of his pure and entire will, in (the) using of the rights which the law (to) him accords, and in the best form which may be able to take place in justice, and by virtue of the freedom which he has reserved (to) himself in his contract of marriage with the lady Thérèse Buard, Widow Pavie, declares and confesses that being satisfied, with the services and fidelity of his mulatto slave named Nicolas Augustin, aged about twenty five years, that his intention is that he should take enjoyment, from this day and for always, from the privilege of (the) enfranchised, (to) him granting to this effect, without any restriction whatsoever, the most extensive and entire liberty, so that he use it peacefully, without being forever disturbed, either by himself, nor his heirs, or having cause, for thus is his will, and (he) promises to hold as firm, stable, and irrevocable the content to the present [i.e. theses presents], and in the contrary case, gives power to the justice of His Majesty to be aware of these affairs and to compel him to the execution of the said presents, this was thus done and passed at the said place of the Natchitoches, the same day and year as at (the) head, in (the) presence of the Sieurs Paul Marcollay and André Rambin, witnesses of assistance here residing, who have signed with the said Sieur Claude Thomas Pierre Metoyer and Me, (the) above-said Commandant of which I do faith.   Pierre Metoyer

André Rambin   Paul Marcollay
                    Louis DeBlanc

Louis Metoyer Granted Liberty[44]

Today the twenty-eight of the month of May of the year one thousand eight hundred and two, I Pierre Metoyer, habitant of this post of Natchitoches, by virtue of my contract of marriage with Therese Buard, presently my spouse, passed before the notary of said post, on date of ten October of the year one thousand seven hundred eighty-eight, by which it is noted that I thereunder reserved for myself the right and the power of giving liberty when it seemed proper to me, without which my said spouse would be able to oppose that in any manner whatsoever, to six young mulatto or mulattress slaves named in the said contract, who are independent of our community property; in consequence of this privilege the name LOUIS, mulatto, son of Marie Therese called Coin Coin, free Negress, having always served me faithfully and exactly, always conducting himself to my satisfaction, wishing to recompense him for the good service that he has rendered me, who was in a position to gain escape everywhere that he found himself; to these considerations I declare in the presence of Sieur Jean Baptiste Ailhaud Ste Anne, and Jean Baptiste Buard, required and undersigned witnesses, to having verbally given the first of January one thousand eight hundred one, liberty to said Louis, the which liberty I confirm this day and irrevocably declare him free before the said date, that he is master to go where it pleases him and enjoy the privileges accorded to franchised slaves; such is my wish, which is irrevocable. Therefore I have signed the present, written with my hand and of my own impulse in presence of witnesses named above and who equally signed. For this end that the present have complete and entire effect, at Natchitoches the said day and year which are there above, twenty-eight May, eighteen hundred and two. Made in duplicate.

/Signed/

Bte Buard witness   Metoyer

Ailhaud Ste anne witness

Pierre Metoyer Granted Liberty[45]

Today the twenty-eight of the month of May of the year one thousand eight hundred and two, I Pierre Metoyer, habitant of this post of Natchitoches, by virtue of my contract of marriage with Therese Buard, presently my spouse, passed before the notary of said post, on date of ten

October of the year one thousand seven hundred eighty-eight, by which it is noted that I thereunder reserved for myself the right and power of giving liberty when it seemed proper to me, without which my said spouse would be able to oppose that in any manner whatsoever, to six young mulatto or mulattress slaves named in the said contract who are independent of our community property; in consequence of this privilege the name PIERRE, mulatto son of Marie Therese called Coin Coin, free Negress, having always served me faithfully and exactly, always conducting himself to my satisfaction, wishing to recompense him for the good service that he has rendered me, who was in a position to gain escape everywhere that he found himself; to these considerations I declare in the presence of Sieur Jean Baptiste Ailhaud Ste Anne, and Jean Baptiste Buard, required and undersigned witnesses, that of this moment I give to him his liberty and declare him to be free at his will, that he is able to go where it pleases him and enjoy the privileges accorded to franchised slaves; such is my wish, which is irrevocable. Therefore I have signed the present, written with my hand and of my own impulse, in presence of witnesses named above and who have equally signed. For this end that the present have complete and entire effect, at Natchitoches the said day and year which there above, twenty-eighth May, eighteen hundred and two.

Made in duplicate

/Signed/

Bte Buard   witness   Metoyer

Ailhaud Ste anne witness

Marie Susanne Granted Liberty[46]

Today the twenty-eight of the month of May of the year one thousand eight hundred and two, I Pierre Metoyer, habitant of this post of Natchitoches, by virtue of my contract of marriage with Therese Buard, presently my spouse, passed before the notary of said post, on date of ten October of the year one thousand seven hundred eighty-eight, by which it is noted that I thereunder reserved for myself the right and power of giving liberty when it seemed proper to me, without which my said spouse would be able to oppose that in any manner whatsoever, to six young mulatto or mulattress slaves named in the said contract who are independent of our community property;

In consequence this privilege the named MARIE SUSANNE, mulattress, my slave, daughter of Marie Therese called Coincoin, free Negress, having always served with zeal, fidelity, and exactness, having conducted herself to my satisfaction, having by her service and her good attentions saved several lives in diverse maladies, also that of my wife and all our infants, having in fact nourished with her milk our son Benjamin, dry-nursed, raised, and managed our other children in their childhood and even to this day and several other important attentions which were rendered to us. In recognition of all her good services I declare by the present in presence of Sieur Jean Baptiste Ste Anne and Jean Baptiste Buard, required and undersigned witnesses, that as of the moment which it is pleasing to God to retire me from this world, that the said Marie Suzanne will be free, because of this my receiver, nor any of my heirs, or assignees will have no claim whatsoever on the product of her industry or savings which have been obtained by any talent and which she will be able to acquire in consequence, she having at all times been authorized and she is authorized by her master by the present to enjoy in appropriate measure the fruit of her economy, that her infants, their successors, born or to be born of her and those who will be born of her said children, to whom at the same time I give equally to them all their liberty, by the clauses which will all apply for their said mother, up to the age of majority or which they are deemed at their maturity, this to her consent. Such is my voluntary wish. It is why I have signed the present of my own initiative in the presence of witnesses above named and who have equally signed. To this end that the present have complete and entire effect. Made in duplicate by my own hand at Natchitoches, the said day and year which are above, twenty-eighth May, eighteen hundred and two

Marie Thérèse, Slave Owner

In the twenty-first century, there are still people unaware that thousands of free Blacks and free people of color owned slaves in the nineteenth century. Because of this lack of awareness, I have often been asked how someone who has experienced the perils of slavery can have the impudence to own slaves. Was it ethical? Was it politically correct? In all her wisdom, Marie Thérèse was probably able to justify her life decisions. She may have promised herself that she would ensure that her slaves had a better life than she and her parents had experienced. Giving slaves a better life, she may have rationalized, meant owning slaves but treating them respectfully. Being an astute businesswoman, she knew that money equated some degree of power, protection, and respect. Slave ownership afforded her the money needed to receive these things. Power, privilege, or empathy—no one but Marie Thérèse can discern her motivation for slave ownership. To second guess her motives would be to make implications I have no right to make. The decisions she made are hers alone. She did make them, and in the process, she forged a place in the chronicles of history for herself and her children.

Historical records indicate that Marie Thérèse continued to purchase land and slaves. In April of 1758, while still a slave, Marie Thérèse's worth was appraised for only $1,000 by her slave owner.[1] Once freed from her tethers, she worked endlessly, and during her lifetime she possessed nearly one thousand acres of land, and she may have owned at least sixteen slaves. At the Natchitoches post, she was the first Black slave owner.[2] Aside from her children and grandchildren who she purchased and immediately freed, she bought three other slaves—an African female and two African males.[3] The female slave, Marguerite, produced ten children who were also the property of Marie Thérèse. Slave records indicate that she sold or donated all her surviving slaves to her children prior to her death. On April 20, 1816, she sold or donated to Pierre, Jean, Louis, Augustine, and Susanne twelve slaves valued at $5,250.[4]

One might reason, because Marie Thérèse was a slave-owner in her own right, there would be no need for her to continue any type of relationship with Pierre. Her children were free and self-sufficient. She was an independent businesswoman and landowner. She had risen to a status that few of her class had dreamed. But it appears her new status did not dilute her fondness for Pierre. He assisted her with several of her business transactions, and her friendship with her lover persisted throughout his lifetime.

As though not to be left in life without Pierre, who died in 1815 at age seventy-one,[5] Marie Thérèse soon followed him. No records exist for the exact date of her death. She was alive in April 1816. This was when she last executed the sale of her property—both land and slaves. In December 1817, when her son, Pierre, drafted his marriage contract he indicated that she was deceased. She would have died between the ages of seventy-three and seventy-four years old. Marie Thérèse's life has been exposed for all to analyze, but her exact time of death is unknown. Descendants have asserted that she was buried in the same cemetery that held her beloved Pierre[6]—a cemetery not far from where she first laughed and cried, lived and loved, and exposed her wide, *perhaps* crooked grin to the world. In life, Marie Thérèse had made her mark as a remarkable woman, but in death, she, and her children would become legends.

Marie Thérèse's First Property and Homestead

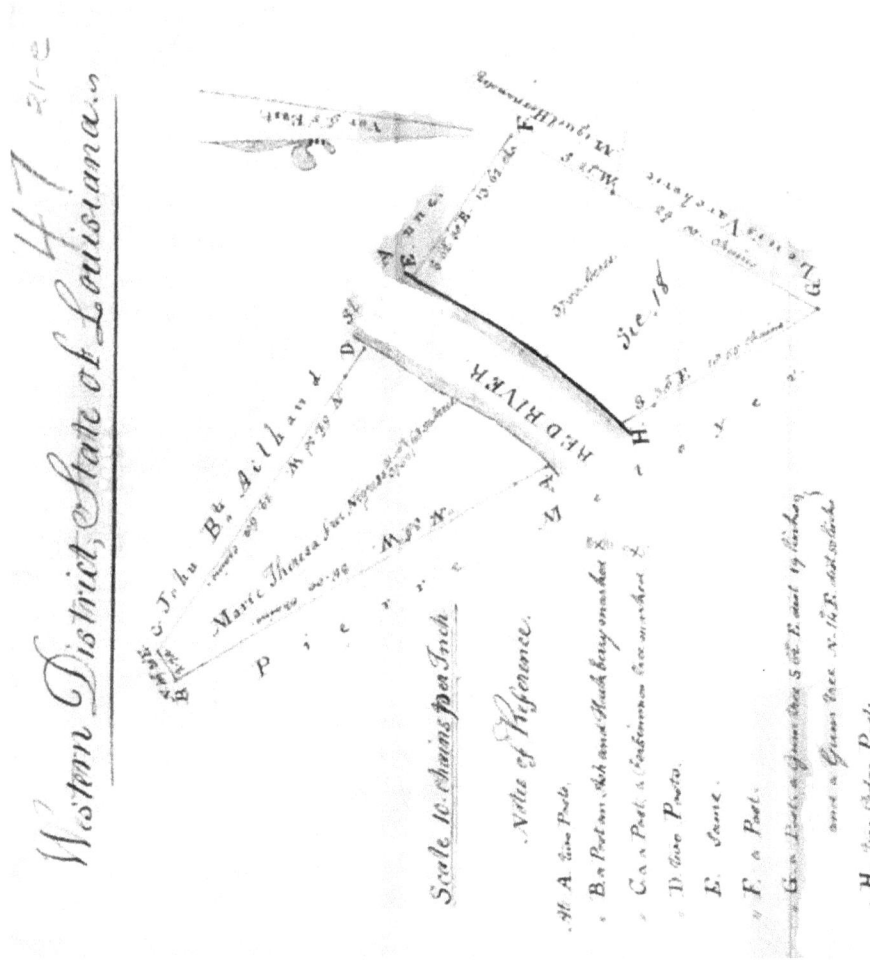

Section 18 and 89 State Land Office

Marie Thérèse's First Property and Homestead Claim[53]

Baton Rouge 07215.

4—1040-B.

The United States of America,

To all to whom these presents shall come, Greeting:

WHEREAS, there has been deposited in the General Land Office of the United States a Certificate of the Register of the Land Office at Baton Rouge, Louisiana, whereby it appears that the Private Land Claim of Marie Therese Metoyer was confirmed by the Old Board of Commissioners for the Western District of Louisiana, under authority conferred upon them by the Act of March 2, 1805 (2 Stat., 324), as evidenced by Certificate B-2146, issued December 15, 1812 (American State Papers, Gales and Seaton's edition, volume 2, page 866), and that the said claim has been duly surveyed to embrace Section fifty-five in Township eight north of Range seven west of the Louisiana Meridian, Louisiana, containing six hundred seventy-seven and ninety-four-hundredths acres, as shown by the township plat approved November 22, 1848:

NOW KNOW YE, That the UNITED STATES OF AMERICA, in consideration of the premises, HAS GIVEN AND GRANTED, and by these presents DOES GIVE AND GRANT, unto the said Marie Therese Metoyer, and to her heirs, the lands above described; TO HAVE AND TO HOLD the same, together with all the rights, privileges, immunities, and appurtenances, of whatsoever nature, thereunto belonging, unto the said Marie Therese Metoyer, and to her heirs and assigns forever.

IN TESTIMONY WHEREOF, I, **Woodrow Wilson** President of the United States of America, have caused these letters to be made Patent, and the seal of the General Land Office to be hereunto affixed.

GIVEN under my hand, at the City of Washington, the **TWENTY-FIRST** day of **OCTOBER** in the year of our Lord one thousand nine hundred and **FOURTEEN** and of the Independence of the United States the one hundred and **THIRTY-NINTH.**

(SEAL)

By the President: Woodrow Wilson

By M. O. LeRoy, Secretary.

S. C. Lamar, Recorder of the General Land Office.

RECORD OF PATENTS: Patent Number 437269

Endnotes

1. Elizabeth Shown Mills, "Demythicizing History: Marie Thérèse Coincoin, Tourism, and the National Historical Landmarks Program," *Louisiana History* 53 (Fall 2012): 410.

2. "Death of Étienne Pavie's Slave/Metoyer Was Witness," 1776 Natchitoches Colonial Archives (NCA) document no. 713, Office of the Clerk of Court, Natchitoches, Louisiana; Mills, E. S., and Mills, G., "Slaves and Masters," 169; Mills, *Natchitoches, 1729-1803*, entries 1347, 1552.

3. Pierre Metoyer to Marie Thérèse Coincoin, Donation, document no. 2119, Natchitoches Colonial Archives, Natchitoches Clerk of Court; Claude Thomas Pierre Metoyer's will (5 May 1801), Folder 1801, Melrose Collection, Cammie Henry Research Center, Watson Memorial Library, Northwestern State University, Natchitoches, Louisiana.

4. Metoyer to Marie Thérèse Coincoin, Donation, 1792, pg. 28, document no. 2119, Natchitoches Colonial Archives.

5. "Marie Thérèse Coincoin Renounces Annuity, 1802," Miscellaneous Book no. 2, pages 206, 207, Natchitoches Colonial Archives.

6. Mills, E. S., *Natchitoches, 1729-1803*, entries 1598, 2051, 2180.

7. 1810 U. S. census, Natchitoches Parish, Louisiana, town of Natchitoches, p. 209 (penned at top right), line 29, Pierre Metoyer; digital image, *Ancestry.com*, accessed December 5, 2010, http://search.ancestry.com/iexec?htx=view&r=0&dbid=7613&iid=4433226_00176&fn=Pierre&ln=Nictoyen&st=r&ssrc=&pid=17537; citing National Archives microfilm publication M252, roll 10.

8. Division of Administration, State of Louisiana, Historical Documents, Land claims, A-1 CLAIM PAPERS N.W.D. T.8N. R.5&6W, pg. 94, Maria Theresa, Free Negress, accessed December 1, 2012, https://wwwslodms.doa.la.gov. Mills, E. S., "Demythicizing History," 417-21.

9. Burton and Smith, *Colonial Natchitoches*, 127-35.

10. Mills, G., *Forgotten People*, 30, citing État de la Cargaison d'un Bateau Apartenant a Pierre Metoyer et d'un Gabarre a Marie Thérèse, in Holmes Collection, Reel 1.

11. Mills, G., *Forgotten People*, 31.

12. Giraud, *History of Louisiana*, 130-32.

13. Burton and Smith, *Colonial Natchitoches*, 139-40.

14. Ibid., 146, 160.

15. Mills, E. S., "Marie Thérèse Coincoin (1742-1816),"; Bureau of Land Management, "Land Patent Search," *U. S. General Land Office Records* accessed May 1, 2008, https://glorecords.blm.gov/PatentSearch, entry for Marie Therese Metoyer (Natchitoches Parish, Louisiana), Bureau of Land Management Serial no. 0007215;.Division of Administration, State of Louisiana, *Historical Documents*, document no. 510.00078, pg. 101, assessed December 1, 2012, https://wwwslodms.doa.la.gov.

16. *Historical Documents*, document no. 510.00078, pg. 101, accessed December 1,

2012, https://wwwslodms.doa.la.gov; Mills, G., *Forgotten People*, 33.

17. LaLande to Marie Thérèse, Natchitoches Original Conveyance Acts, book 42, document no. 501; Coincoin to Toussaint Metoyer, Natchitoches conveyance, book 3, 308-09.

18. Mills, E. S., "Marie Thérèse Coincoin (1742-1816)," 18; Giraud, *History of Louisiana*, 265-66.

19. Mills, E. S., "Marie Thérèse Coincoin (1742-1816)," 17, 18.

20. "Marie Thereze Coinquin Purchases and Frees Marie Louise, 1795"; Natchitoches Colonial Archives, book 26-A, document no. 2596, trans. Transcription Services, Ltd.

21. Mills, G., *Forgotten People*, 35

22. "Marie Thereze Coinquin Purchases and Frees Marie Louise, 1795."

23. Marie St. Denis to Marie Thérèze Coincoin, document 2807, Natchitoches Colonial Archives; Marguerite LeRoy, Widow LeComte to Marie Thérèze Coincoin, 1794, document no.2550, Marie Thérèze Coincoin to Catiche, 1794, documents no. 2552, Natchitoches Colonial Archives.

24. Mills, E. S., and. Mills, G., "Slaves and Masters," 171-72 ; "Proceedings concerning Nicolas Augustin's Petition to redeem his brother Nicolas Chiquito, a negro slave of Antonio Gil Ibarvo," 23-25 September 1797, Blake Collection, Vol. III, Supplement, 355–58, Bexar Archives, University of Texas, Austin, Texas.

25. Mills, E. S., and Mills, G., "Slaves and Masters," 171.

26. Mills, G., *Forgotten People*, 40, 41.

27. *U. S. General Land Office Records*, accessed May 1, 2008, https://glorecords.blm.gov/PatentSearch; *Historical Documents*, accessed December 1, 2012, https://wwwslodms.doa.la.gov.

28. Mills, G., *Forgotten People*, 33.

29. Mills, E. S, "Marie Thérèse Coincoin (1742-1816)," 22.

30. Burton and Smith, *Colonial Natchitoches*, 100.

31. Mills, E. S., and Mills, G., "Slaves and Master," 170.

32. "Marie Thereze Coinquin Purchases and Frees Marie Louise, 1795."

33. Burton and Smith, *Colonial Natchitoches*, 94-95.

34. Ibid.; "Manumission of Augustin Metoyer, 1792"; Natchitoches Colonial Archives, Document no. 2409.

35. Traer, *Marriage and the Family*, 139.

36. Mills, E. S., *Natchitoches 1729-1803*, entry 3389.

37. "Manumission of Dominique Metoyer, 1795," Natchitoches Colonial Archives, document no. 2584, trans. Gary B. Mills and Elizabeth Shown Mills, 1972.

38. Mills, E. S., *Natchitoches 1729-1803*, entry 3401.

39. "Manumission of Louis, Pierre, and Marie Susanne Metoyer," Miscellaneous Book no. 2, 208-10, Natchitoches Parish Records, Office of the Clerk of Court, trans. Gary B. Mills and Elizabeth Shown Mills, 1972.

40. "Metoyer Purchases His Two Slave Children Dominique and Sister from St. Denis' Daughter," document no. 1473, Natchitoches Colonial Archives.

41. Claude Thomas Pierre Metoyer's will (1783), Acts of Leonardo Mazange, vol. 78, 187-91, Notarial Archives, New Orleans, Louisiana.

42. Claude Thomas Pierre Metoyer's will (5 May 1801), Folder 1801, Melrose Collection, Cammie Henry Research Center, Watson Memorial Library, Northwestern State University, Natchitoches, Louisiana, specifically page 7, paragraph 3. Pierre reiterates term of 1788 marriage contract to Marie Thérèse Buard that concerns his six mulatto slaves.

43. "Manumission of Nicolas Augustin," Bundle 1792, Book of Conveyances no. 22, document no.2409, Natchitoches Colonial Archives, Office of the Clerk of Court, Natchitoches, Louisiana, translation 2013 by Translation Services Limited with minor corrections by Linda S. Manuel.

44. "Louis Metoyer Granted Liberty," Miscellaneous Book 2, 208, Clerk of Court's Office, Natchitoches, Louisiana, trans. Gary B. Mills and Elizabeth Shown Mills, 1972.

45. "Pierre Metoyer Granted Liberty," Miscellaneous Book 2, 209, Clerk of Court's Office, Natchitoches, Louisiana, trans. Gary B. Mills and Elizabeth Shown Mills, 1972.

46. Marie Suzanne Metoyer Granted Liberty," Miscellaneous Book 2, 209, Clerk of Court's Office, Natchitoches, Louisiana, trans. Gary B. Mills and Elizabeth Shown Mills, 1972.

47. "Names of Slaves of St. Denis and their values before division," April 1, 1758, succession of Widow of St. Denis, document no. 206, Clerk of Court Office, Natchitoches, Louisiana.

48. Mills, E. S., and Mills, G., "Slaves and Masters," 170.

49. Mills, E. S., "Marie Thérèse Coincoin (1742-1816)," 20.

50. Marie Thérèse Coincoin to [children], Natchitoches Parish Conveyance Book 3: 524-549, Clerk of Court's Office, Natchitoches, Louisiana.

51. Claude Thomas Metoyer headstone, American Cemetery, Natchitoches Parish, Louisiana.

52. Mills, G., *Forgotten People*, 48, citing Pierre Metoyer and Marie Henriette, Marriage Contract, Books 2 and 3, Natchitoches Clerk of Court.

53. Private land claims were granted in Louisiana by the Spanish Crown to individuals who requested them with a guarantee that they would make improvements as stated by the Crown.

Chapter 8

The Children Make Their Marks

The children of Pierre and Marie Thérèse (only one of them educated and able to read or write) set out to make their marks in the world. Making their marks included slave ownership. Theories flourish about why they, like thousands of other people of color, owned slaves. As one researcher so aptly analyzed, resources were needed for their protection. These resources came in the form of slave ownership. Because they had the resources, they were able to appoint attorneys when their land and livelihood were being jeopardized. Several times family members had to resort to going to court to safeguard their land. In the early 1800s, one of the sons of Pierre and Marie Thérèse had to spend $40,000 protecting the land he possessed. Without the resources that slave ownership provided, he would not have been able to employ lawyers to defend the property he had labored on for years to improve and maintain. Property and livelihood would have been lost. Resources were also needed for education. Although only one of the children of Pierre and Marie Thérèse could read and write, these resources enabled them to educate their children and subsequent generations. By doing so, their children were cognizant of the laws and the protection they were afforded under the fluctuating laws of the colony. It also enabled them to support others in their community who did not have the resources to protect themselves.[1] Even more so than their white counterparts, people of color needed the education and protection that slave ownership provided them.

Also, as it did for their white counterparts, slave ownership afforded the children of Pierre and Marie Thérèse the lives of luxury they would subsequently lead. Their homes were said to be elegant and included imports from France, their father's homeland. They imported glassware, china, silverware, and pianos. Several of the children possessed plantation homes. One of these plantation homes was equipped with a billiard parlor. French books in the homes were passed down to their descendants. Wine collections were in the home. When their children married, the newlyweds were given property and money. Their children were taught by private tutors.[2] Most of the first generation Metoyers, born into slavery, without formal education and without an inheritance from their father, acquired wealth that surpassed that of their free white half-siblings, Pierre Victorin and François Benjamin Metoyer. Born into an elitist life and not bound by slavery, the white Metoyer sons inherited the wealth of their father.[3] Undoubtedly, having observed the hard work and initiative of his Franco-African children, in Pierre's will he beseeched these children to take care of their white siblings if the need arose. Pierre's 1801 will stated, "If by some unforeseen event, my children come to be in a state of poverty, I hope that the said mulattoes [his Franco-African children] mentioned herein above, will be willing to relieve them according to their abilities."[4]

From all accounts, the lives of Pierre and Marie Thérèse's Franco-African children went well. Their lives were easier than most because of the place in which they lived. Louisiana differed from other states because the governments were constantly revolving. During the era when the Metoyers were establishing their wealth, the Spanish controlled the land. Little oversight into what was happening in the rural settlement gave leeway as to how the settlement was governed. Land was abundant, and any able-bodied white or free person of color who was prepared to work and improve the land could petition for a land grant. When there were land disputes, the courts afforded free people of color (with the resources to hire a lawyer) the same opportunity to sue as whites. Privy to equal treatment under Louisiana laws, the Metoyer children made their marks. Most of them led profitable lives and left sizable estates when they died.

François, the last born child of Pierre and Marie Thérèse, was born free and never received a Spanish land grant, but he bought and sold several tracts of land. Dominique, the fifth-born of Marie Thérèse and Pierre, acquired several land grants. Born a slave in 1776, he was a slave until 1795 when he turned 19. In 1839, after supporting seventeen children and granting them dowries and donations, he left an estate of $42,405. In 2011 the value of his estate would have been $1,060,000. Pierre, the fourth born son, the only child that could read or write, died in 1834. He had been married twice and had at least seven children. After he divided the estate among his children and made donations to them, he left an estate valued at $19,969. If valued in 2011, his estate would have been worth $541,000.[5] His younger brother, Joseph Antoine (bought and freed as an infant by his father) was the father of nine children. He bought and manumitted his mother-in-law. Joseph

Antoine left an estate of $31,000 when he died in 1838. His estate valued in 2011 would have been worth $773,000[6].

In an era when the majority of people of color were slaves or entrenched in poverty, the children of Marie Thérèse and Pierre achieved lives of affluence. Oil paintings, wine collections, and fine mahogany furnishings were portions of the older children's estates.[7] Though born in slavery, the first generation Metoyer family, with hard work and financial savvy, was able to rise above it as they each made their mark in the world.

The first three children of Marie Thérèse and Pierre—Augustin, Marie Susanne, and Louis (the branches of the tree from which Bertha sprang) would also live profitable lives and leave a legacy in the small rural town of Isle Brevelle along the meandering Cane River.

Endnotes

1. Elizabeth Shown Mills, "*Isle of Canes* and Issues of Conscience: Master-Slave Sexual Dynamics and Slaveholding by Free People of Color," *Between Two Worlds: A Special Issue of* The Southern Quarterly: A Journal of the Arts in the South 43 (Winter 2006): 158-75, specifically 162-64; digital image at Elizabeth Shown Mills *Historical Pathways, accessed December 4, 2012,* http://www..HistoricPathways.com.

2. Sister Frances Jerome Woods, C. D. P., *Marginality and Identity; A Colored Creole Family through Ten Generations* (Baton Rouge, Louisiana: Louisiana State University Press, 1972), 33-35, 68-69.

3. Mills, G., *Forgotten People,* 137–38, citing succession of Pierre Victorin Metoyer, Succession Book 11, 393. Natchitoches Clerk of Court Office, Natchitoches.

4. Claude Thomas Metoyer's 1801 Will.

5. Mills, *Forgotten People,* 137, citing succession of Dominique Metoyer, No. 375, citing succession of Pierre Metoyer, no.193, Natchitoches Parish Records; Lawrence H. Officer and Samuel H. Williamson, "Purchasing Power of Money in the United States from 1774 to 2010," *MeasuringWorth., accessed November 26, 2012,* http://www.MeasuringWorth.com/usgdp/.

6. Woods, *Marginality and Identity,* 35; Officer and Williamson, "Purchasing Power," *MeasuringWorth, accessed November 26, 2012,* http://www.MeasuringWorth.com/usgdp/ ; Mills, E. S., and Mills, G., "Slaves and Masters," 180-183.

7. Woods, *Marginality and Identity,* 33-35, 68-69.

Three Third Great-Grandparents
What a Tangled Web We Weave

To understand the dynamics of Bertha's ancestral tree, you must understand the time, place, and circumstances into which her ancestors were born. Isolated in rural Louisiana, her forefathers began their lives as slaves and worked assiduously to develop wealth and opportunities for their families. Few free people of color, in the rural Isle Brevelle community of Natchitoches, during the 1800s, achieved the degree of success that the Metoyers achieved. Like many in a privileged social stratum, not wanting to jeopardize the wealth and position they had worked so hard to achieve, Bertha's ancestors chose not to marry those with less social status. Their other alternative for marriage was to marry creoles of color from the city of New Orleans. Creoles of color in New Orleans, though not too far away geographically, considered themselves more culturally advanced and may not have been as receptive to their rural counterparts. For reasons never shared, marriage by the Metoyers outside the Natchitoches colony was not a choice that most second generation Metoyers made. Therefore, the children of Marie Susanne and Nicolas Augustin begin to intermarry; unaware of the role that genetics might play in such a close relationship. Because of these kindred affairs, Bertha has not one, but three sets of third great-grandparents on her maternal tree. Her third great-grandparents are the first three born children of Marie Thérèse and Pierre Metoyer—Nicolas Augustin, Marie Susanne, and Louis. As I traveled in the footsteps of these ancestors, like the lowly caterpillar, I went through a metamorphosis that gave me the wings of a butterfly and dared me to fly.

Chapter 9

Nicolas Augustin Metoyer and Marie Agnes Poissot
Partners for Life

In a submission to *The Natchitoches Genealogist*, Dr. Gary Mills writes of Bertha's third great-grandfather, Nicolas Augustin Metoyer, "There have been but few men, in the course of Natchitoches history whose names are legend, whose contributions are eternal, whose memories are revered. The Chevalier Louis Juchereau de St Denis, founder of Poste Saint Jean Baptiste des Natchitoches, surely leads the ranks. But just as surely there stands close behind him the cavalier form of a freed slave of the St. Denis family, Nicolas Augustin Metoyer."[1]

It was this man, Bertha's third great-grandfather, Augustin Metoyer, who initially reached for the sky as the branches of her family tree stretched towards the sun. Whether he was the first to venture into the world or the second is not known because he was born a twin, but he was the first born son of Marie Thérèse and Pierre Metoyer. On January 22, 1768, Augustin forced his way into the world. Born a slave, he was officially the property of his mother's mistress, Madame de Soto. Despite knowing the precarious position into which their child was born, it must have been a wondrous event for young Marie Thérèse and Pierre as they gazed into the tiny brown face they had created. Marie Thérèse was already an experienced mother of five, but this would be the first confirmation of Pierre's manhood. He surely must have beamed with pride. One gesture performed by Pierre that exhibited the obvious love he felt for his son was to invite the commandant of the nearby Rapides post, Nicolas Maraffret Laisard, to serve as Augustin's godfather. An even larger gesture was the christening of his first born son. Pierre gave him the name of his father, Nicolas.[2] He was christened Nicolas Augustin Metoyer, but would become known as Augustin.

Until the age of eight, from 1768 to 1776, Augustin was the property of Madame de Soto. His father bought him, along with three other siblings, on March 31, 1776.[3] From the day he became the property of his father, until he evolved into a young man, Augustin traveled in Pierre's footsteps and absorbed

77

the wisdom of his experience. He was the genesis of a new generation. Unlike his parents, his generation would not be defined by black or white, free or slave, but would become uniquely its own. To some, they would become known as mulattoes, to others, they would be creoles of color, but to them, they were the children of Marie Thérèse and Pierre Metoyer.

During the primary years of his life, Augustin had the undivided attention of Pierre. He was the first born son; the one whom most men dote on. As the first boy-child of Pierre Metoyer, he had plenty to learn. As Pierre and his father walked among the slaves, surely Augustin recognized how the shade of his skin differed from that of his father. If questioned, did Pierre just tease him about playing too long in the sun, or did he explain that love has no color? If we knew his answer to this question, we could tell a lot about the character of the man. Unfortunately for us, his response was only meant for a son learning about the ways of the world from his father. Like most young boys, Augustin probably aspired to emulate his father. As Pierre honed his skills as a merchant, Augustin, in all likelihood, was nearby peering over his shoulder and learning his father's trade. When Pierre became a planter, it was young Augustin who first sauntered beside him in his fields hanging onto his every word and asking endless questions—questions he needed answers to before he tackled the world alone. Augustin would have depended on Pierre to learn how to sow and reap the rewards of his seeds. One day, Pierre would rely on Augustin to protect his mother when he went off to fight in the Revolutionary War. More son, than his father's slave, the words spoken by his father would become ingrained in his heart and mind. The bond shared in the early years between father and son would never be broken, and the sage advice during those formative years would be taken to heart. After twenty-four years of walking in the footsteps of his father, on August 1, 1792, when Pierre sensed the time was right, he granted his son freedom.[4] With his new freedom, Augustin began to make plans for his future. Although much was on his agenda to accomplish, foremost was to marry the love of his life, Marie Agnes Poissot. With only three weeks of freedom under his belt, Augustin and twenty-one year old Agnes began their marital journey together.[5]

Marie Agnes Poissot was a free German-Franco-African girl who had a story of her own. Unlike Augustin, she was declared free at the age of six. Despite her freedom, she endured irreparable damage from her father's wife. Her story is one of sadness interwoven with familial love.

Agnes and her mother, Françoise, were the slaves of the French-Native American planter, Pierre Derbanne. Pierre's father, François Derbanne, had been St. Denis' compatriot. He had fought with St. Denis during the Chitamache Campaign in 1703, and he later married a Chitamache slave. This Native American slave was the mother of Pierre Derbanne. Agnes' mother, Françoise, was the cook for the Derbanne family. While a slave in the Derbanne household, between 1770 and 1772, Françoise had a liaison with the neighboring white planter, Athanase Poissot.[6] Agnes was the product of this affair.

In 1773, Athanase married Manuela de Soto, the granddaughter of Louis Juchereau de St Denis.[7] But, in 1775, when Agnes was about six years old, Athanase decided he wanted possession of his daughter. Athanase's father, the paternal grandfather of Agnes, Remy Poissot, arranged for Athanase to exchange a seven-year-old slave for his granddaughter. Remy granted Agnes freedom that same year. This gesture caused contention in the Poissot household. Aware that the young Agnes must have been the daughter of her husband, Manuela punished her relentlessly. Remy, undoubtedly, very fond of his young granddaughter, learned she was being mistreated by Athanase's wife, and he repeated his manumission three years later. In 1778, in his second manumission, Remy indicated that he would "go to whatever lengths necessary to enforce her freedom over all objections."[8] His words are those of a grandfather who truly loved and cherished his granddaughter.

Despite his undeniable love, the painfully devastating mental and physical abuse Agnes sustained at the hands of Manuela always haunted her. In 1784, as a young woman aged sixteen or seventeen, Agnes filed charges of ill treatment against her father's wife.[9] Due to the passage of time, the records that contained the outcome of the suit have vanished. However, in 1787 Agnes continued her life in the household of Dominique and Jean Baptiste (Barthelemy) Rachal on the upper Isle Brevelle. A child born in September of the previous year, named Jean Baptiste, is believed to be the child of Marie Agnes and Jean Baptiste (Barthelemy) Rachal. Fortunately for Augustin, the relationship with Rachal did not endure. In 1795, Agnes married her lifelong soul mate and found solace and protection as Augustin's wife.[10]

With Agnes by his side, Augustin began propelling beyond the stars. He requested a concession for land from the Spanish colonial government. On May 6, 1795, three years after his marriage to Agnes, the Spanish colonial government gave him the authorization to settle on the land and have it surveyed. Augustin would soon be granted his first tract of land— 395 acres.[11] Exactly when he physically occupied the land is not known. It may have been prior to requesting the concession in 1795 or soon after. But this property, on the Isle Brevelle, was a narrow strip of land that was bordered by the Old River and the

Cane River, south of Natchitoches, Louisiana. It was now up to him to make his mark in the world. Augustin, Bertha's most pragmatic ancestor, initially lived on his land in a small cabin. But one day he would live in a mansion home. It would not be long before he, like his father and mother before him, would realize his dreams of security and self-reliance.

Augustin realized early the significance of land ownership, and he began to obtain hundreds of acres of land. On March 3, 1807, Augustin received land patent B1955 for two tracts of land. One tract was 428 acres and the other was 66 acres. In January of 1836 he acquired 206 acres of land. Later that year, land certificate 2710 verifies that he purchased two more tracts of land, one was 72 acres and the other was 26.[12] After much buying and selling of land, over a period of time, Augustin owned a significant amount of property.

At the age of 29, two years after his petition had been approved for the surveying of and settlement on the Isle Brevelle land, Augustin purchased his first known slave—a young adult male. The initial acquisition of slaves was typically made to help with their master's chosen occupation. In the case of Augustin, his new land had to be cleared, and this was not a job for a lone man. Augustin's rationale for his purchase was no different from that of his fellow Creole planters. Unlike most planters, though, some of his subsequent acquisitions were made out of love and compassion for family. Augustin's second purchase was his wife's young sister, Marguerite, who he immediately freed. In 1800, with $300 in hand, he bought his young niece, Marie Rose, the daughter of his brother, Louis. She, too, was immediately granted her freedom. In 1801, he bought Marie Perine for $600 and freed her. Perine would later become the wife of his brother Pierre.[13] As Augustin's property expanded so did his slave ownership. The 1810 census revealed that Augustin owned 17 slaves,[14] but by 1820, he possessed 25.[15] Between 1820 and 1830, his slaves had doubled.

By 1830, slave ownership was widespread among free people of color, especially in Louisiana. Of the 753 free persons of color in New Orleans, twenty-five owned at least ten slaves. Eulalie de Mandeville Macarty, a free business woman of color in New Orleans, owned thirty-two slaves. Perhaps, because of more farmland and the need for more manual labor, slave ownership was more widespread in the rural regions of Louisiana. In rural Louisiana, where Augustin resided, forty-three free persons of color collectively owned 1,327 slaves. Three plantation owners in St. John the Baptist Parish averaged 46 slaves each. In Pointe Coupee Parish, 297 slaves were owned by eight planters giving them an average of 37 slaves each. One hundred eighty-four slaves were owned by six planters in Iberville Parish. This amounted to approximately

31 slaves for each planter.[16] In comparison, the 1830 census recorded Augustin with a total of 54 slaves.[17] No one can say how many slaves Augustin bought out of love and compassion or how many were bought for profit, but his record of emancipating slaves surpassed most of the planters in the region.

As Augustin's slave labor increased, so did his wealth. When Agnes died and their possessions were inventoried, the extent of his wealth was disclosed. Inventoried in 1840, among his numerous possessions were a plantation house, a small house, twenty-two cabins, two pigeon houses, two cisterns, a barge, and a pirogue. His main plantation had two cotton gins, a gin for grain, known as a gristmill, and a pounding mill. Very few planters owned and operated cotton gins, and in 1840 there were only three gristmills in the entire parish.[18] Augustin, the former slave, had exceeded most of his fellow planters, and he had finally earned the prestige and respect of his peers.

Augustin, like most planters, was concerned with building his wealth. But unlike the white planters he competed with, the new American regime was becoming increasingly antagonistic towards free people of color. The American government, unlike the French and Spanish Crown, began placing restrictions on free people of color. Legislation was passed forbidding them to insult or strike a white person. Free people of color were not to "conceive themselves as equal to whites." The right to free one's slaves was restricted by the new government. Offenses, such as arson, poisoning of whites, and rape of whites, meant the death penalty for free people of color, but not for whites.[19] With such laws legislated towards his people, it was paramount that Augustin insulate his family against these hostilities. Monetary resources gained through slave ownership allowed him the means to do this.[20]

In 1835, a portion of Augustin's land (a section of a 640 acre tract that had been approved in 1825) was claimed by his neighbor François Roubieu. According to Roubieu, he had inherited and therefore owned the 640 acres of land that bordered Augustin's land on the north. Augustin, Roubieu alleged, illegally had his land surveyed. This survey showed that 200 acres of his land actually belonged to Augustin. Because the survey placed the land on Augustin's property, Roubieu claimed that Augustin took possession of the land and proceeded "to cut and destroyed the timber on it." The damage he estimated was $5,000. He also alleged that because of this damage the rest of his land was valued at less; therefore, he could not complete the construction of a cotton gin that he had in progress. He requested that a new survey be done of his land and wanted $10,000 worth of damages from Augustin.[21] Not one to be intimidated by a legal confrontation, Augustin retaliated.

In 1836, because Augustin had the financial means to afford an attorney and defend his property ownership, he countersued. He stated that it was Roubieu who was encroaching on *his* land. According to Augustin, he had a valid title to the land, and he was the legal owner. He stated that he had been in possession of the land for ten years. He further alleged Roubieu enclosed the land and had cut and removed cypress and other trees that belonged to him. To prevent Roubieu from trespassing, Augustin requested an injunction to prevent him from taking his timber. The case went to court, and after years of court appearances and delays, due to his patience and persistence, Augustin prevailed. He did not have to pay the $10,000 in damages as requested by Roubieu, and he was proven to be the rightful owner of the property.[22] Without the wealth he had amassed due to slave ownership, his land and livelihood would have been lost. Protection of his family and his holdings were Augustin's primary concerns, but he also had another dream he wanted to fulfill. He wanted a place for him and his family to worship—a place that he was determined to make a reality.

Family tradition holds that while Augustin was abroad in France with his father he envisioned a special place for his family to worship and find solitude. Exactly where the vision originated has been lost with the passage of time, but Augustin did realize his dream. Although exact dates have been disputed, by July 19, 1829 his vision had become a reality, and the St. Augustine Church (built with the aid of his brother, Louis Metoyer, on land owned and donated by Augustin) was blessed by Father J. B. Blanc.[23] St. Augustine is believed to be the first Catholic Church built for and by free people of color. Despite being built for free people of color, its doors were opened to all ethnic groups who wished to worship there. Situated directly behind Augustin's pew were eight pews he reserved for his white friends. White marriages were held in the church and whites also had their slaves and children baptized there.[24] The love for his church can be seen in a life size painting Augustin had commissioned in 1836. In the painting, Augustin stands proudly on the veranda at his plantation home pointing to the church. This painting hangs in the church today. In 1856, before Augustin's death, his beloved St. Augustine was decreed to be a parish in its own right. At that time, in the state of Louisiana, it was the only known church with authority over a mission for whites.[25] In Augustin's will, he stated that he wanted the land on which the church was built to never be used for anything other than a church and cemetery.[26] His wishes are still being honored.

Despite starting his life handicapped by slavery for 24 years, Augustin was once the wealthiest man in the Cane River colony.[27] He made loans to his counterparts, both white and free men of color, and he was well respected by the leaders in his community. He was the voice of reason and considered the patriarch of the family. Although he was generous with his children, he did not squander his money. In 1840, after many long years of togetherness, Agnes, his wife, companion, and confidant died. At her death, the estate was assessed at $140,958 despite a depression that had bankrupted many Americans.[28] Among his possessions were his two cotton mills. The one on the right bank of the river was valued at $1,200, and the one on the left bank was valued at $2,000. The land on which he lived on the Red River consisted of 1,484 acres. Another property on the Little River was 640 acres. Calculations made by using the United States historical standard of living equated the value of his estate at $3,780,000 in 2011. His slaves were worth $44,560 in 1840. Because slaves were considered commodities, as commodities, their worth in 2011 would amount to $1,140,000 using the CPI (Consumer Price Index). In 1840, Augustin's movable assets were worth $8, 465.50. In 2011, those same assets would have been valued at $217,000 using CPI.[29]

    Bertha's third great-grandfather, Nicolas Augustin Metoyer, never learned to read or write and was a slave for 24 years. Despite beginning his life as a slave and his lack of a formal education, he knew that he could succeed, and he persevered. During the time in which he lived, slave ownership was a means of becoming successful. This success gave him and his family security and protection. Like his mother before him, he made choices that many of his peers of color and not of color made. Like his mother before him, they were *his* choices to make. Augustin lived a long and prosperous life with much time to reflect on the decisions he made. Regrets or not, we will never know. On December 19, 1856, at the age of 88, Augustin died at his home on Isle Brevelle. His funeral was attended by those without power as well as those in power. In attendance among his family and slaves were the bishop, all the pastors in the civil parish, and the Sisters of the Holy Cross.[30] After the death ritual was over, Augustin was laid to rest in the same tomb occupied by his beloved Agnes behind the St. Augustine Church he had so lovingly built for the people of Isle Brevelle.

    The examples of Nicolas Augustin Metoyer, Bertha's third great-grandfather, and Marie Agnes Poissot, her third great-grandmother, taught me a very valuable lesson. For better or worse, you make your own choices in life. If you are willing to watch, listen, and learn from those who come before you, life is filled with promise and possibilities. It is up to you to discover where the promise and possibilities lie. It was these two partners for life, Augustin, the family patriarch, and Agnes, his faithful and loving wife, who gave life to

Bertha's second great-grandmother, Marie Louise Metoyer; a woman whose forbidden love for her first cousin would help to contribute to the interweaving of our bloodlines.

Known Slaves of Nicolas Augustin Metoyer[31]
Waiting for their Stories to be told

Baptized 18 April 1802
Antoine, Congo Negro, aged 20 years

Baptized 8 June 1815
Marie Pelagie, daughter of Jeny, aged 8 years
Jacque, daughter of Jeny, aged 5 years
Marie Celeste, daughter of Jeny, aged 3, years
Rose, daughter of Marie Fany, aged 2 ½ years

Baptized 11 February 1816
L Silben, son of Charlot, aged 10 months

Baptized 19 April 1819
Rafael, daughter of Charlot aged 2 ½, years

Baptized 20 March 1820
Marcelite, born 10 May 1819, daughter of Jeny

Baptized September 3, 1821
Charles Mertil, born 3 September 1821, son of Charlot

Baptized 17 December 1821
Lendor, Guinea Negro, aged 26 years
Gavriel, Guinea Negro, aged 24 years
Jean Btte., Guinea Negro, aged 24 years
Antoin Fortun, Guinea Negro, aged 12 years
Nicolas, Guinea Negro, aged 21 years
Charles, Guinea Negro, aged 18 years

Atanas, Guinea Negro, aged 19 years
Paul, baptism, Guinea Negro, aged 22 years
Jeann Ned, Guinea Negro, aged 18 years
Joseph Bron, English Negro, aged 15 years
Henry, English Negro, aged 23 years
Jean Pierre, English Negro, aged 12 years
Andres, Guinea Negro, aged 24 years
Jeann, Guinea Negro, aged 17 years
Me. Zalye, English Negro, aged 23 years
Me. Zephany, English Negro, aged 25 years
Marie Charlot, English Negro, aged 20 years
Me. Felicite, Guinea Negro, aged 18 years
Marie Genye aged 32 years

Baptized 6 July 1822
Manuel, son of Saly, aged 7 months

Baptized 27 May 1826
Merry daughter of Phebie, aged 4 years
Desire Dezilie, born 15 December 1826, daughter of Phebie
Marie Agathe, daughter of Phebie

Additional slaves from Augustin's 1840 Donation Inventory (some deleted so as not to repeat list above)

Baptism dates unknown
Males
Jessie aged 33
Linoor aged 60
Lubin aged 26
Januel aged 30
Wade aged 28
Beau Jim aged 25
Tom aged 22
Sam aged 28
Ben aged 25
Sandy aged 20
Piccaillen aged 30
Jacquite aged 35

Francois aged 50
Arore aged 50
Boniface aged 11
Jacques aged 22
Peter aged 40
Joe aged 18

Females
Victoria aged 25
Carmelite aged 16
Fanny aged 35
Jenny aged 28
Helene, daughter of Jenny, aged 18 months
Labelle aged 26
Cecelia, daughter of Labelle, aged 5 years
Caroline, daughter of Labelle, aged 2 years
Filia, child of Marie, aged 8 months
Cecile aged 50
Jeanne aged 35
Rose aged 35
Doralize aged 28
Rigobert, child of Doralize, aged 2 years

Some names may be duplicated or omitted, but I hope this list brings closure for someone looking for their missing link.

Augustin Metoyer and Marie Agnes Poissot's Family

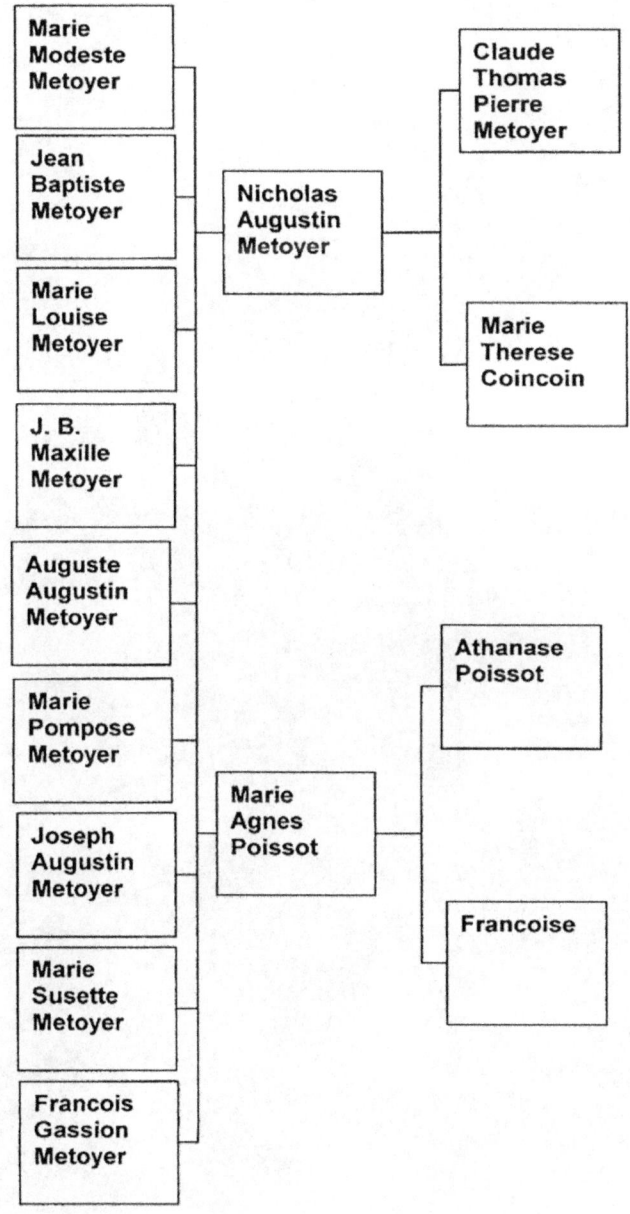

Nicholas Augustin Metoyer
Family Patriarch

Photograph, courtesy of Cammie G. Henry Research Center

Marie Agnes Poissot
Wife of Nicholas Augustin Metoyer

Photograph, courtesy of Cammie G. Henry Research Center

Auguste Augustin Metoyer
Son of Nicolas Augustin Metoyer

Photograph, courtesy of Cammie G. Henry Research Center

Linda S. Manuel

Plate commissioned by Francois Mignon in honor of Augustin Metoyer and Louis Metoyer

Endnotes

1. Gary B. Mills. "The Ancestry of Sieur Nicolas Augustin Metoyer, fmc, Patriarch of Isle Brevelle," *The Natchitoches Genealogist* (October 1984) 28.

2. Mills, E. S., *Natchitoches, 1729-1803*, entry 3389.

3. "Purchase of Nicolas, Marie Suzanne, Louis, and Pierre," 1776 Natchitoches Colonial Archives (NCA) Document no. 1161; Office of the Clerk of Court, Natchitoches, Louisiana.

4. "Manumission of Augustin Metoyer," 1792, Natchitoches Colonial Archives, Document no. 2407. Office of the Clerk of Court, Natchitoches, Louisiana.

5. Mills, E. S., *Natchitoches, 1729-1803*, entry 3389.

6. Elizabeth, Shown Mills, *Isle of Canes* (Provo, Utah: Ancestry Publishing, 2006), "Lecomte-Dupré-Poissot Connections."

7. Mills, E. S., *Natchitoches, 1729-1803*, entry 1011.

8. Pierre Derbanne to Athanase Poissot, p. 84, Bundle 1775, Document no. 1052; Agnes, slave of Remy Poissot, Emancipation p. 3, Bundle 1775, Document no. 1093; Agnes, Slave of Remy, Poissot, Emancipation, p.4, Bundle 1778, Document no. 1357; Natchitoches Colonial Archives, Office of the Clerk of Court, Natchitoches, Louisiana.

9. Agnes v. Mrs. Athanase Poissot, listed in "Index to French Archives"; Office of the Clerk of Court, Natchitoches, Louisiana.

10. Mills, E. S., *Natchitoches Colonials,* 55: Elizabeth Shown Mills, "Information regarding her research done on Jean Baptiste (Louis)Rachal and Jean Baptiste (Barthelemy) Rachal," email to author from eshown@comcast.net, December 30, 2010; Mills, E. S., *Natchitoches, 1729-1803*, entries 1479, 3389.

11. Mills, G., *Forgotten People*, 53, citing File B1960, Augustin Metoyer, State Land Records.

12. State Land Office, Baton Rouge, Natchitoches District Tract Books, Section 75, Township 10N, Range 7W, p. 46; Section 39, Township 10N, Range 7W, p. 44; Sections 70 and 71, Township 7N, Range 6W, p. 49; Section 67, Township 8N. Range 6W, p. 52.

13. Widow Lecomte to Nicolas Augustin, 1800, Old Natchitoches Data, No. 279, Cammie G. Henry Research Center, Northwestern State University, Natchitoches, Louisiana; Mills, G., *Forgotten People*, 65, citing Ambroise LeComte to Nicolas Augustin, Sale and Manumission of Marie Perine.

14. 1810 U. S. census, Natchitoches Parish, Louisiana, town of Natchitoches, p. 214 (penned at top right), line 21, Augustin Meteyer [Metoyer]; digital image, *Ancestry.com,* accessed July 12, 2011, http://search.ancestry.com/iexec?htx=view&r=0&dbid=7613&iid=4433226_00181&fn=Augustin&ln=Meteyer&st=r&ssrc=&pid=17673; citing National Archives microfilm publication M252, roll 10.

15. 1820 U. S. census, Natchitoches Parish, Louisiana, page. 98 (stamped), line 67, Augustin Metoyer [erroneously indexed as Angst Metoyer]; digital image, *Ancestry.com,* accessed July 12, 2011, http://search.ancestry.com/iexec?htx=View&r=0&dbid=7734&iid=4433165_00096&fn=Angt&ln=Metoger&st=r&ssrc=&pid=1493593; citing National Archives microfilm publication M33, roll 142.

16. Loren Schweninger, "Antebellum Free Persons of Color in Postbellum Louisiana," *Louisiana History*, 30 (Fall 1989): 345-64, especially 347.

17. 1830 U. S. census, Natchitoches Parish, Louisiana, page 69 (penned) line 5, Augustin Meytoier [Metoyer]; digital images, *Ancestry.com,* accessed July 12, 2011, http://search.ancestry.com/cgi-bin/sse.dll?indiv=1&db=1830usfedcenancestry&rank=1&new=1&MSAV=1&msT=1&gss=angs-d&gsln=metoyier&dbOnly=_F0006BC0%7c_F0006BC0_x%2c_F0006BD3%7c_F0006BD3_x%2c_F0006BD4%7c_F0006BD4_x%2c_F0006BD5%7c_F0006BD5_x%2c_F0006BD6%7c_F0006BD6_x%2c_F0006BD7%7c_F0006BD7_x&uidh=bmr&pcat=35&fh=16&h=1898855&recoff=7+19+33; ; citing NARA microfilm publication M19, roll 201.

18. Mills, G., *Forgotten People*, 116.

19. Laura Foner, "The Free People of Color in Louisiana and St. Domingue: A Comparative Portrait of Two Three-Caste Slave Societies," *Journal of Social History*, 3, (Summer, 1970): 422, 423.

20. Mills, E. S., "*Isle of Canes* and Issues of Conscience," 161-63.

21. Roubieu v. Metoyer, District Court Suit 1395 (1835), Office of the Clerk of Court, Natchitoches Parish, Louisiana.

22. Metoyer v. Roubieu, District Court Suit 1473 (1836).

23. Mills, G., *Forgotten People*, 145.

24. Ibid., 146, 151, 153.

25. Mills, E. S., and Mills, G., "Slaves and Masters," 175.

26. Last Will and Testament of Nicolas Augustin Metoyer, in Natchitoches Parish Records, Book 25, Notarial Records, 77-80.

27. Mills, G. *Forgotten People*, 139.

28. Augustin Metoyer Succession, No. 395, Natchitoches Parish Records.

29. Mills, G., *Forgotten People*, 137–38, citing succession of Agnes Metoyer, No. 395, Natchitoches Clerk of Court; Officer and Williamson, *MeasuringWorth*, accessed November 26, 2012, http://www.MeasuringWorth.com/usgdp/ .

30. Mills, E. S., and Mills, G., "Slaves and Masters," 175.

31. Elizabeth Shown Mills, *Natchitoches, 1800-1826 Translated Abstracts of Register Number Five of the Catholic Church Parish of St François des Natchitoches in Louisiana* (New Orleans: Polyanthos, 1980), entries 1153, 1217, 1440, 1455-1473, 1548, 1642, 1643, 1645, 1817, 2305-2308, 2413; "Act of Donation by Augustin Metoyer," The Natchitoches Genealogist (April 1984):, 32-33, citing Book of Donations, vol. 70, 1840.

Searching For Bertha

Chapter 10

Marie Susanne Metoyer and Dr. Joseph Conant
Ships Passing in the Night

As Augustin sauntered toward the sun in the footsteps of his father, his twin, Bertha's third great-grandmother, Marie Susanne Metoyer, was inspired by their mother to dance among the stars. Like Augustin, she was the slave of Madame de Soto until the age of eight. Unlike her brother, it would not be her father, but her determined mother who would teach her the ways of their world. Susanne had observed as her mother transitioned from slave to slave owner. Day after day, as Marie Thérèse attended the needs of her mistress, her oldest daughter wasn't far from her side observing and learning the skills of her mother's trade. These talents would someday prove to be a blessing and a curse for the young girl. When Pierre decided it was time to release her mother from the burden of slavery, Susanne would have been there to cheer him on. After Pierre and Marie Thérèse parted ways, Susanne witnessed her mother tackle the wilderness and make it her own. From her mother, she learned how to cross the threshold of slavery into freedom with dignity and grace. As Susanne began to make her way in the world, everything she needed to know about the workings of freedom and slavery, she had already learned from her mother.

On May 31, 1776, Pierre decided it was time for him to gain possession of Susanne and three of her siblings. At the tender age of 8, Susanne was no longer the slave of Madam de Soto; she had become her father's slave. This transfer of power was meaningless to such a young child. As her father's slave, life may have been easier, but this would not have deterred her from assisting her mother (who was still a slave) as her mother continued to care for her mistress.

It would be twenty-six years later, On May 2, 1802, at the age of 34, when pen would be put to paper declaring Susanne quasi-free. Unlike the instantaneous emancipation granted to his sons, Louis and Pierre, on that very same day, Pierre's daughter's freedom would be conditional. In the document that was written to render Susanne free, Pierre stated, "In recognition of all her good services I declare ... in [the] presence of Sieur Jean Baptiste Ste. Anne and Jean Baptiste Buard, required and undersigned witnesses, *that as of the moment which it is pleasing to God to retire me from this world,* that the said Marie Susanne will be free."[1] With this said, she would not be freed until the death of her father regardless of the fact that she had "served with zeal, fidelity, and exactness, ... conducted herself to [his] satisfaction, having by her service and her good attentions saved several lives in diverse maladies, [including] that of [his] wife and all [their] infants, having in fact nourished with her milk [their] son Benjamin, dry-nursed, raised, and managed [their] other children in their childhood and even to this day and several other important attentions which were rendered to [them]."[2] The skills Susanne had learned from her mother were so essential to the well-being of her father and his family that they derailed her freedom. Perhaps she found some solace in the fact that her father also stated, "My receiver, nor any of my heirs, or assignees will have no claim whatsoever on the product of her industry or savings which have been obtained by any talent… she having at all times been authorized and she is authorized by her master ... to enjoy in appropriate measure the fruit of her economy…"[3] Unlike his sons, working hard and being loyal had not paid off for Pierre's girl-child. Because of her father's provisions, Susanne would technically be a slave until her father died.

Susanne was bonded by law to her father and his wife, but because she was the daughter of Pierre Metoyer (one of the wealthiest men in Natchitoches) she was virtually able to conduct her affairs as though she was a free woman. Being quasi-free and with the stipulations fixed by her father, she would have the right to charge for any services she provided. As time passed and Susanne grew to understand the nuances of her world, she would use her quasi-free status to her advantage. This beneficial status would someday help her circumvent certain laws and elevate her social status.

In the meantime, around 1793 or 1794, Susanne was introduced to Bertha's third great-grandfather, Dr. Joseph Conand from New Orleans.[4] Like her father, Dr. Conand had ventured to Louisiana from France. Five years her senior, the doctor was born August 24, 1763 at Serrieres in the Canton of Shis (Ain) in France to Dr. François Conand and Marie Anne Brillat.[5] Family records indicate that Joseph's father and his family lived in Kaskaskia, Illinois in the late 1700s. His father was employed as a surgeon major for the United States troops at Fort Clark.[6] Precisely how Susanne first encountered Dr. Joseph Conand is unknown. It is feasible that the doctor may have been visiting relatives when he became acquainted with Pierre Metoyer. This meeting may have been the beginning of an arranged relationship between Susanne and Dr. Conand.

It was not unusual for white fathers, of slave daughters or free daughters of color, to arrange for the financial well-being of their daughters by placing them with suitors they felt could financially support them. This act of placement was known as *plaçage.* The system of *plaçage,* although not restricted to, is well-known for taking place in New Orleans. One example of a father overseeing such an arrangement is the case of Eulalie de Marigny de Mandeville of New Orleans whose *plaçage* lasted fifty-years. Eulalie's white father, Pierre Enguerrand de Marigny de Mandeville, made such an arrangement with Eugene Macarty. Macarty was from a wealthy aristocratic family and would be beneficial for de Mandeville's daughter. The relationship between Eulalie and Macarty was condoned and chaperoned by her white father and her father's mother. Land, slaves, and gifts were given to the young *plaçee* by her white father and his family members. Eventually, Eulalie became one of the wealthiest women in New Orleans.[7]

Such an agreement by a father for his daughter may well have been the situation with Susanne. She, like Eulalie, had a white father of means. In the rural area of Natchitoches, there were no free men of color who had achieved the financial or social status of the free Metoyer's of color. Although Susanne was a slave, she was a Metoyer, and the thought of her becoming the wife of a slave was objectionable. Pierre, conceivably, made this arrangement anticipating his first-born daughter would be properly cared for. Or, perhaps, it was just a coincidence that in January of 1794 Dr. Conand and Susanne welcomed their son Juan Francisco Florentin into the world,[8] and two months later Conand bought land from Susanne's father.[9] Whether it was a familial arrangement, temporary love, or pure and simple lust, we may never discern. But the two did share an intimate connection and a son for a period of time.

Despite his obligation to Susanne and their child, Dr. Conand's stay in Natchitoches was brief, and he eventually moved to New Orleans. The reason for his parting is up for speculation. But, a series of violent incidents in the post may have hastened his departure. In 1795 there was a rebellion at the outpost. This rebellion, known as "The Natchitoches Revolt," was instigated by the Spanish government's attempt to remove the post's beloved French priest, Father Jean Delvaux. The rebels, known as *le Revenants* (the Ghosts) attacked citizens using weapons. Spanish supporters were a target of the rebels. Whether or not Dr. Conand supported Louisiana's Spanish government is not known, but he was attacked twice. These attacks may have spearheaded his departure.[10]

Not long after his move, while continuing her life in Isle Brevelle with their son Florentin, Susanne met a new suitor. This time it was a widowed planter by the name of Jean Baptiste Anty. In 1798, while Susanne cemented her relationship with Jean Baptiste, Dr. Conand chose a wife of his station, a white French wife, Thérèse Jourdan.[11] As Susanne's father had done with her mother, Dr. Conand had conformed to society's mores. But unlike her father, by doing so, he abandoned Florentin, his first born son.

In 1805, Dr. Conand and his family called house #33 on the Rue de Chartres in New Orleans home,[12] but in 1808 the doctor was doing so well he bought the 6,385 feet Conand Mansion at 722 St. Louis Street in the French Quarters.[13] This mansion was equipped with slave quarters, a flagstone patio, and carriage way. During a forty year period, he practiced medicine in New Orleans and then moved to Ascension Parish in Louisiana where he died on June 30, 1830.[14] His succession disclosed he owned several acres of land in addition to a sugar plantation. Included among his possessions was a brick sugar house, two stables, a sugar mill with a steam engine, a main dwelling, a store, slave cabins, and other buildings. The Conand estate was valued at $120,815 in 1830. The value in 2011 would have been $3,040,000.[15] Dr. Joseph Conand had done quite well for himself, but, considering the circumstances of her birth and her late start in life, Susanne did not lag too far behind.

By 1797, Susanne and Jean Baptiste Anty had formed a mutually satisfying alliance. With him, she began a lengthy relationship which produced four daughters.[16] Although still a slave and the caretaker of her father, along with his wife and children, Susanne had discovered someone who would integrate some happiness into her life. Unfortunately for her, this happiness would be laced with pain. Susanne became pregnant with another boy-child, but in 1805 she lost this son.

Determined to move forward, in 1810, Susanne did something that she was strictly forbidden to do according to the laws of Louisiana. While still a slave, she bought her first slave. Louisiana Code Noir twenty-two specifically stated, "We declare that slaves can have no right to any kind of property, and that all that they acquire, either by their own industry or by the liberality of others, or by any other means or title whatever, shall be the full property of their masters."[17] Somehow, *quasi-free* Susanne was able to circumvent this law, and she purchased her first slave for $600.00.[18] Perhaps, drawing on the words of her father in his emancipation stipulation, she felt she would not lose her property. He had stated, "*My receiver, nor any of my heirs, or assignees will have no claim whatsoever on the product of her industry or savings which have been obtained by any talent... she having at all times been authorized and she is authorized by her master ... to enjoy in appropriate measure the fruit of her economy...*"

Knowing that her father, also her master, had promised not to take her property, the following year, in 1811, she defied the law again and bought her second slave.[19] Susanne, still a slave, but with property of her own, was positioned to make further strides. But tragedy touched her life again. In 1814, another son, eight year old Valsain, died from a fever. As though this was not sufficient pain for one person, the very next year, when Susanne was forty-seven, her father died. This lost, though tragic, gave her the freedom to live the remainder of her life unfettered.[20]

Now that she was truly free, in 1815 Susanne bought land from her brothers Augustin and Louis.[21] It was the same year that her son Florentin and her niece Marie Louis decided to marry.[22] Surely, happiness was on the horizon. But, as fate would have it, between 1816 and 1817, there was more heartbreak—Susanne lost her mother.[23] Her mother, her role model, the family matriarch, Marie Thérèse had died. Not to be deterred and determined to walk in her mother's shoes, Susanne, and her only son, Florentin, went about the business of developing their plantation. Everything she needed to know about being a successful slave holder and plantation owner, she had already learned from her mother.

Susanne was among the few free women of color in the rural south that belonged to the planter class, a class that was dominated by men. She, like her female peers, managed her plantation and made it profitable. Some women of color inherited or were given a financial start by their white fathers or lovers. This was not Susanne's fate; she received very little, if any, financial assistance from her wealthy white father. Unlike Margaret Mitchell Harris who inherited twenty-one slaves from her father, Susanne was in her forties, still a slave, before she bought her first slave. Yet she, like her female counterparts became one of the most prosperous single women in her parish. Similar to some of her peers, Susanne did not marry. It has been asserted that the reason free business women of color did not marry was because courts favored the male when it came to property rights; thus the female could lose everything if she did not choose her mate wisely.[24] In Louisiana, though, free women of color, who could afford it, were given the same protection under the law as men. Louisiana court cases demonstrate that free females exercised those rights without restraint.[25]

In the early 1800s Natchitoches did not have a pool of suitors that were socially acceptable to the Metoyers, and this alone may have been the reason Susanne elected not to enter into a formal marital arrangement. Whatever the circumstance may have been for the new entrepreneur, she decided to remain a single female. With the help of her son, and the numerous slaves she acquired through hard work and cash payment, Susanne operated a successful plantation that afforded her and her family a secure lifestyle; a lifestyle as secure as that of her male counterparts.

Like her brother, Augustin, Susanne owned a plantation that was equipped with a cotton gin and a gristmill. Also, like her brother, she must have been an astute business person, because, in 1820, she only owned seven slaves,[26] but that amount tripled by 1830; she owned twenty-one.[27] In spite of operating a plantation, Susanne also found time to enjoy life's feminine luxuries. A business account she opened before her death indicated she had purchased silk stockings, perfume, and "workmanship of a gown."[28] It appears that Susanne worked hard and enjoyed the well-deserved fruits of her labor. When she died, in 1838, she was one of the wealthiest unmarried females in the parish.[29] Her estate was valued at $61,600. Her estate would have been valued at $1,540,000 in 2011. Her slaves brought $25,735 at auction and her movables were worth $1,616. The combined worth of slaves and movables in 2011 CPI value would have been $682,000.[30]

Two ships passing in the night, Bertha's indomitable third great-grandmother, Marie Susanne and her third great-grandfather, Dr. Joseph Conand, introduced Juan Francisco Florentin to the world. It would be their son, Florentin, and his first cousin, Marie Louise, who would throw caution to the wind and tread where few people dared. Marie Louise and Florentin, the children of the Metoyer twins, Augustin and Marie Susanne, would create the initial web of tangled bloodlines that would touch our ancestors for generations to come.

Known Slaves of Marie Susanne Metoyer[31]
Waiting for their Stories to be told

Angelique, born 20 October 1819, baptized 20 March 1820
Agnes (mother of Angelique) aged 37 in 1838, value $900
Francois, born 10 November 1819, baptized 20 March 1820
Pelagie, mother of Francois
Jean Baptiste Ziphorine, born 10 September, 1821
Marie Felicite, (mother of Jean Baptiste Ziphorine) aged 37 in 1838, value $700
Marianne, baptized 18 December 1821, English slave, aged 13
Marie Modeste, baptized 10 August 1822, aged 15 in 1838, value $1000
Marie (mother of Marie Modeste) aged 36 in 1838, value $400
Joseph Lucas, baptism 18 April 1802, 6 months old
Jeanne, mother of Joseph Lucas
Jn [Jean] Louis, baptized 28 January 1817, Guinea Negro, 25 years old
Jn [Jean] Btte. [Baptiste] Senvil [St. Ville] baptized 8 January 1818, 4 months old,
Anries, mother of Jean Baptiste Senvil
Pierre, born *about* 1795, aged 45 in 1838, value $600
Jean Baptiste, born *about* 1794, aged 43 in 1838, value $800
Evils aged 18 in 1838, value $1,000
Bob aged 36 in 1838, value $1,000

Denis aged 32 in 1838, value $1,200
Henry aged 30 in 1838, value $1,000
Symphorien aged 16 in 1838, value $900
Priscilla aged 30 in 1838, value $800
Wine or Wene [sic] aged 20 in 1838 and infant son, value $1,000
Azelie aged 16 in 1838, value $1,000
Lazie [sic] aged 40 in 1838, value $800
Felicite aged 37 in 1838, value $700
Marguerite aged 11, value $400
Derzile [sic] aged 11, value $400
Nanette aged 9, value $300
Elsy aged 22, value $1,000
Victorin aged 15, value $900
Lucas, aged 36 in 1838, value $1,200 (this may be Joseph Lucas, mentioned above)
Omissions and repetitions in this list are possible. To err is only human. But I hope this list brings closure for someone looking for their missing link

Marie Susanne Metoyer's Family

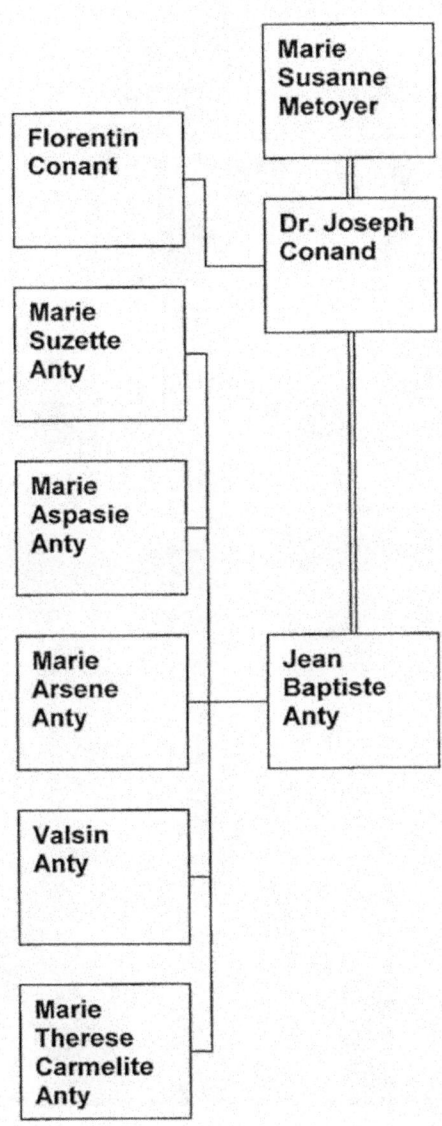

Marie Thérèse Carmelite Metoyer
Daughter of Marie Susanne Metoyer
(Half Sister of Florentin Conant)

Photograph Courtesy of Cammie G. Henry Research Center

Linda S. Manuel

Endnotes

1. Marie Suzanne Metoyer Granted Liberty," Miscellaneous Book 2 p. 209, Clerk of Court's Office, Natchitoches, Louisiana, trans. Gary B. Mills and Elizabeth Shown Mills, 1972.

2. Ibid.

3. Ibid.

4. Conant is a variant of Conand. Conant came into use after Florentin Conant, son of Susanne Metoyer, came of age. Other records in Natchitoches, Ascension, and New Orleans record the spelling Conand.

5. Albert J. Robichaux Jr., *Civil Registration of Orleans Parish Births, Marriages and Deaths, 1790-1833*(Rayne, LA: Hébert Publications, 2000), 192.

6. "Family note cards about Jacques Francois Conand living in Kaskaskia, includes sell of house and profession," deposited by Ruth Winston, File CF. 812.52, Creole Heritage Center.

7. Penny Johnson, "Eulalie de Mandeville: An Ethnohistorical Investigation Challenging Notions of Plaçage in New Orleans as revealed through the Lived Experiences of a Free Woman of Color" (master's thesis, University of New Orleans, 2010), 7, 11, 13-21, accessed January 10, 2012, http://scholarworks.uno.edu/td/1285.

8. Mills, E. S., *Natchitoches, 1729-1803,* entry 2764.

9. "Pierre Metoyer to Joseph Conand," Natchitoches Parish Records, doc. 2518, Natchitoches Parish Courthouse.

10. Gilbert C. Din, "Father Jean Delvaux and the Natchitoches Revolt of 1795," *Louisiana History* 40 (Winter 1999): 5-33; Mills, Elizabeth and Mills, Gary B., *Tales of Old Natchitoches* (Tuscaloosa, Alabama: Mills Historical Press, 1994), 38.

11. Robichaux Jr., *Civil Registration of Orleans Parish,* 192.

12. "1805 New Orleans City Demographics," submitted by Judith Vinson and Colleen Fitzpatrick *USGenWeb Archives, accessed December 21, 2012,* http://files.usgwarchives.net/la/orleans/history/directory/1805demo.txt, citing New Orleans in 1805 a directory and a census, published by The Pelican Gallery, Inc. New Orleans, La. 1936.

13. Stanley Clisby Arthur, *Old New Orleans: A History of the Vieux Carré, Its Ancient and Historic Buildings* (1936; reprinted, Westminster, Maryland: Heritage Book Company, 2007) 56.

14. New Orleans, Louisiana Death Records Index, 1804-1949 for Joseph Conand, accessed December 24, 2012, http://search.ancestry.com/cgi-bin/sse.dll?rank=1&new=1&MSAV=1&msT=1&gss=angs-c&gsfn=joseph&gsln=conand&cpxt=0&uidh=bmr&cp=12&pcat=34&h=991&recoff=10+11&db=NewOrleansDeaths1&indiv=1; citing State of Louisiana, Secretary of State, Division of Archives, Records Management, and History, Vital Records Indices, Baton Rouge, LA. Robichaux, Civil Registration of Orleans Parish, Births, Marriages and Deaths-Period 1790-1838, 192, Folder CF-812.56, Creole Heritage Center, Northwestern State University, Natchitoches, Louisiana.

15. Pie Lanoux, "Joseph Conand's Estate," Folder CF-812, article details items in succession, date and publisher of article not recorded. Iris-Louise "Pie" Lanoux wrote articles for the Ascension Parish Newspaper, *The Ascension Citizen*. This article may have been taken from there, Creole Heritage Center.

16. Mills, E. S., *Natchitoches, 1800-1806,* entries 720, 785, 1887, 2058; Mills, E. S. *Natchitoches, 1729-1803*, entry 3179

17. "Louisiana's Code Noir (1724)," Taylor, et al., *BlackPast.org*.

18. Marie Susan buys slave from Thomas Carhan, p. 302, bundle 1810, Register no. 3813, Natchitoches Colonial Archives.

19. Mills, G., *Forgotten People*, 66.

20. Mills, E. S., *Natchitoches, 1800-1806,* entries 415, 1724, 1745.

21. Marie Suzanne buys land from Augustin Metoyer, pg. 312, bundle 1815, Register 4449; Marie Suzanne buys land from Louis Metoyer, pg. 312, bundle 1815, Register 4451, Natchitoches Colonial Archives.

22. Marriage contract, Marie Louis Metoyer and J. B. Florentin Metoyer, page, 312, bundle 1815, register 4464, Natchitoches Colonial Archives.

23. Mills, G., *Forgotten People*, 48, citing Pierre Metoyer and Marie Henriette, Marriage Contract, Books 2 and 3, Natchitoches Clerk of Court.

24. Loren Schweninger, "Property Owning Free African American Women in the South, 1800-1870," *Journal of Women's History* 1 (Winter 1990): 13-44.

25. Johnson, "Eulalie de Mandeville," 40-41.

26. 1820 U. S. census, Natchitoches Parish, Louisiana, population schedule, p. 99 (stamped) line 64, Susanne Metoyer; digital image, *Ancestry.com,* accessed July 12, 2011, http://search.ancestry.com/iexec?htx=View&r=0&dbid=7734&iid=4433165_00096&fn=Susanne&ln=Mitager&st=r&ssrc=&pid=1493590; citing National Archives microfilm publication M33, roll 142.

27. 1830 U. S. census, Natchitoches Parish, Louisiana, page 69 (penned) line 7, Susan Metoyier [Susanne Metoyer]; digital images, *Ancestry.com,* accessed July13, 2011, http://search.ancestry.com/cgi-bin/sse.dll?indiv=1&db=1830usfedcenancestry&rank=1&new=1&MSAV=1&msT=1&gss=angs-d&gsfn=susan&gsln=metoyer&dbOnly=_F0006BC0%7c_F0006BC0_x%2c_F0006BD3%7c_F0006BD3_x%2c_F0006BD4%7c_F0006BD4_x%2c_F0006BD5%7c_F0006BD5_x%2c_F0006BD6%7c_F0006BD6_x%2c_F0006BD7%7c_F0006BD7_x&uidh=bmr&pcat=35&fh=0&h=1898857&recoff=6+7+18+19+31+32; citing NARA microfilm publication M19, roll 201.

28. Mills, G., *Forgotten People*, 129.

29. Mills, E. S., and Mills, G., "Slaves and Masters," 177.

30. Succession of Marie Suzanne Metoyer no. 355, Natchitoches Colonial Archives, Natchitoches, Louisiana; Officer and Williamson, *MeasuringWorth*, accessed December *21, 2012,* http://www.MeasuringWorth.com/usgdp/.

31. Mills, E. S., *Natchitoches 1800-1806*, entries 1214, 1215, 1439, 1477, 1562, 1816, 2524, 2597; "Succession of Marie Suzanne Metoyer."

Linda S. Manuel

Chapter 11

Marie Louise Metoyer and Florentin Conant
A Family Affair

Marie Louise Metoyer and Florentin Conant (Bertha's second-great grandparents) ignited a passion that would last a lifetime. Louise and Florentin (the children of Augustin and Marie Susanne Metoyer), about three years apart in age, had shared life experiences since they were small children. Because their mother and father were twins, from the moment Louise was born she would not have been far from her cousin, Florentin. Sharing Sunday suppers and holidays and frolicking in the same yards as they teased and fought with one another must have made the two inseparable. Love, it seems, was inevitable, and the next step, marriage, would have seemed logical if they were not first cousins. Precisely when they recognized it was more than familial love is anyone's speculation, but at some time and place it crossed that familial threshold, and the two decided they wanted to become one.

Although Louise and Florentin had dared to cross the familial threshold, they were not alone. They shared this bond with some renowned people. Among them were Johann Sebastian Bach, Albert Einstein, H. G. Wells, and Charles Darwin. As forbidden as the prospect of marrying ones cousin may appear, it is not now, and was not then, a new phenomenon. One only has to look back through the annals of history to recognize that cousin marriages have existed since biblical times. In the Old Testament there was a marriage between Abraham's son and his first cousin, once removed. Abraham's grandson, Jacob, also married his first cousin.[1] For centuries, Christian countries have been accustomed to cousin marriages. Yet, the debate about cousin marriages is a constant. Some scholars theorize that children of these marriages are more apt to have physical and mental disabilities, while others propose that inbreeding has produced vigorous offspring.[2] A recent study by geneticist, Alan H. Bittles, suggests that the risks are not

107

as pronounced as they were purported. In a worldwide study, Bittles discovered the risks to be only seven percent higher than persons not married to cousins. The greatest risks appear to be for those who are carriers of extremely rare disorders.[3] The Metoyers, according to Sister Jerome Woods, who did a sociological study on the Metoyer family, "have not been a sickly people. On the contrary, they have shown an immense vitality, a high fecundity, a comparatively balanced sex ratio, and a determination to maintain themselves as a people."[4] From what this author has observed, despite the countless cousin marriages among the Metoyers during the 1800s and early 1900s, physical and mental disorders among them, as Bittle established in his study, appear to be equivalent to those in the general population.

One motivation for cousin marriages between the Metoyers during the 1800s may have been because suitable mates could not be found for their children in the isolated colony of Isle Brevelle. The colony, when the second generation Metoyer children were born, mostly consisted of white Frenchmen or slaves. In Natchitoches in 1810 there were 1,213 Whites, 1,476 slaves, and only 181 free people of color.[5] There were very few, if any, free people of color who had the wealth and social standing of the Metoyer family. Since the Metoyer offspring were the descendants of a slave and a Frenchman, they were forbidden by law to marry someone from the white race. The thought of marrying a slave was inconceivable because of the social class into which they were born and because their parents were slave owners. Another reason for cousin marriages may have been to retain the wealth in the family. As one researcher revealed, families instinctively draw together as a method of survival. Part of this survival is pooling finances and passing those finances down. Relatives marrying create strong family bonds that enable the family to accumulate and retain wealth. This encouragement, by families for their offspring to marry cousins, guarantee that the property will be retained by the family assuring continued prosperity.[6] Therefore, the Metoyer cousin marriages would have been advantageous for the growth of wealth and the protection of the family. The exact rationale behind the Metoyer marriages, like the earlier Metoyers, has long departed. But for reasons that were their own, and with no voice from the church, the Metoyers intermarried.

For the parents of Florentin and Louise, the acceptance of marriages between first cousins must have been a cogent solution for the circumstances into which they were born. Several of their children would follow the path that Florentin and Louise had taken. In 1816, the same year Florentin and Louise married, Louise's oldest brother, Jean Baptiste Augustin, married Florentin's half sister, Marie Suzette. In 1817, Louise's brother, J. B. Maxille, married Florentin's half sister, Marie Aspasie Anty,[7] and in 1824, her other brother, Auguste Augustin, married Florentin and Aspasie's sister Marie Therese Carmelite Anty.[8] Therefore, with the blessing of their parents and the church, in 1816, at the age of seventeen, Louise Metoyer married her first cousin and lifelong love, twenty-one year old Florentin Conant.[9]

If witnesses are to be believed, Florentin had been in the process of making arrangements for a family prior to 1816. In 1814 (though still a slave according to the provisions of Pierre's arrangements in his mother, Susanne's, manumission agreement), Florentin had submitted a land claim for 640 acres of land. The claim was submitted under the premise that he had occupied the land when it was under Spanish rule, but he had failed to complete the grant process during that period. In order to substantiate his claim, Florentin brought forth two witnesses, a free man of color, Michel Papillon, and Marcellet Martin. Presumably, Martin was white, although his race was not identified in the records. On May 15, 1814, Papillon testified that Florentin had been living on the land and cultivating it for approximately ten years. He also further proclaimed that about two years ago he "was in that neighborhood, and found the claimant still there." On August 3, 1814, Martin stated that Florentin had "inhabited and cultivated the land for fourteen consecutive years…" He also indicated that Florentin was about thirty-five years old and had no family. Inaccuracies in the testimonies abound. Born in 1795, it would have been impossible for Florentin to cultivate the land for the period of time his witnesses specified.[10] Despite these fallacies, Florentin was granted his claim which permitted the couple to begin their new lives with an immense amount of property.

Florentin's contribution to the family's portfolio was reinforced by Louise. It was customary for Louise's father, Augustin, to make donations to his children when they married. He provided each of his oldest children with 600 piasters and property in the range of 200 to 400 arpents as wedding gifts. Louise would have conveyed property to the marriage in the form of slaves, money, land, or a combination of these gifts.[11] One plantation, not considered as community property, exclusively belonging to Marie Louise, was five arpents front on each side of the Red River.[12] With the generosity of their parents and the ingenuity of Florentin and his witnesses, the young couple would have begun their lives together without the financial burdens that most young couples have to endure.

It would be four years before the couple would introduce their first child to the world. But, finally, on June 17, 1820, Florentin Jr. made his appearance.[13]

Two years later, in 1822, a girl-child, Florentine, was born. In 1825, their second son, Charles, arrived. He was soon followed by another boy-child, Augustin.[14] On May 3, 1828 the couple presented their last child, another girl-child, to the world, Marie Agnes Conant.[15]

In 1837, after twenty two years of marriage, when Agnes was only nine years old, Florentin lost his life-mate, Louise. Tragedy must have struck the family twice previously because when Louise's succession was held, the only children included in the succession were Florentin, Florentine, Jean Baptiste, and Agnes. There was no declaration to Charles and Augustin. The following year, Florentin lost his mother, Marie Susanne Metoyer. He was now a single father without the support of his mother in the rearing of his children. One of those children, Agnes, was Bertha's great-grandmother.

By the time Agnes was born, the Metoyers were becoming aware of the complications that were possible due to the intermarriage of close relatives, especially first cousins. Advice was purportedly given to Augustin Metoyer by a priest that he should make an effort to make more marital choices available for the family.[16] An influx of free people of color from neighboring areas and New Orleans began to migrate to the Isle. As Agnes came of age, there were more free people of color from which she could select a mate. By 1820, the population of free people of color would have increased immensely, but it still lagged far behind that of slaves and whites. There were 4,725 whites, 2,326 slaves, and 415 free people of color.[17] Though the number of free people of color had more than tripled, most were not as affluent as the Metoyers. But, some were measured as socially acceptable for the Metoyers to marry. One of those families was the Christophe family from New Orleans.

The head of the family, Firmin Capello Christophe Sr., and his wife, Marie Françoise Mayeux relocated to the Isle Brevelle from New Orleans during the 1830s.[18] Firmin had served in the War of 1812 from 1814 to 1815. He was not an extremely prosperous man, but he brought a vocation with him. He was a tailor, and he remained in this profession for thirty years. By 1850, his prosperity had advanced, and he was the proprietor of fifty hogs and nineteen heads of cattle. He also possessed twenty acres of established property and three hundred forty acres of undeveloped parcels. By 1860, he had an income of $12,000 that surpassed most Americans.[19] Measured by the historical standard of living value in 2011, his income would have been $33,500.[20] His son, Firmin Capello Christophe Jr., also resided on the Isle and held a respectable job as a teacher.[21] Firmin Jr. married Agnes' cousin, Marie Julia Metoyer. Agnes pursued Julia's lead and introduced another Christophe into the family. By doing so, she married in her social stratum and assured that the wealth and family continued to flourish.

It was the second son of Firmin Sr., Charles Christophe, who garnered the attention and seized the heart of Agnes. On November 18, 1845, after two banns (church announcements), Marie Agnes Conant pledged her love to Charles Christophe.[22] The union of Bertha's great-grandparents, Agnes and Charles Christophe, would soon produce a daughter, Marie Laura Christophe. Laura, like her grandparents before her, would one day step over the familial line and discover more than familial love with a cousin, Félicien Balthazar—the great-grandson of Bertha's other third-great grandparent, Louis Metoyer.

Slaves owned by Florentin Conant and Marie Louise Metoyer[23]
Waiting for their stories to be told

(Ages of these slaves and value placed on them is at the time of Louise's 1837 Succession)
Frank aged 40, $500
William aged 37, $1000
Manuel aged 37, $1000
Sam aged 30, $600
Charles aged 28, $1000
Santy aged 30, $1000
Julien aged 23, $1000
William, carpenter, aged 35, $1700
Maria aged 25, $700
Adeline aged 20, $700
Nora aged 40
Henriette, daughter of Nora, aged 11
Lolette, daughter of Nora, aged 9
Jules, Son of Nora, aged 7
Acula, child of Nora, aged 4
(Nora's family value was appraised together for $1,125)
Betsey aged 20, $800
Lovy aged 35, $1000
I hope this list brings closure.

Marie Agnes Conant Christophe
Bertha's Great-Grandmother

Photograph Courtesy of Kathleen Balthazar Heitzmann

Linda S. Manuel

Florentin Conant and Marie Louise Metoyer's family

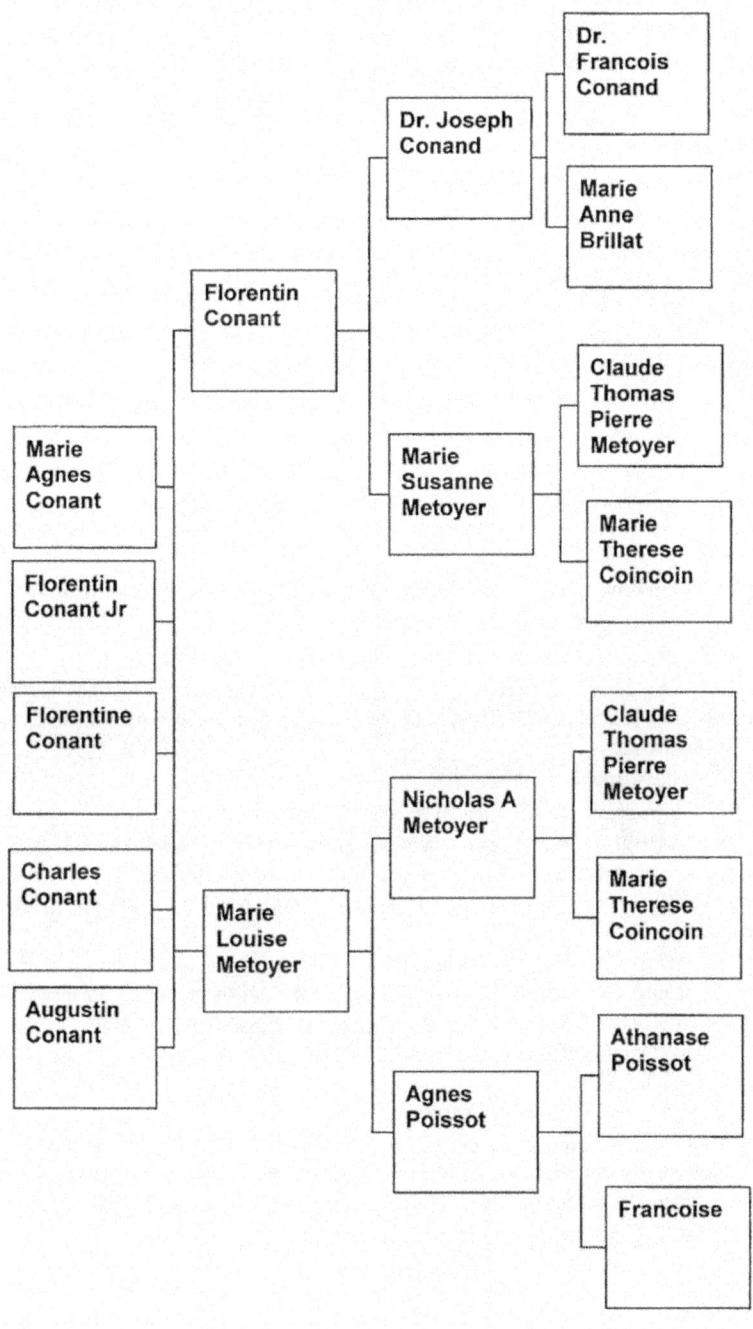

Endnotes

1. Genesis 24, 28, 29.
2. Jill Durey, "The Church, Consanguinity and Trollope," 127, 136, accessed March 25, 2013, http://www.docstoc.com/docs/74736776/The-Church_-Consanguinity-and-Trollope.
3. Alan H. Bittles, *Consanguinity in Context* (New York: Cambridge University Press, 2012), 3, 147, 213, 227.
4. Woods, *Marginality and Identity*, 49.
5. *Biographical and Historical Memoirs of Northwest Louisiana, Comprising a Large Fund of Biography of Actual Residents, and an Interesting Historical Sketch of Thirteen Counties,* (Chicago: Southern Publishing Company, 1890), 294, accessed January 15, 2013, http://books.google.com/books?id=ZucxAQAAMAAJ&printsec=frontcover#v=onepage&q&f=false.
6. Durey, "The Church," 128.
7. Mills, E. S., *Natchitoches, 1800-1826*, entries 720, 721,773.
8. Mills, E. S., *Natchitoches Church Marriages, 1818-1850*, entry 172.
9. Mills, E.S., *Natchitoches, 1800-1826*, entry 721.
10. American State Papers: Public Lands, 3:175, accessed January 19, 2013, http://memory.loc.gov/cgi-bin/ampage?collId=llsp&fileName=030/llsp030.db&Page=175.
11. Woods, *Marginality and Identity*, 34; Mills, E. S., and Mills G., "Slaves and Masters," 175.
12. Succession of Marie Louise Metoyer, no. 323, Natchitoches Colonial Archives.
13. Mills, E. S., *Natchitoches, 1800-1826*, entry 1274.
14. Ibid., entries 1274, 1632, 1633.
15. Agnes Conant's birth record, Saint Augustine's Catholic Church baptismal, marriage, death records, book beginning 1880, Priest A. Dupré, pp. 18,19; Saint Augustine's Catholic Church, Natchez, Louisiana.
16. Woods, *Marginality and Identity*, 67.
17. *Biographical and Historical Memoirs of Northwest Louisiana*, 294.
18. "War of 1812 Pension Application Files Index, 1812-1815," Marie Francoise Christophe, widow's pension application no. SC 3743; service of Firmin Christophe (Private, 1st Battalion, Fortiers, Louisiana Militia); Department of Veterans Affairs, Record Group Number 15; National Archives, Washington, D C.
19. 1860 U. S. census, Natchitoches Parish, Louisiana, population schedule, p. 48 (penned), dwelling 378, family 378, Firmon Christopher [Firmin Capello Christophe, Sr.]; digital image, *Ancestry.com*, accessed March 21, 2009, http://search.ancestry.com/iexec?htx=View&r=an&dbid=7667&iid=4231225_00050&fn=Firmon&ln=Christopher&st=r&ssrc=&pid=38481502; citing NARA microfilm publication M653, roll 414.
20. Officer and Williamson, *Measuring Wealth*.
21. 1850 U. S. census, Natchitoches, Parish, Louisiana, Natchitoches township, p. 99, Firman Christophe, owner; digital images, *Ancestry.com*, accessed February 12, 2013, http://ancestry.com; citing NARA microfilm publication M432; Mills, G., *Forgotten People*, 99, 114, 134, 185.
22. Mills, E. S., *Natchitoches Marriages*, entry 611.
23. Succession of Marie Louise Metoyer.

Chapter 12

Louis Metoyer and Françoise
Young and Tenacious

The last of Bertha's third great-grandparents, Louis Metoyer, is the branch from which our limbs began to unfurl as they gravitated towards the warmth of our life-source, the sun. Evidence uncovered tends to indicate that it was a mighty strong branch. Having been surrounded by the freedom of one's mother and brothers, but unable to taste that liberty for one's self is enough to break the strongest of men. But Louis would be an exception. With wit, ingenuity, and hard work, he proved that one is not destined to remain in the station into which one is born.

Wedged between two worlds, one black and one white, one free and one enslaved, Louis' life was an enormous paradox. He relished the freedom that his father's whiteness afforded him, but he was his slave. His mother cherished and nourished him, but she could not protect him. Reflected from his mirror was neither the image of his mother nor his father. Unlike his father, his skin was shades of brown, and unlike his mother, his skin was shades of white. Exactly who was this boy-child, and how would his world of ambiguity define who he would become?

Before being acquired by his father, when he was about five, Louis was a slave in the house of Madame de Soto. After possibly picking worms from tomato plants, or feeding the chickens and gathering their eggs, he was likely free to play, wander, and imagine life's possibilities. To a child, at such an early age, the concepts of slavery and freedom are beyond ones scope of comprehension. Louis' innocence was his salvation. His recollections, as a slave with Madame de Soto, may have just been whispers in the wind speaking to him on occasion to remind him of things endured. As the young child gravitated towards adolescence and finally emerged into manhood, did the nagging winds that whispered to him as a child transform into a raging storm when he became the slave of his father?

Adolescence alone wreaks havoc on the soul, but what goes through the mind and heart of an adolescent when he recognizes it is his father, not a stranger, who possesses the key to his freedom? Were questions asked and tears shed? Were there times when Louis pleaded to his mother to talk to his father about granting him his freedom, or was he content with the degree of independence he had due to his familial ties with his father? One might debate that his life was better than most under his father's ownership. But was "better" enough to silence the longing that all people have for freedom? Yet, for thirty-two years, Louis stood in the shadows of the freedom possessed by his mother, his oldest brother, Augustin, and his younger brothers François, Toussaint, Joseph Antoine, and Dominique, and he appeared to have emerged unbroken. Did he seethe inside knowing his mother and brothers were free, or did he wish them well as he fantasized of one day possessing his own freedom? Only Louis could discern the thoughts he kept within. But what we do know is that long before Louis tasted the tantalizing sweetness of freedom there was one constant in his life—Françoise Lecomte, the illegitimate daughter and slave of the neighboring planter, Jean Baptiste Lecomte.[1]

Both Françoise and Louis were familiar with the constraints of slavery. Although Françoise's father died when she was young, like Louis, her father had owned her. She was subsequently the property of her father's widow and her white half-brother, Ambrose Lecomte.[2] She, similar to Louis, had a French father, and her mother was his slave. This may have been the glue that bonded them together. The couple may have sought solace in one another on those hot, humid afternoons as they went about their mundane lives cursing the system and parents that enslaved them. As the sun faded behind the clouds and the cloak of darkness took its place, did they rush into each other's arms beneath some magnificent oak, beside a trickling stream for comfort? The meandering Red River and the mighty oaks are not releasing their secrets. But it is from the loins of these lovers that two daughters were conceived: Marie Louise Catiche, born in 1790, and Marie Rose, born in 1792.[3]

Bertha's third great-grandmother, Françoise, the mother of the girls and perhaps the first love of Louis, would not become his wife. Although he did not wed Françoise, she found love and acceptance with someone else. Around 1796, four years after the birth of Marie Rose, Françoise, had an affair with a young white planter, Jean Baptiste Louis Rachal. This affair would eventually produce three children, Jean Baptiste Espalier, Adelaide, and Pierre. In 1799, Jean Baptiste bought his first born son, and namesake, from the heirs of the Widow LeComte. In 1803, when Françoise was thirty, she, along with the other children, was sold to Jean Baptiste. Two years after purchasing Françoise and the children, Jean Baptiste freed the children. Eventually, Françoise was also freed because the 1810 census shows that all the persons in the home of Jean Baptiste were white or free people of color. As a couple, Françoise and Jean lived together and had several more children. Around 1816 or 1817, Françoise, Bertha's third great-grandmother, the mother of Louis' first offspring, Catiche and Marie Rose, died.[4]

Though little was published about Françoise, her daughters would grace the pages of history. Louis' mother, Marie Thérèse, Coincoin, would pay the price for the freedom of his first daughter, Catiche. In 1794, Catiche was bought from her maternal grandfather's widow. The price of four-year-old Catiche was set at $150.00, a price her paternal grandmother proudly paid. As Marie Thérèse did with all her kin, soon after the purchase, Catiche was given her freedom. She lived from the age of two with her grandmother.[5] Louis' brother, Augustin, would ensure that his other enslaved niece, Marie Rose, would experience a life her mother had never known as a child. It may have been the pleadings of his brother that triggered Augustin to liberate Rose, or the familial love of an uncle for his niece. Nonetheless, with $300 in hand, Augustin purchased seven-year-old Marie Rose from her maternal grandfather's widow on November 18, 1800. She like, Catiche, was almost immediately freed.[6]

Louis Makes His Mark

Determined to better understand Louis, I retraced the decisions he made in life. By doing so it became evident to me that he was tenacious and ambitious. At the age of twenty-five, before freedom was a reality, Louis had set in motion plans for his future. In 1795, while he was still his father's slave, he reportedly petitioned the Spanish government for approximately 900 acres of land. In 1796, the land was granted to Louis because its previous owner, Silvestre Bossier, had abandoned it.[7] Louis' ability to obtain property as a slave is one of history's unsolved mysteries. Property ownership by a slave was against the law in colonial Louisiana. Furthermore, how could a slave buy property? Unlike his sister, Susanne, who had bought a slave while she was still a slave, Louis was not *quasi-free*. Was his father assisting his son to prepare for the freedom he would eventually grant him, or did his free mother have a hand in the transaction? How a slave was able to become the owner of such a large tract of land will always be in dispute, but ownership of the property by Louis was not a moot point.

In 1801, liberty was footsteps away from Louis. He had a substantial amount of land that he was working hard to maintain. Louis was the father of two daughters; Catiche and Marie Rose, (the daughters of Françoise) who were now free from slavery and under the watchful eyes of his mother. And he was the father of Thérèse, another daughter he had conceived with Madeleine Grappe. On October 10, 1800, his first-born son, Jean Baptiste Louis was born. Life could not have been better for a man who was about to grasp his freedom and capitalize from it. The only thing he lacked was a wife to share his first moments of freedom and be a mother to his children. His wife of choice was the mother of his first son, Marie Thérèse Lecomte. [8]

Marie Thérèse had stolen the heart of Louis and conceivably broken the hearts of Françoise and Madeleine, the mothers of his three daughters. Marie Thérèse's mother was an enslaved Lipan Apache of the Canneci tribe of Native Americans.[9] She was the slave of the planter, Ambroise Lecomte. While she was enslaved by Ambroise, she had a liaison with him that resulted in the conception of Marie Thérèse. Ambroise was also the father of Jean Baptiste Lecomte: the man who had fathered Louis' first love, Françoise. Marie Thérèse, a French-Native American child, would become Louis' wife. Ironically (due to the father/son kinship between Ambroise and Jean Baptiste Lecomte) by becoming his wife, Marie Thérèse would be the stepmother, as well as the first cousin, of Louis' daughters, Catiche and Marie Rose.[10]

Despite this awkward kinship, on February 9, 1801, a year before he officially became a liberated man, and after three banns, thirty-one-year-old Louis stood at the altar with his eighteen-year-old bride. Among those witnessing the nuptials were Louis' older brother, Augustin, and Thérèse's brother, Jacques.[11] Louis' best man, Julien Besson, unlike Louis and his new bride, was white.[12] It would be Louis' ability to forge diverse friendships, like the one with Julien, which would serve him well as he maneuvered through the complexities of life.

Years behind the accomplishments and hard labor of his mother and older brother, Louis wasted no time in catching up to their social status. He accomplished this by engaging in the business that came with land ownership in the colonial south. He cultivated his land and contemplated slave ownership. His land, on the Isle Brevelle, in Natchitoches parish, imbedded between the ever changing Red River (today known as the Old River) and Cane River was a picture-perfect place to construct a home. The land was fertile and the wildlife was abundant. This untamed virgin land must have once been paradise on earth despite the annoying mosquitoes, cane brakes, and stinging yucca plants. Built from cypress beams held together with a mixture of mud, deer fur, and Spanish moss,[13] Louis's original home could have been the foundation for ideas that would blossom into his plantation home that he would later design on the other side of the river—a home grander than Louis could have possibly envisioned.

In 1802, when Louis was officially emancipated, (possibly as a rite of passage) he bought his first slave, thirty-five year old George.[14] He was certainly necessary to help clear the cane brakes, root out cypress trees, and cultivate the land on Louis's vast amount of property. For four years, George, Louis, and possibly Louis' brothers and their slaves worked incessantly to develop his land into a successful property. It would be four years later, in 1806, before Louis acquired his second slave, Marie. By 1810, Louis owned 15 slaves:[15] more than most inhabitants on the Isle Brevelle. In the two years that followed, he continued to sell and buy property. Louis had experienced freedom for only eight years, but he was more successful than free men who had never been enslaved and were not of color. Was he just a driven spirit, or was this Louis' method for making up for the time he had lost while being enslaved? Perhaps he equated slave ownership with manhood and acceptance. Or was it just the natural progression of things in his world? His mother, father, and brothers were slave holders. Nothing less could be expected of him. With ambition, tenacity, and hard work, Louis seemed destined to become a very prosperous man.

Unfortunately, along the way to prosperity, there are unavoidable crevices in the road. In 1813, while Louis was buying land and slaves, the original 912 acres that he had acquired while still enslaved came into question. Because of this land, Louis discovered himself embroiled in a lawsuit. But, Louis, as his opponent would soon determine, would be anything but passive about his property, and he would defend it even if it meant taking his case to the state's highest court.

According to the lawsuit, filed by Silvestre Bossier, the parcel on which Louis had built his plantation house belonged to Bossier. In 1789, Bossier had petitioned the government for the land, and the petition had been approved. But when Bossier failed to clear the land (as specified by the Spanish government), in 1795 Louis petitioned for it. Louis improved the land as was stipulated, and an order of survey and settlement were ordered in 1796. In 1806 Louis filed his claim with the U. S. Land Office. For approximately three years, from 1817-1819, the two men found themselves in court. In the original trial, which occurred in district court, the land was granted to Bossier. Louis, with the resolve of his mother, and perhaps the influence of his father, decided a battle lost was not a war won. In 1818, Louis appealed to the Louisiana Supreme Court, and the decision of the lower court was overturned.[16] His persistence had prevailed, and Louis was declared the rightful owner of the land. He was now free to continue on his carefully orchestrated path to success.

With the lawsuit behind him, Louis continued on his ambitious journey. But once again his progress was temporarily derailed by another lawsuit that transpired less than two years after the first. This lawsuit was filed by Louis against Geneviève and Clay, two free people of color. They had decided to become squatters on Louis' property and attempted to claim his title. As with the previous lawsuit, Louis fought their claim and was successful. The court ordered the couple to vacate his property and pay his court costs.[17] With another triumph in court, Louis continued with the progression of his life. In 1820, he possessed 22 slaves.[18] Louis must have been a religious man because between 1800 and 1826 he had 29 of his slaves baptized.[19] Of his slaves, there is only one record that has surfaced regarding a runaway. In 1825, the *Natchitoches Courier* published an advertisement for the capture of a slave named Charles owned by Louis Metoyer. Louis offered $50 if the slave was captured east of the Sabine and $150 if captured to the west.[20] Whether this slave was apprehended is not known.

As history goes, dates are often disputed. An exact date cannot be verified, but amid the lawsuits, and the buying of land and slaves, Louis began designing his dream plantation home. Supposedly, commissioned to build the house was Seraphin Llorens, a carpenter who resided in the area.[21] This plantation home, known today as Melrose, was one of the finest homes of its era. The walls of the house were built two feet thick, and the floors were made from bricks made by slaves.[22] The veranda's pillars were made of brick that were attached to a wide gallery. The gallery was enclosed with banisters. Four dormers with arched windows were built on the main house. Two dormers faced the front and two were in the back.[23] The kitchen was built detached from the main house, and there was also a separate storeroom.[24] The interior of the house was furnished with mahogany woods. The house was adorned with imported art and glassware from France.[25] Despite the fact that he had been a slave for 32 years, he was now a rich Creole planter, and this home would be the crème de la crème for his wife, Thérèse, and his son, Jean Baptiste Louis.

During the development of his plantation, Louis continued to buy slaves, and in 1830 he owned 54. In 1830, there were approximately 800 heads of households counted in Natchitoches Parish, and less than half owned slaves. Louis and his brother, Augustin, were among the top fifteen largest slaveholders. His two white half-siblings (who had the benefit of inheriting their father's estate) ranked ninth and eleventh with 58 and 63 slaves.[26] A wealthy landowner, Louis had all the privileges afforded free people of color. Trips to France and visits to New Orleans were not beyond his grasp. Louis Metoyer had finally attained an extraordinary lifestyle— a lifestyle exceedingly far beyond the grasp of most former slave's dream. Although he had lived a long lifespan for the era in which he lived, his lifestyle of wealth and privilege would be short-lived. On March 11, 1832, a year before his beloved plantation house was completed, Louis died at the age of sixty-two.[27] He would never know the pleasures of living in the home he had so lovingly designed. That home is still standing almost 200 years after his death, and has been declared a *National Historical Landmark* by the National Park Service's landmark program. Upon Louis' death, his estate was inherited by his son, Jean Baptiste. When Louis passed away, the estate was valued at $113,000.[28] This was an incredible amount for the period in which he lived. Valued in the 2011 market it would have been worth $2,840,000.[29] "Included in his property were 63 slaves, a flatboat, a barouche (type of carriage), a stud horse, silverware, mahogany furniture, and a plantation home near completion."[30] Surpassing the accomplishments of many of his peers, Louis led a lucrative and rewarding life.

Louis Metoyer was born a slave and kept in bondage for 32 years. Unshackled, and with tenacity and sagaciousness, he was able to achieve more during his 30 years of freedom than most people attain in a lifetime. His endeavors have been debated and will continue to be debated long after my demise. But, in a world defined by black and white, freedom and slavery, he bowed but was never broken. It is from this unwavering branch that Bertha's second great-grandmother, Marie Rose Metoyer, the daughter of Françoise and Louis Metoyer, was born.

Known Slaves of Louis Metoyer
Waiting to be Discovered

Slaves Owned by Louis Metoyer and Baptized
Baptized 6 July 1822
Joseph, aged 6 months, son of Marianne.
Romain, son of Marie.
Baptized 30 November 1821
Marie Asely, born 22 April 1821, daughter of Marie.
Marie Loyse, born 25 August 1821, daughter of Delphine.
Baptized 17 December 1821
Henry, aged about 28, English Negro.
Charles, aged about 26, English Negro.
Francoise, aged about 28.
Zenon, aged 25, English Negro.
Manuel Chasmé (? Charmé), aged 17, Guinea Negro.
Athanas, aged 18, Guinea Negro.
Philipe, aged 17, Guinea Negro.
Jacque, aged 19, Guinea Negro.
Cezar, aged 12, English.
Marie, aged 22, Guinea Negro.
Rosaly, aged 24, Guinea Negro.
Delphine, aged 20, English.
Mariane, aged 34, Guinea Negro.
Marie Laysa, aged 16, English Negro.
Baptized 20 March 1820
Severinne, 3 months old, daughter of Delphine
Baptized 27 June 1820
Dorselin, born 22 March 1820, infant, son of Marie.
Modest Marie, born 19 Mary 1820, daughter of Marianne.
Baptized 28 January 1817
  Me. Jeanne Bernadiet, born 26 December 1816, daughter of Marianne.[31]
Baptized 8 June 1815
Francisca, born 10 March 1807, daughter of Mariana.
Marie Felicite, born 22 March 1808, daughter of Maria.
Onore, baptized 8 June 1815, born 10 August 1809, son of Maria.

Jose Sensir, born 26 May 1813, son of Rosaly.
Bernard, born 25 August 1813, son of Mariane.
Antonio, born 6 December 1814, son of Marie.
Baptized 26 June 1815
Marie Louisse, born January 1815, daughter of Marie.

Slaves Owned by Louis Metoyer, Baptism (if any) Unknown
George, age 35 in 1802
Marie Congo, age 20 in 1806, from Congo
Jasmin, Islamic, Black male
Baba, age 45, liberated 1810
Françoise, age 55, liberated 1810
Jascinine? Jascinité? Male
Sam
Henry
Toussaint, about age 15 in 1813 *nègre* Creole
Charlotte, Cankau, or Caukau
Marie, age 28 in 1816, from Congo
Belle, age 3 in 1816
Mascannie? Marianne, age 19 in 1816
Mario? , child of Marianne
Babette, about age 45 in 1816, from Guinée
Brigitte, about age 14 in 1817, female, *Negress*, Creole
Françoise, age 50 in 1818, Black
Eliza age 12 in 1819
Pierre, born 5 April 1826, son of Marie Luisa
Marie Lolitte, born 16 July 1824, daughter of Marie Laiza
Charles, born 5 August 1823, son of Marie
Jean Baptiste Ludgeiare, born 26 May 1825, son of Marie
Antoin, born 6 June 1825, son of Marianne
Caroline, age 5 years in 1826, daughter of Rose
Colas, about 30 in 1827, Negro
Deneige, about 26 in 1827, *Negress*[32]

May these lists bring closure to someone searching for their missing link.

Searching For Bertha

Louis Metoyer's Family

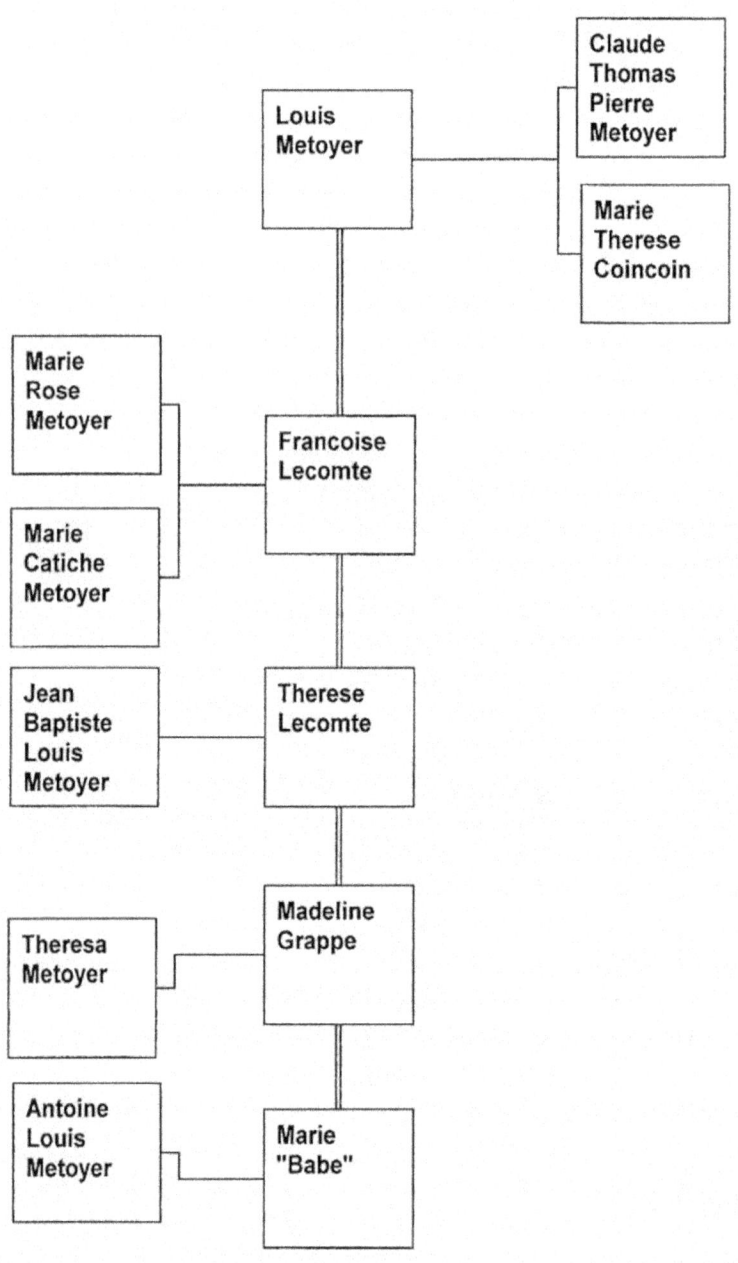

Main House at Melrose Plantation

Photo by Jack Boucher, Courtesy of U.S. Department of the Interior, National Park Service, Historic American Building Survey.

African House at Melrose Plantation
Photo by Lester Jones, Historic American Building Survey

The Yucca House at Melrose Plantation
(Home where Louis Metoyer died.)
Photo by Lester Jones, Historic American Building Survey

Endnotes

1. Mills, E. S., *Isle of Canes*, see book's genealogy charts for, "The Lecomte Slave Roots."

2. Mills, E. S., (shown@comcast.net) to author, (aceteach13@wideopenwest.com), December 30, 2010, "Balthazar Slaves"; citing Lecomte Heirs to Jean Baptiste Rachal, sale of slaves, 1803, Doc. 2913, Natchitoches Colonial Archives.

3. Mills, E. S., *Natchitoches, 1729-1803,* entries 2623, 2749.

4. Mills, E. S. (shown@comcast.net) to author, (aceteach13@wideopenwest.com) ; Mills, *Isle of Canes*, "The Lecomte Slave Roots."

5. Mills, G., *Forgotten People*, 38.

6. Widow Lecomte to Nicolas Augustin, 1800, Old Natchitoches Data, No. 279, Cammie G. Henry Research Center, Northwestern State University, Natchitoches, Louisiana.

7. Louis Mettoyer Land Claim Certificate B1953, Reg. no.7 Natchitoches, Old Board Commissioner's Certificates for Act 1805, no. B 1810-2278, pp.90-91, State Land Records, Baton Rouge; Sylvestre Caezer Bossier, S. Bossie, curator ad bona, and Isaac Baldwin, Curator ad litem of Pamela Bossie vs. Louis Metoyer, District Court suit 186, bundle 5 (Dec. Term 1817), Natchitoches Parish, Louisiana.

8. Mills, E. S., *Natchitoches, 1729-1803*, entry 2992.

9. Ibid.

10. Mills, E. S., *Isle of Canes*, see preface, Genealogy Tree, "Lecomte Slave Roots."

11. Mills, E. S., *Natchitoches, 1729-1803*, entry 3448.

12. Mills, G., *Forgotten People*, 212.

13. Herman de Bachellé Seebold, *Old Louisiana Plantation Homes and Family Trees* (Gretna, Louisiana: Pelican Press, 1941) vol.1, 362.

14. Fiona J. L. Handley, "Cane River Historic Documents Project" (File No. 377.N4 No. 363, April; 2004, Louisiana Collection, Northwestern State University, Cammie G. Henry Research Center, Natchitoches, Louisiana), entry Individual Resume: Louis Metoyer #1.

15. 1810 U. S. census, Natchitoches Parish, Louisiana, town of Natchitoches, p. 214 (penned at top right), line 23, Louis Metoyer; digital image, *Ancestry.com,* accessed December 5, 2010, http:// http://search.ancestry.com/iexec?htx=view&r=0&dbid=7613&iid=4433226_00181&fn=Louis+M&ln=Metoyer&st=r&ssrc=pt_t3131577_p82111866&pid=17675 ; citing National Archives microfilm publication M252, roll 10.

16. Louis Mettoyer Land Claim Certificate B1953, Reg. no.7 Natchitoches, Old Board Commissioner's Certificates for Act 1805, no. B 1810-2278, pp.90-91; "Bossier et al. vs. Metoyer."

17. Mills, E. S., and. Mills, G., "Slaves and Masters," 177.

18. 1820 U. S. census, Natchitoches Parish, Louisiana, population schedule, p. 99 (stamped) , line 1, Louis Metoyer; digital image, *Ancestry.com,* accessed December 4, 2010,

http://search.ancestry.com/iexec?htx=View&r=0&dbid=7734&iid=4433165_00097&fn=Louis&ln=Metoyer&st=r&ssrc=&pid=1493595; citing National Archives microfilm publication M33, roll 142.

19. Mills, E. S., *Natchitoches, 1800-1826,* entries 1213, 1255-1256, 1546-1547, 1635-1641, 1680-1695, 2292-2294, 2297-2298, 2318, 2464, 2521.

20. Mills, G., *Forgotten People,* 119, citing *Natchitoches Courier*, July 19, 1825.

21. Mills, G., *Forgotten People,* 178.

22. Woods, *Marginality and Identity,* 68.

23. Seebold, *Louisiana Plantation Homes,* 361.

24. Woods, *Marginality and Identity,* 68.

25. Ibid., 69.

26. 1830 U. S. census, Natchitoches Parish, Louisiana, population schedule, page 69 (penned), line 4, Louis Metoyier; page 67 (penned), line 13, Benjmine Meytoyier; page 77 (penned), line [illegible] Pr Mytour [Pierre Victorin Metoyer], digital images, *Ancestry.com*, accessed December 27, 2010, http://www.ancestry.com; citing NARA microfilm publication M19, roll 201. For total number of slaves see 1830 census at *Ancestry.com.*

27. Louis Metoyer, death record, Saint Augustine's Catholic Church baptismal, marriage, death records, begins 1880, Priest A. Dupré, p. 162; Saint Augustine's Catholic Church, Natchez, Louisiana.

28. Woods, *Marginality and Identity*, 35.

29. Office and Williamson, *MeasuringWorth.*

30. Ibid.

31. Mills, E. S., *Natchitoches, 1800-1826,* entries 1213, 1255, 1256, 1546, 1547, 1680-1695, 2292-2294, 2297, 2298, 2318, 2464, 2521.

32. Handley, "Individual Resume of Louis Metoyer."

Chapter 13

Marie Rose Metoyer
A Life Laced with Tragedy

The blood of Bertha's second great-grandmother, Marie Rose Metoyer, the love child of Louis Metoyer and Françoise Lecomte, quickly pulsates through our veins. While Rose's first cousins, Florentin and Louis, ignited a fire that endured a lifetime, Rose flitted from flame to flame. If Louis was one of the branches from which we sprang, Marie Rose was the bud from that branch which bred in us the adventurous spirit that beckons us to leap and reason just before we plummet to the ground. But who was this Rose? What molded her existence and how? To appreciate the woman, I attempted to analyze the conditions that prepared her for womanhood and fashioned her existence.

During the era in which Rose was born, she lived a life of freedom that most people of color in Louisiana never fathomed. But, with freedom comes responsibility. After examining Rose's life, some might argue that Rose sought the rewards, but avoided the burdens of responsibility required of freedom. Others may conclude that circumstances beyond her control damaged her young psyche and steered her down a somewhat destructive path. To whichever conclusion one may arrive, I feel most will agree that the path Rose chose led not to sustained love but to a life filled with heartbreak and tragedy.

Rose and her sister, Catiche, were the love children of slaves, Louis Metoyer and Françoise Lecomte. Their mother, Françoise, was the product of a sexual relationship that had occurred between the French planter, Jean Baptiste Le Comte, and his slave, Marguerite Victoire; therefore, Rose and Catiche were the grandchildren of Sieur Le Comte. This would have afforded the girls privileges other children on his plantation did not possess. This may have also been a double-edged sword because Madame Le Comte may not have been as giving. Rose, born in 1792, was the younger of the two girls. In 1794, at the age of four, her sister, Catiche, was purchased and emancipated by Marie Thérèse "Coincoin" their paternal grandmother with whom Catiche was already living. It would be five years later, in 1799, after the death of the Widow Le Comte, that eight-year-old Rose would be bought and liberated by her father's brother, Augustin.[1]

In all likelihood, after Rose's manumission she went to live with her paternal grandmother and her older sister, Catiche. Bonding between Catiche and her grandmother had years to evolve before Rose became a member of the household. This could have triggered animosity in Rose towards her sister and resentment for her grandmother. During Rose's formative years, these negative feelings possibly tainted her future life decisions. I cannot say with absolute certainty that these feelings existed or that they had a lasting effect, but it is plausible.

Around 1796, perhaps rejected or neglected by Louis, Rose's mother had begun a new family with the French planter Jean Baptiste Louis Rachal. Because Louis Metoyer was still enslaved, this affair would afford Françoise possessions that Louis could not. Françoise and Jean Baptiste's relationship would blossom into a twenty year affair—an affair which would eventually lead to the purchase and manumission of Françoise and her new children.[2] This relationship, during Rose's formative years, may have alienated Rose from her mother and may have adversely affected her young spirit.

Not knowing the reality of what happened between her father and mother, as Rose blossomed into womanhood, she may have perceived that her father abandoned her mother and married another woman. While her mother suffered the austerity of slavery and had an affair to escape it, for this other woman, her father constructed a plantation. This could have tarnished the daughter-father relationship and influenced her perception of men. Strained relationships between fathers and daughters sometimes cause daughters to become immersed in a succession of affairs as they search for father figures. Rose's choice of mates was usually older, and she did have several. Deep within, Rose might have been searching for the father she did not find in Louis. Although not verifiable, jealousy, resentment, and daughter-father issues may have been the catalysts that helped to create Rose the woman.

From all accounts, the fusion of French and African blood in Rose created a desirable woman. She appeared to be the type of woman who women envied and men desired. Did she knowingly use her natural assets to entice men, anger her father, and further her status in life? Or was she unaware of her mesmerizing effect on men? I can only reflect on these questions. However, history does show that she led an unconventional lifestyle—a lifestyle that was questioned by some.

There was something about Marie Rose that must have captivated the men she encountered because she was seldom without their company. Perhaps, gifted with beauty and charisma, she had a natural ability to attract men. A portrait of her daughter, Thérèsine, is a two dimensional image to which one can compare the seemingly delightful femme fatale. But an image does not reflect character and cannot express the passion that burns within ones soul; therefore, it leaves much to the imagination. Rose may have been the norm in French colonial Louisiana, or perhaps she was a spirited release in an otherwise humdrum agricultural society. Was it the French-African blood that coursed through her veins that made her irresistible to men, or was it the freedom from slavery that gave her the impetus to stare caution in the face and challenge it to win? I can only speculate about what motivated Rose, but I do know she had no trouble capturing the hearts and souls of countless men.

The first man to be enamored by Rose was a man eighteen years her senior, Jean Baptiste Balthazar-Monet. Jean Baptiste owned property in Monette's Bluff in Natchitoches Parish, Louisiana. It was around 1810 when thirty-six-year-old Jean Baptiste succumbed to the charms of eighteen-year-old Rose.[3] The two had similar backgrounds. He, like she, had been emancipated at a very young age. Both their fathers were slave owners. Jean Baptiste was the son of the French planter, Jean Baptiste Dupré. His mother, Catherine, was a Native American and the servant of Dupré;[4] therefore, Jean Baptiste Balthazar-Monet was of French-Indian heritage. In Dupré's will, written in 1781, he freed his seven-year-old son.[5] As an adult, Jean Baptiste became a property owner and planter. When or where he met Rose has not been established, but they soon began creating a life together.

It was about 1810 when Rose married Jean Baptiste.[6] Together they produced two children, a son, Jean Baptiste Louis, and a daughter, christened Marie Rose, after her mother. No records have been found to substantiate the exact date of their son's birth, but in 1811, Rose gave birth to her namesake.[7] From similar backgrounds, this marriage could have been long and stable. It may have afforded Rose the life for which she was searching. Unfortunately, the marriage was short lived. In May 1812, after only two years of marriage, Jean Baptiste died leaving Rose alone with an estate and two children.[8]

After Jean Baptiste's death, Rose and her young children went to live with her father, Louis Metoyer, on the Isle Brevelle. Along with her children, she brought the remains of her husband's estate. This property included twenty-three heads of cattle, oxen for plowing, four horses, animals that were roaming the woods, and other items indicative of a farmer's life.[9] Rose, residing with her father and stepmother and widowed at the age of twenty, had to rethink her objectives in life. From the day Balthazar died and onward, Rose would be defined by the choices she made. Perhaps, because she longed for a life of love and privilege and had been molded in an environment that may have filled her with jealousy and resentment, she chose a path few journeyed. The path she selected was the path of the *placée*.

The term *plaçage* comes from the word *placer* meaning "to place with." The women were known as *placées* and their unions were recognized among free people of color as *"mariages de la main gauche"* or left-handed marriages. In the *plaçage* system, Anglo-American, French, and Spanish men entered into extra-legal common-law marriages with women that were African, Indian, or of mixed heritage.[10] This system was quite common during the French and Spanish colonial period and well into the early 1900s. Before 1808, Louisiana law allowed a part of a male's estate to go to his *placée* (concubine) but in 1808 a new Civil Code was put into place. The new code specified that those who have lived together in open concubinage are incapable of donations inter vivos [during the person's lifetime] or mortis causa [during a person's approaching death] that are immovable and only up to one-tenth of a movable portion of an estate.[11] Despite the laws, the *plaçage* system continued to flourish.

In the more sophisticated city of New Orleans, the *plaçage* system was flaunted. Extravagant balls were organized so that well-to-do men could find a *placée*. The *placées* were cared for financially, and they were afforded many privileges.[12] In rural Natchitoches, Louisiana, in the Metoyer family, this system was the exception instead of the norm. As I tried to understand Rose, the revelation that she was drawn into the world of *plaçage* was not surprising. I believe that in her search for love and acceptance she would have taken any path that filled that void in hopes that it might lead to security and adulation.

With her ambitions not to be deterred by her husband's demise, Rose, in her early twenties, soon became the *placée* of Jacques Antoine Coindet. Coindet was a much older French associate of her father. Like Rose's grandfather, Pierre Metoyer, Antoine had migrated to Louisiana from France.[13] In 1811, Antoine had provided an affidavit for Rose's father in his U. S.

Land Office claim against Silvestre Bossier.[14] While a guest in her father's house after the death of her husband, Rose may have been introduced to Antoine. Or perhaps, Antoine became enamored with Rose while he was involved with his first placée, Marie Louise Coindet—the godmother of Rose's daughter.[15] Could Antoine have abandoned Marie Louise for Rose? The circumstances of their initial encounter are uncertain, but within a few years Rose and Antoine's arrangement had produced the first of their three children. In 1815, three years after the death of Balthazar, Rose produced her first child with Antoine, Marie Antoinette. Three years later, in 1818, Marie Doralise was born. Completing her family with Antoine was his namesake, Antoine Lucien, born in 1821.[16] As fate would dictate, for the second time in Rose's life, happiness was derailed. Not long after the birth of their son, tragedy visited the now thirty-year-old Rose. In 1822, Antoine died.[17] Once again Rose was alone with additional children to rear. Life certainly was not proceeding as she had anticipated.

In Louisiana, it was against the law for the man to place his mistress and/or their children in his will. But, in Antoine's will he had specified that his entire estate was to go to his children. This would have given Rose some sense of security. Despite the fact that it was against the law for the children to be included in Antoine's will, initially, his wishes were upheld. The estate was settled with the help of Rose's half-uncle, Benjamin, the white son of Pierre Metoyer. But, when Antoine's relatives in France became cognizant of the estate, litigations arose because they were legally entitled to it. According to France's civil code, Code Napoleon, under which Antoine's relatives lived, a person could freely dispose of only one-third of his property *if* there were two (*legitimate*) children. Being born out-of-wedlock, Rose's children were not considered legitimate by French law: in Louisiana, being from a concubine relationship, they were not legally considered at all. In France, in line for the portion of the property guaranteed by law stood the direct descendants, paternal and maternal ascendants, and then collateral relatives. Collateral relatives included cousins, uncles, aunts, etc. If there were no blood relatives, children that were illegitimate could inherit. Last in line would be the wife of the deceased.[18] Because relatives existed in France, Antoine's final wishes were ignored, and Rose and her children could not inherit his estate. An out of court settlement was agreed upon, and Rose had to abandon the children's share of Antoine's estate. She was required to pay his relatives the money she had been awarded with additional interest.[19]

Not to be deterred, with a survival instinct (probably learned through slavery) and with head held high (possibly due to her French heritage), Marie focused her attention on a new suitor. Naïve, perhaps, about the affairs of state and unaccustomed to being alone, Rose wasted no time charming another Frenchman, Dr. Jean André Zépherin Carles.[20] With Dr. Carles, Rose produced two daughters, Thérèsine and Françoise Rosine. Thérèsine was born January 28, 1825,[21] and Françoise Rosine was born June 25, 1827.[22] Being a woman conditioned by the society in which she lived, she trusted her financial affairs to her new lover. The doctor had an office constructed on the land of her ex-lover and became a member of her household. As though fate had not thrashed her enough, when she missed a payment on the money owed to the Coindet heirs, they were granted the land given to her by Antoine and the office that Carles had built.[23] As if losing a home and property were not sufficient retribution, for the third time fate shook its fist at Rose—her lover, Dr. Carles died. December 22, 1827, six months after the birth of their daughter, Rosine, the inventory of his remaining possession took place.[24] The death of Carles, like the death of Antoine, found Rose in litigations again fighting for her livelihood.

In 1830, the case went to trial. The curators for the estate of Dr. Carles alleged that Rose was indebted to "Dr. Carles in his lifetime for the sum of eighteen hundred and twenty dollars for Negroes, his medical attendance, and his service as agent in the management of her affairs, besides the amount of a note of three hundred dollars [signed] by her in favor of the deceased." Rose, tenacious like her father and uncles before her, fought back. She went to court and petitioned for "eight hundred and seventy-five dollars and twenty-five cents for work…done for the said Doctor Carles in his life time for board, washing, also furnishing to said Carles for himself and others in his account..." Witnesses for both Rose and Dr. Carles testified in the trial.

Louis Vercher, who had been an overseer on Rose's plantation, testified that Dr. Carles had his washing done and had made use of fodder and corn for his two or three horses. He also stated that he did not know if Carles was a physician on the plantation and had not witnessed him administer any medicine. Another witness testified that the Negress (who belonged to Carles and lived on the plantation) "worked in the field but did not do enough work to suffice for her boarding." The man who had built an office on Rose's plantation testified that the doctor had boarded there along with some of his slaves. He also offered estimates of what he felt the price of their boarding should be worth.

In favor of Dr. Carles' estate, Dr. Normand, who had worked with

Carles, stated that he had witnessed a Negro boy name Raphael belonging to Carles working in the fields on Rose's plantation. He also saw the slave, Minerva, belonging to Carles waiting upon the tables, and "it appeared she did a great deal about the house." An old Negro woman, Dr. Normand testified, attended and took care of Rose's children. He also stated that the doctor frequently got intoxicated. Mr. Silvestre Rachal testified that the services for work done by Minerva were worth eighty to one hundred dollars per year. Minerva he stated was there for three years. He also indicated that he felt fifteen dollars per month was reasonable for the work that Carles had done for Rose as her agent for five years. Another witness stated that the last two years of Carles life he "was almost helpless owing to his drinking and three-fourths of the time he was intoxicated."[25]

Because several documents were illegible, the totality of the trial cannot be reiterated and the exact amounts rendered by the plaintiff and the defense could not be deciphered. But in one document, the court ruled in favor of Rose for "the sum of two hundred and eight dollars and twenty-five cents with legal interests from the 24th day of November 1829 until now (July, 26, 1830) and the costs of this suit [were] to be taxed."[26]

Life had delivered Rose blow after blow. After three tragic blows, most would probably admit defeat. But Rose, determined woman that she must have been, fought her battles and continued her life with her children (Marie Rose and Louis Balthazar; Antoinette, Doralise, and Antoine Lucien Coindet; Thérèsine and Rosine Carles) making the most of what was willed to her by her husband, Jean Baptiste Monet-Balthazar, and the eleven slaves she had acquired.[27] Along the way, she found comfort with her fourth lover, a married man from North Carolina, Dr. James Hurst.[28]

Little is known about the mysterious relationship between Dr. Hurst and Rose, except that he was one of her many devotees. For a period of time life must have gone well for Rose. In 1830, with the companionship of her latest conquest, Rose had the service of fifteen slaves to help her maintain her lifestyle.[29] Between 1831 and 1832, she gave birth to another daughter, Amanda. Another child, Sarah, is also thought to have been born either before or after Amanda.[30] Of course, with Rose, life does not proceed as intended. This time, it was not Rose, but her lover who would find himself in court, not once, but twice. His first wife, whom he had abandoned before becoming Rose's suitor, sued him for divorce. Having been married in North Carolina to Dr. Hurst since 1812, his first wife had come to Louisiana a year before she filed for divorce. Her hopes were that he would "take her to his bed and board again," but she found him living with Rose. "And he continued to live so within three weeks before the suit." In the initial ruling, Dr. Hurst won the case and a divorce was not granted. His wife fought the case all the way to the Louisiana Supreme Court. Hurst's wife's law suit alleged that Hurst was living in "open concubinage and adultery with a free woman of color named Rose Metoyer." Although there was no proof of how long he had lived with Rose, there was proof that he did live with her "a considerable length of time making the house of his concubine his home." Because Hurst lived in the home of Rose and she fed and housed him, the court rendered "the plaintiff more degraded and despicable." The wife was granted a divorce and Hurst was ordered to pay costs in the Supreme Court and the lower court.[31]

After Hurst's marriage and his affair with Rose ended, he remarried. In the mid-1830s, his second wife also found reasons to divorce and sue Hurst. In this instance, Rose and the financial arrangements made by Hurst for their children were detailed in the lawsuit. Year after year, it appears that Rose had failed at achieving her happy ending as a *placée*. After over twenty years of witnessing life hampered by unforeseen land-mines, Rose finally decided to tackle life alone.

In 1840, Rose's household consisted of a white male, between the ages of ten and fourteen, and two of her children. The child between the ages of 10 and 14, identified as white, was possibly her son, Antoine Coindet, and the other children were probably Amanda and Sarah— children fathered by Dr. Hurst.[32] At the age of 48, without a suitor in the home, Rose continued to maintain her household with the service of eight slaves and financial contributions from Dr. Hurst.[33] Long after the departure of Dr. Hurst, Rose remained independent. In 1850, Rose and her daughter, eighteen-year-old Amanda, lived together with the assistance of six slaves.[34] But life is not eternal, and on March 7, 1856, at age 64, Rose, the unconventional enchantress, died.[35]

It was Rose who bestowed upon us that bodacious gene that causes us to go full speed ahead and throw caution to the wind. We will never know why she chose the path she did, but her choices were hers to make. Though her escapades were unconventional and laced with tragedy, Marie Rose Metoyer, slave, slave owner, wife, mother, and *placée* is that adventurous bud from which we sprang. She was the mother of Bertha's great grandfather, Jean Baptiste Louis Balthazar. It was Louis who would find the stability in family that appeared to have eluded Rose throughout her lifetime.

Baptism of Marie Rosa Metoyer

*"Maria Rosa [Metoyer]**
June 15, 1793, baptism of Maria Rose, about eleven months old, mulata daughter of Franca, a mulata slave of Madame LeComte. Godparents: Josef and Maria Luisa Marta.*

*According to Father A. Dupré (a priest assigned to Isle Brevelle in the mid -1900s), "Metoyer Family Genealogy...local tradition held that Marie was the natural daughter of Louis Metoyer, mulatto. This infant was purchased and manumitted in 1800 by Louis's older brother Augustin Metoyer." (See Widow Lecomte to Nicolas Augustin, Old Natchitoches Data, Doc. 279, Cammie G. Henry Collection, Northwestern State University Library, Natchitoches).[36]

Purchase and Manumission of Marie Rose

Today, this eighteenth day of the month of November of the year one thousand eight hundred, before me Felix Trudeau, civil and military commander of the Post of Natchitoches and dependencies, notary public ex officio for want of a public scrivener, and in presence of Nicolas Lauve and François Dubois, assisting witnesses, has appeared the widow Lecomte, who, by these presents, has sold and ceded all property rights to the free mulatto, Nicolas Augustin, a young mulatto girl, named Marie Rose, aged about eight years, which mulatto girl has been sold on condition that she enjoys full and entire freedom with all the attached privileges, for the price and sum of three hundred dollars, which have been paid upon the spot and for which the said widow Lecomte gives good quittance and receipt to the purchaser, who waves from the present and for the future all rights of bondage on said mulatto, Marie Rose. Therefore the parties have signed, one of them knowing not how to write, has affixed a cross, in presence of the witnesses already mentioned and with me commander the day and year above specified: in witness thereof,[37]

Widow Lecomte Dubois Mark of
Felix Trudeau   Nicolas Augustin

Searching For Bertha

Marie Rose Metoyer's Family

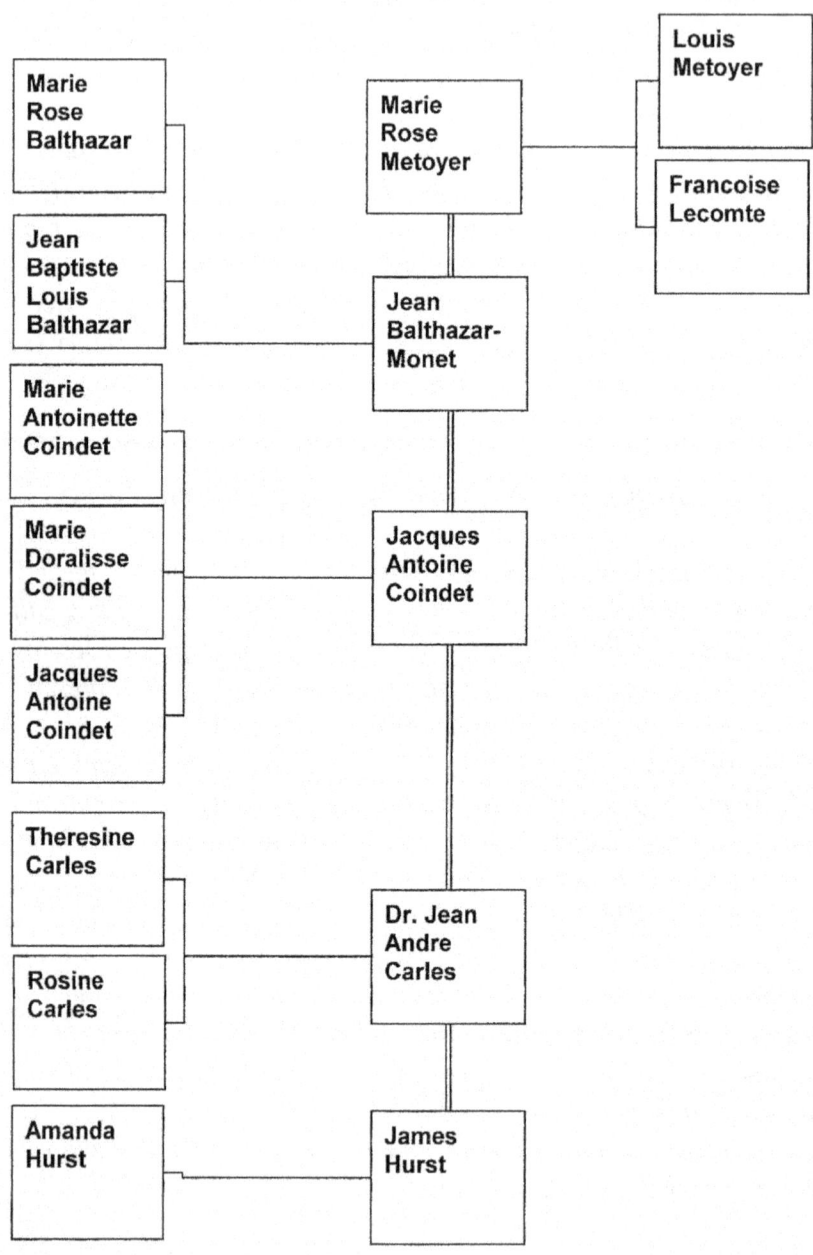

Thérèsine Carles

Daughter of Marie Rose Metoyer and Jacques Antoine Carles[38]

Endnotes

1. Marguerite LeRoy to Marie Thérèse Coincoin, document 2550, Marie Thérèse Coincoin to Catiche, document 2552, Office of the Clerk of Court, Natchitoches, Louisiana; Mills, G., *Forgotten People*, 38.

2. Manumission of Jean Baptiste Espallier, 1799, Natchitoches Colonial Archives, Doc. No. 2913; Purchase of "Fanchon," Marie Adelaide, and Pierre, 1805, Natchitoches Colonial Archives, Docs. 3115 and 3313.

3. Mills, G., *Forgotten People*, 98.

4. Jean Baptiste Dupré and Marguerite Lecomte marriage contract, 7 September 1769, Natchitoches Colonial Archives, Doc. 593, Office of the Clerk of Court, Natchitoches, Louisiana.

5. Natchitoches Parish, Louisiana, Parish Court Files: Dupré vs. Alexis Cloutier (1825), Natchitoches Parish Court microfilm PO, 22; Office of the Clerk of Court, Natchitoches.

6. Mills, G., *Forgotten People*, 89.

7. Mills, E. S., *Natchitoches, 1800-1826, entry* 2099 (638).

8. Jean Baptiste Baltasar's Will (2 April 1812), Microfilm roll VS1 (1813), Office of the Clerk of Court, Natchitoches, Louisiana.

9. Fiona J. L. Handley, "A Social History of the Isle Brevelle, Natchitoches Parish, Louisiana 1795-1920," p. 4; Cane River Historic Documents Projects (File no. 377. N4, H36354, December 2004; Louisiana Collection, Cammie G. Henry Research Center, Northwestern State University, Natchitoches, Louisiana).

10. Joan M. Martin, "Plaçage and the Louisiana Gens de Couleur Libre: How Race and Sex Defined the Life of Free Women of Color," ed. Sybil Klein, *Creole, The History and Legacy of Louisiana's Free People of Color*, (Baton Rouge: Louisiana State University Press, 2000), 68.

11. Edwin T. Merrick, *The Revised Civil Code of the State of Louisiana, with References and Acts of the Legislature Up to and Including the Session of 1912*, (1899; reprint, New Orleans: F. F. Hansell and Brothers, Ltd., 1913), 410 digital images, Googlebooks.com, accessed, 5 April 2013.

12. Ibid.

13. Guillaume Coindet et al. vs. Marie Rose Metoyer, District Court suit 942, Office of the Clerk of Court, Natchitoches.

14. Mills, G., *Forgotten Peopl*e, 55; File B1953, Louis Metoyer, State Land Records.

15. Mills, E. S., Natchitoches, 1800-1826, 2099 (638).

16. Mills, E. S., *Natchitoches 1800-1826,* entries 2406, 2619, 1397.

17. Guillaume Coindet et al. vs. Marie Rose Metoyer.

18. Traer, *Marriage and the Family*, 179.

19. Ibid.

20. Mills, G., *Forgotten People*, 101.

21. Saint Francois Catholic Church (Natchitoches, Louisiana), Register 7, baptism of Theresine Carles; records unpublished and untranslated, information provided by E. S. Mills (shown@comcast.net) to author (aceteach13@wideopenwest.com), 4 November 2010.

22. Saint Francois Catholic Church (Natchitoches, Louisiana), Register 7, baptism of Françoise Rosine Carles; records unpublished and untranslated, information provided by Mrs. E. S. Mills.

23. Mills, G., *Forgotten People*, 101, citing Rose Metoyer to J[n]. A. Z. Carles, D. M., Procuration, No. 109, and Rose Metoyer J[n] P[re] M[ie] Dubois, Procuration unnumbered document, in DeBlieux Collection.

24. Elizabeth Shown Mills, (shown@comcast.net) to author (aceteach13@wideopenwest.com), November 4, 2010; comments on date of Dr. Carles succession inventory in markups on original manuscript.

25. Rose Metoyer, f. w. c. vs. Curators of Andre Z. Carles, Natchitoches Parish Court House, Natchitoches, Louisiana.

26. Ibid.

27. Mills, G., *Forgotten People*, 101.

28. Ibid., 74.

29. 1830 U. S. census, Natchitoches, Parish, Louisiana, Natchitoches township, p.60, Mary R. Metyier (*sic*); digital images, *Ancestry.com*, accessed February 1, 2011, http://search.ancestry.com/iexec?htx=View&r=an&dbid=8058&iid=4409528_00119&fn=Mary+R&ln=Metyier&st=r&ssrc=&pid=1898624; citing NARA microfilm publication M19, roll 44.

30. Adams vs. Hurst, 9 Louisiana 243 (1836), Box 4, Folder 62, Natchitoches Parish Records, Louisiana State University Archives, Baton Rouge, Louisiana; 1850 U. S. census, Natchitoches Parish, Natchitoches, population schedule, [illegible], p. 498 dwelling, 884, family 884, Amanda Metoyer ; digital images, *Ancestry.com*, accessed December 5, 2010 http://search.ancestry.com/iexec?htx=View&r=an&dbid=8054&iid=4198706_00249&fn=Amanda&ln=Metoyer&st=r&ssrc=&pid=2767989; citing NARA microfilm publication M432, roll 1009.

31. Ibid, Adams vs. Hurst; *Report of Cases Argued and Determined in the Supreme Court of the State of Louisiana, Western District, Opelousas, 1835*; digital images, *Google books*, accessed January 19, 2013, http://books.google.com/books?id=yToLAAAAYAAJ&printsec=frontcover&source=gbs_ge_summary_r&cad=0#v=onepage&q&f=false, citing 243-245.

32. Ibid,, Adams vs. Hurst; Marriage records of Sarah and Amanda Hers [Hurst] , Saint Augustine's Catholic Church Baptismal, Marriage, Death Records Book, beginning year 1880, Priest A. Dupré, p. 197; Saint Augustine's Catholic Church, Natchez, Louisiana.

33. 1840 U. S. census, Natchitoches, Parish, Louisiana, Natchitoches township, p.127, Rose Metozer [*sic*], owner; digital images, *Ancestry.com*, accessed February 1, 2011,

http://search.ancestry.com/iexec?htx=View&r=an&dbid=8057&iid=4409529_00309&fn=Rose&ln=Metozer&st=r&ssrc=&pid=1306486; citing NARA microfilm publication M704, roll 149.

    34. 1850 U. S. census, Natchitoches, Parish, Louisiana, Natchitoches township, p.931, Rose Metoyer, owner; digital images, *Ancestry.com*, accessed February 1, 2011, http://search.ancestry.com/iexec?htx=View&r=an&dbid=8054&iid=4198706_00249&fn=Rose&ln=Metoyer&st=r&ssrc=&pid=2767988; citing NARA microfilm publication M432, roll not identified.

    35. Death record of Rose Metoyer, Saint Augustine's Catholic Church Baptismal, Marriage, Death Records Book, beginning year 1880, Priest A Dupré, p. 197; Saint Augustine's Catholic Church, Natchez, Louisiana.

    36. Mills, E. S., *Natchitoches, 1729-1803*, entry 2749.

    37. Widow Lecomte to Nicolas Augustin, 1800; Old Natchitoches Data, No. 279; Cammie G. Henry Research Center, Northwestern State University, Natchitoches, Louisiana.

    38. Mills, G., *Forgotten People*, photo opposite p.55.

Chapter 14

Jean Baptiste Louis Balthazar and Marie Antoinette Coton-Maïs
Stability at Last

Marie Thérèse and Pierre Metoyer will always be known as the original progenitors of Cane River's creoles of color. Augustin Metoyer will be recalled for his contribution of the St. Augustine Church to the Catholic community of Isle Brevelle. Louis Metoyer will always be remembered because of his slave holdings and Melrose Plantation. Marie Rose Metoyer may be recalled because of her part in a *plaçage* system, common for the place and time in which she lived, but strongly disapproved of by her family. My story could have ended with those that came before Rose, Florentin, and Louise. Most accounts written about the Metoyer family did not venture beyond the earlier generation. As the second generation came to an end and the third generation began, the era of wealth and privilege came to a close. I chose to go further because no matter how minute the contributions of our ancestors were, they did exist, and do exist, in our hearts, minds, and souls, and their lives should be rewarded with remembrance. Therefore, my story continues with Jean Baptiste Louis Balthazar, Bertha's great grandfather, and the first-born son of Marie Rose Metoyer.

My mind runs rampant as I try to visualize what Rose's first born, Jean Baptiste Louis Balthazar (known later as just Louis) experienced as a child. The eldest of Rose's children, born between 1807 and 1809, Louis, it appears, was one of two boys in a household filled with girls. At an early age, he lost his father and witnessed his mother experience numerous affairs that ended in tragedy. Being the oldest child he would have been expected to shoulder a great deal of responsibility. Along with working on the land, he would have had a hand in rearing the children. This lifestyle, I suggest, had an effect on this young boy.

Some children thrive to emulate their parents. Others learn from their parents' mistakes. Louis must have been the latter because it appears that he had a very stable relationship with his wife, Antoinette Coton-Maïs. This relationship gave him the security of family that he may have longed for with his mother. When Louis decided it was time to choose a wife, he may have peered down two paths. He may have looked for the image of his mother, as some boys tend to do, or he may have been smitten by someone who made him feel the sense of security he may not have felt as a child. What determined his choice we will never know, but his choice was well known to the family and gave him a life of stability.

The woman Louis selected for his wife, Antoinette Coton-Maïs, was already a member of the Metoyer clan. Louis' sister-in-law, Désirée Coton-Maïs, had married his mother's first cousin, Joseph François Metoyer. Antoinette's father, Antoine, like Louis' mother, was a property owner and a man of reasonable means. In 1830, Antoine owned three slaves,[1] and despite the economic Panic of 1837, which cost a loss of livelihood for many of his neighbors, he was able to increase his slave holdings. This was a phenomenal feat in a market which had triggered a downward spiral for many and had profoundly affected most families in the area. When Antoine's succession was held in February of 1840, among his property were thirteen slaves valued at $5, 400.[2] In 2011 this would equate to $145, 000.[3] Some of this wealth would have been inherited by Antoinette. Like Louis, Antoinette had come from a family with some means and would bring those means to her new family.

Having made his choice for a life mate, on May 1, 1830, after three banns, in the chapel of St. Augustine, on the Isle Brevelle,[4] Louis Balthazar took his solemn vows with Antoinette. With allegiance pledged to his new wife, Louis began to establish himself in his community as a farmer. The couple began having children soon after the marriage. Like his mother and grandparents before him, slave ownership was an expected part of his life. Despite the fact that the wealth of his earlier ancestors had escaped him, in 1830 Louis did own two slaves.[5] It's impossible to know how long the family had the benefit of their slave labor, but in 1840 they were no longer a part of their household. The economic Panic of 1837 could very well have taken a toll on the couple's finances causing them to sell their slaves.

Many families in the United States and the Cane River area became heavily indebted during the Panic of 1837. Credit was very limited, and land had to be paid for with gold or silver, of which there was a shortage. Banks began failing, and businesses followed. Many families, who had invested in land, lost it. Coupled with the financial woes of the Panic was the subsequent and consistent failure of the families' mainstay—their crops. In a rural setting, agriculture determined the livelihood of most of the families in Natchitoches. In 1839, a drought hit the area stunting the performance of crops, and the next year their harvests were inundated with caterpillars. The following year, 1841, the price of cotton toppled to nine cents per pound. As though Mother Nature had not caused enough havoc, in 1842 bud worms destroyed the crops of cotton. Not only was the yield of cotton insufficient, but in 1843 the price of cotton was only four to six cents per pound.[6] Crop failures, decrease in profits, and an economic panic that was unrelenting for approximately ten years could have financially devastated the family. Despite the hardships, with a commitment to each other, Louis and Antoinette farmed their land and supported their family. In a span of twenty years, there were twelve new Balthazar family members.

Unfortunately, by 1850, misfortune had visited the family again. The 1850 census listed Louis, and his oldest son, Prosper, under the heading "Deaf and Dumb, Blind, Insane, Idiotic, Pauper, Convict." From which affliction they suffered and when their misfortune began were not recorded.[7] Despite this setback, with twelve children, Bertha's great-grandparents, Louis and Antoinette, had made a significant contribution with children who would become productive citizens in their own rights. One of those contributions was child number nine (Bertha's grandfather), Pierre Félicien Balthazar, who would fight in the Civil War, helping to unite our country and assure our bloodline continued to thrive. This in itself is enough to give tribute to Jean Louis Baptiste Balthazar and his wife, Marie Antoinette Coton-Maïs.

Searching For Bertha

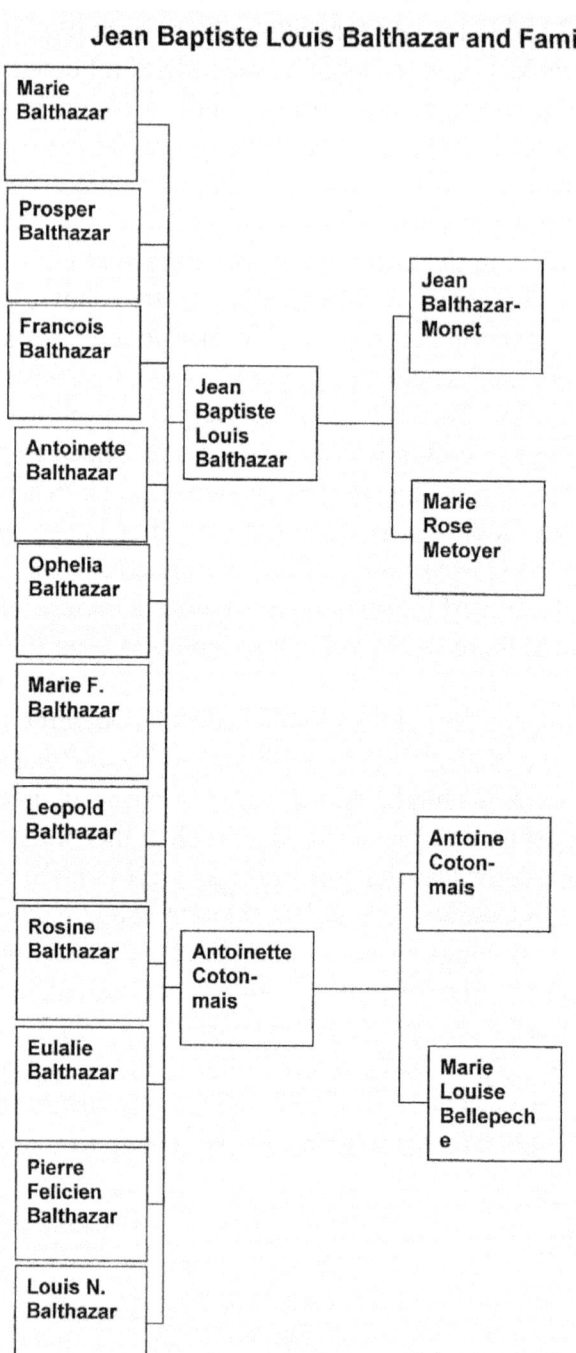

Endnotes

1. 1830 U. S. census, Natchitoches, Parish, Louisiana, Natchitoches township, p.70 (penned), line 9, Antonius Cottonmie [Antoine Coton-Maïs] digital images, *Ancestry.com,* accessed February 1, 2011, http://search.ancestry.com/iexec?htx=View&r=an&dbid=8058&iid=4409528_00139&fn=Atonius&ln=Cottonmie&st=r&ssrc=&pid=1898885: citing NARA microfilm publication M19, roll 44.

2. Natchitoches Parish, Louisiana, Succession vol. 14: 41-43, Inventory of Antoine Coton-Maïs, 17 February 1840; Office of the Clerk of Court, Natchitoches.

3. Officer and Williamson, M*easuringWorth*, accessed January 19, 2013, http://www.MeasuringWorth.com/usgdp/.

4. Mills, E. S., *Natchitoches Marriages, 1818-1850,* entry 171.

5. 1830 U. S. census, Natchitoches Parish, Louisiana, p. 60 (penned), line 9, Louis Batthasar [Balthazar] ; digital image, *Ancestry.com,* accessed March 21, 2009 http://search.ancestry.com/iexec?htx=View&r=an&dbid=8058&iid=4409528_00119&fn=Louis&ln=Batthasar&st=r&ssrc=&pid=1898625; citing NARA microfilm publication M19, roll 201.

6. Mills, G., *Forgotten People,* 221-222.

7. 1850 U. S. census, Natchitoches Parish, Louisiana, population schedule, p. [illegible], line 14, Louis Belthesuire [Balthazar] ; digital image, *Ancestry.com,* accessed March 21, 2009 http://search.ancestry.com/iexec?htx=View&r=an&dbid=8054&iid=4198706_00275&fn=Louis&ln=Belthesuire&st=r&ssrc=&pid=2769068; citing NARA microfilm publication M432, roll 233.

TO COLORED MEN!

FREEDOM,
Protection, Pay, and a Call to Military Duty!

On the 1st day of January, 1863, the President of the United States proclaimed FREEDOM to over THREE MILLIONS OF SLAVES. This decree is to be enforced by all the power of the Nation. On the 21st of July last he issued the following order:

PROTECTION OF COLORED TROOPS.

"WAR DEPARTMENT, ADJUTANT GENERAL'S OFFICE,
WASHINGTON, July 21.

"*General Order,* No. 233.

"The following order of the President is published for the information and government of all concerned:—

EXECUTIVE MANSION, WASHINGTON, July 30.

"'It is the duty of every Government to give protection to its citizens, of whatever class, color, or condition, and especially to those who are duly organized as soldiers in the public service. The law of nations, and the usages and customs of war, as carried on by civilized powers, permit no distinction as to color in the treatment of prisoners of war as public enemies. To sell or enslave any captured person on account of his color, is a relapse into barbarism, and a crime against the civilization of the age.

"'The Government of the United States will give the same protection to all its soldiers, and if the enemy shall sell or enslave any one because of his color, the offense shall be punished by retaliation upon the enemy's prisoners in our possession. It is, therefore, ordered, for every soldier of the United States, killed in violation of the laws of war, a rebel soldier shall be executed; and for every one enslaved by the enemy, or sold into slavery, a rebel soldier shall be placed at hard labor on the public works, and continued at such labor until the other shall be released and receive the treatment due to prisoners of war.

'"ABRAHAM LINCOLN."'

'"By order of the Secretary of War.

'"E. D. TOWNSEND, Assistant Adjutant General."'

That the President is in earnest the rebels soon began to find out, as witness the following order from his Secretary of War:

"WAR DEPARTMENT, WASHINGTON CITY, August 8, 1863.

"SIR: Your letter of the 3d inst., calling the attention of this Department to the cases of Orin H. Brown, William H. Johnston, and Wm. Wilson, three colored men captured on the gunboat Isaac Smith, has received consideration. This Department has directed that three rebel prisoners of South Carolina, if there be any such in our possession, and if not, three others, be confined in close custody and held as hostages for Brown, Johnston and Wilson, and that the fact be communicated to the rebel authorities at Richmond.
"Very respectfully your obedient servant,

" EDWIN M. STANTON, Secretary of War.

"The Hon. GIDEON WELLES, Secretary of the Navy."

And retaliation will be our practice now—man for man—to the bitter end.

LETTER OF CHARLES SUMNER,
Written with reference to the Convention held at Poughkeepsie, July 15th and 16th, 1863, to promote Colored Enlistments.

BOSTON, July 13th, 1863.

"I doubt if, in times past, our country could have expected from colored men any patriotic service. Such service is the return for protection. But now that protection has begun, the service should begin also. Nor should relative rights and duties be weighed with nicety. It is enough that our country, aroused at last to a sense of justice, seeks to enrol colored men among its defenders.

"If my counsels should reach such persons, I would say: enlist at once. Now is the day and now is the hour. Help to overcome your cruel enemies now battling against your country, and in this way you will surely overcome those other enemies hardly less cruel, here at home, who will still seek to degrade you. This is not the time to hesitate or to higgle. Do your duty to our country, and you will set an example of generous self-sacrifice which will conquer prejudice and open all hearts.

"Very faithfully yours, "CHARLES SUMNER."

Chapter 15

Pierre Félicien Balthazar
Civil War Soldier

On February 22, 1845, on what may have been a cold, damp winter's day, Bertha's grandfather, Pierre Félicien Balthazar (the ninth of eleven children) kicked his way into the world.[1] The sounds of the eight children before Félicien would have given him a premonition of what awaited him outside the warmth of his mother's womb. Of course, circumstances as he awaited his début are only privy to those who anticipated his arrival, but I have no doubt that Félicien entered into what must have been a chaotic Balthazar household. Once there, he began to forge his position in the family. A home filled with stair-step siblings, jockeying for attention, had to teach Félicien a thing or two about survival. This was fortunate for him because, unbeknownst to this young lad, one day his survival skills would be tested.

Félicien had entered the world in a time when financial turmoil was felt all around him, especially in the rural area in which he was reared. His family, like most, downriver from Natchitoches, probably experienced challenging times. In May of 1842, all but four banks in the state were insolvent.[2] As a farmer, Felicien's father's struggles in the dirt would not reap the rewards as those that had come before him. Hard work and perseverance were lessons Félicien would have to learn as he made his way towards manhood—lessons that would serve him well later in life.

As Félicien was coming of age, his community and our nation were coming apart. In January of 1861, he would have witnessed Louisiana follow other southern states as they seceded from the Union. Félicien, a fifteen-year-old adolescent (about to turn sixteen) must have wondered what was going to happen to the life he had come to know. He had grown up around slavery and had known slaves and slave owners. Unlike most African Americans, generations of his ancestors had been slave owners. In 1830, his father had owned two slaves.[3] Allegiance in the community (spoken or unspoken) was divided between whites and free people of color, slaves and slave-owners. Félicien would have felt the unrest as his community debated Union and Confederate ideals. He would have witnessed his neighbors providing food and other supplies to the Confederate Army. The young man probably knew slaves who had been sent by their slave owners to work on defenses on the Red River for the Confederates. As Félicien observed the formation in Natchitoches of the two confederate militias, the Augustin Guards and the Monette Guards, the shift from loyalty to the Union to allegiance to the Confederate would have become apparent. The Augustin Guards had named themselves in honor of Félicien's great uncle, Augustin Metoyer, and the Monette Guards had been named for his cousin, Louis Monette.[4] Watching the militias drill in preparation for war must have made an impression on young Félicien as he and the nation waited for the inevitable. Would his allegiance be with the Confederates who believed in the system of slavery from which his ancestors had profited? Or would he pledge his allegiance to the Union who wanted to abolish the way of life his ancestors had taken for granted? Félicien looked freedom and slavery in the face and decided to make a choice. How he made his decision when his ancestors had experienced both forks in the road may have once been a subject of debate. But once his choice was made, with integrity, he followed through with his commitment.

On July 17, 1862, two acts were passed by congress permitting the enlistment of African Americans to fight in the Civil War, but official enrollment occurred only after the preliminary September 1862 issuance of the Emancipation Proclamation.[5] On January 1, 1863, President Abraham Lincoln issued the proclamation freeing slaves in the parts of the rebellious states that were actually under Federal control. Included in this proclamation of freedom were portions, but not all, of Louisiana; included was the City of New Orleans.[6] Although it was not until December 1865 that slavery officially ended, this was the official end of slavery in some parts of Louisiana.

The system of slavery had been beneficial for generations of Félicien's family. His ancestors, the Metoyers, had owned hundreds of slaves and were wealthier than most people, both African American and white. Their prosperity was directly correlated to the number of slaves they owned. Abolishing slavery would obliterate much of their wealth. Félicien may have felt turmoil because he had to decide if he would be for or against slavery—something his ancestors believed in. As with many southern families during the Civil War, family connections may have been severed. If this was the situation with Félicien, family never revealed. But we do know, at the tender age of eighteen, Félicien did make a decision. He answered President Lincoln's call to serve his country, and he enlisted in the Union Army.

In hopes of recruiting free men of color, in August of 1862, the commander of the Union troops, Benjamin Butler, appealed to men of color to join the army. These recruits would make up the first official regiment of Black soldiers in the Union army. Mustered in on September 27, 1862, it would be called the 1st Regiment of the Louisiana Native Guards.[7] Their captains and lieutenants were considered, creoles of color. The Louisiana Native Guards was the only unit in the Civil War that was permitted to have their own officers. This regiment, the offspring of white politicians and wealthy, prominent, free men of color from New Orleans, was said to have some of the "best blood of Louisiana."[8] On May 27, 1863, these soldiers proved themselves worthy opponents as they battled against the Confederate troops at Port Hudson, Louisiana. After the courageous battle of Port Hudson, there was an aggressive campaign to recruit more men of color in the Union army. With the successful recruitment of these men, on June 6, 1863 it was decided that the Native Guards would change its name to Corps d'Afrique.[9] Two months later, on August 29, 1863, Félicien joined for three years as a recruit at Fort Macomb, Louisiana. He was assigned to the 1st Regiment Infantry, Corps d'Afrique, Company A which had been formed by P. B. S. Pinchback, who would later become the first Black governor of Louisiana.[10] On October 12, 1862, when his regiment was commissioned into service, Pinchback was captain of Company A.[11] This regiment later became the 73rd United States Colored Infantry.

Unfortunately, the same month that Felicien made his commitment to defend his country, Major General Nathaniel Banks, who had recruited the black troops, decided to purge the officers of color who commanded the men. Among the explanations Banks identified for getting rid of the officers was that he felt they were an embarrassment and an annoyance, and he decided their presence demoralized the white and Negro troops. Although white troops had been violent against the officers of color, Banks asserted that it was the officers' "arrogance and self-assertion" which prompted the violence.[12]

In an effort to eliminate the officers, Banks set up examining boards to evaluate their proficiency in military matters. White officers, though tested, were excluded from passing a rigorous exam. Banks also decided to pay Black enlisted men and their white field officers, but excluded pay for officers of color. Consequently, many of the recruits decided to desert. On September 25, 1863, when Captain Émile Detiége, an officer of color, resigned because of prejudice, a fourth of his company deserted.[13] Prior to Detiége's resignation, on September 11, 1863, Pinchback had also resigned due to prejudice. That same month, on the 16th, Félicien deserted. He later rejoined, by choice or force, and he was transferred to the 74th Regiment, United States Colored Infantry, Company D.[14] This regiment not only had African American lieutenants and captains, but also had an African American major, Major Frances E. Dumas.[15] Félicien would be a member of this regiment until he mustered out.

During the timeframe that Félicien was in the 1st Regiment and the 73rd, the regiment's responsibilities included duty at Port Hudson, the Red River Campaign, and the Mobile Campaign. During his stint in the 74th, responsibilities of the regiment included the Defense of New Orleans and garrison duty at Ship Island. [16]

Determination and survival skills, learned as a child, must have served Félicien well because although many of his comrades were killed and some succumbed to disease, he survived. Not only did he survive death and disease, he, like his fellow African American servicemen, had to survive the racism that was ever present during their enlistment. Though African Americans had enlisted to fight for their country, they were often assigned work as common laborers digging and drudging. Brigadier General Daniel Ullmann of the Corps d'Afrique complained "…months have passed, at times, without the ability of any drill at all." Treatment of the soldiers was sometimes cruel. On an expedition, which included the 73rd Regiment, a chaplain witnessed cursing, kicking, and beatings of the soldiers.[17] Another disparity was pay for the African American troops. In early 1863 their salary was $13 per month— the same amount paid to white soldiers. But, in June of 1863, the pay for African Americans was reduced to $10 dollars per month, with $3 of that going towards clothing. It would not be until mid-June 1864 when equal pay would be reinstated for African Americans provided they had been free on April 19, 1861. Félicien had been born free, so he would have been compensated. But it would not be until March 1865 that all African Americans would get equal compensation.[18]

Linda S. Manuel

The Corps d'Afriques at Port Hudson

Photograph, courtesy of the U. S. National Archives

Despite the injustices that Félicien must have suffered as he volunteered for his country, he survived. Young Félicien had entered military service as an unproven adolescent with rudimentary life experiences, but he returned to Natchitoches as a twenty-one-year-old veteran prepared to take on the responsibilities of a wife and family. On November 11, 1865, after serving in the military for almost three years, he was mustered out of what had become the 74th Regiment of the U. S. Colored Infantry, Company D, in New Orleans. A record of his service can be found on plaque 81 of the African American Civil War Memorial.[19]

Returning to Natchitoches, Félicien was prepared to begin a new chapter in his life. He soon took a wife. His wife of choice was his third cousin, Marie Laura Christophe—the daughter of Charles Christophe and Marie Agnes Conant and the granddaughter of Florentin Conant and Marie Louise Metoyer.

Having grown up with Félicien, Laura may have finally been charmed by his handsome physique in his cavalry uniform. Or, maybe it was he who first became captivated by her smile. My imagination is my own; only they know their secrets. But one day, they made the decision to become one.

After three banns, on July 17, 1866, a year after Félicien had finished his commitment to his country, he married Laura.[20] By 1870, Félicien and Laura owned a farm in Natchitoches' Tenth Ward valued at $300, and they were the proud parents of three children. While Félicien cultivated the land, Laura worked as a mother and housekeeper.[21] Having been part of a large family, Félicien set out to create the type of family from which he had come. By 1880, their family had doubled, and they were the parents of six children.[22] By 1900 the couple had given life to eleven children. Between 1880 and 1900, Félicien and Laura experienced several life changes. The couple lost two of their children. Félicien abandoned the life he knew as a farmer, moved his family from the farm, and settled in downtown Natchitoches on Amulet St. There, in 1900, at the age of 55, Félicien was employed as a cobbler, making and repairing shoes.[23] By 1910, Félicien had died, and Laura lived with her second oldest son, Charles Arthur.[24] It would be nineteen years later, on October 29, 1929, when Laura, who had never left her husband in life, would join him in death. She was buried in the American Cemetery in Natchitoches. Inscribed on her tombstone, as prescribed by her daughter, Marie Odalie Roque, are the words, "In Loving Memory." [25]

For over thirty years, Félicien and Laura had known the stability of family. The couple had been productive citizens and contributed to their community. Félicien had fought to defend his country while Laura maintained the family. Despite Félicien's fight for freedom and equality, during his lifetime he witnessed the erosion of both. After the war, between 1868 and 1876, forty of the members of the Louisiana House were Black. Of those, five had served in the Native Guards as officers. But by 1898, the political gains that had been made, including voting rights, were lost. Félicien saw the nation he had fought to reunite force the races farther apart. Although Blacks and whites in the Union Army had battled together, after the war white veterans did not want their local chapters (posts) integrated by Blacks. Whites did not recognize Black volunteers "in the same sense" as whites.[26] In 1889, social and economic tensions caused a dramatic increase in Black lynching in the South.[27] Félicien lived long enough to witness a death in his daughter's family— a death in all likelihood triggered by discord between the races.

One can only imagine the disillusion he must have felt with the country he had fought to defend. It appears as though the principles and the stability that Félicien and Laura had worked so hard to maintain would elude their children, especially their first born daughter, Marie Resida Balthazar.

Marie Resida Balthazar is the mother of Bertha: the child who ignited the flame that initiated this soul-searching journey. Marie Resida is that elusive puff of smoke that seems to have disappeared never to be found.

Felicien Balthazar, Laura Christophe, and Family

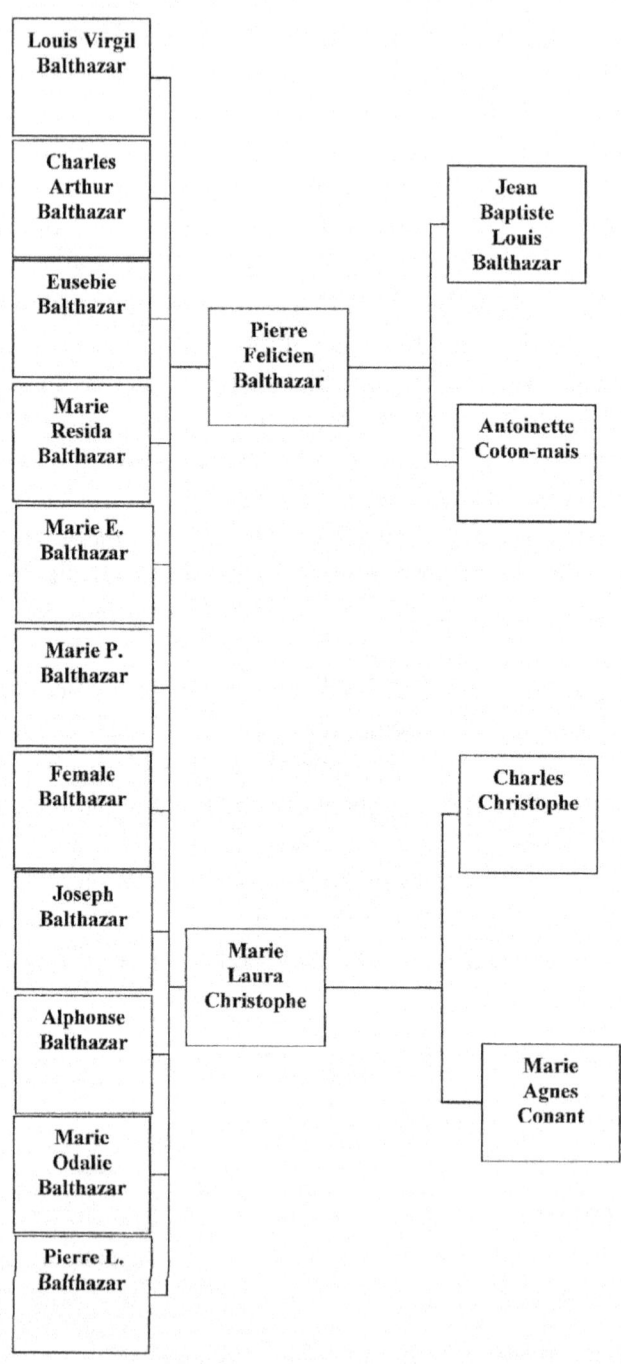

Linda S. Manuel

Pierre Felicien Balthazar
Civil War Soldier

Courtesy of Renee Roque

Endnotes

1. "Creole Family History," database, "Louisiana Creole Heritage Center," Pierre Felicien Balthazar, accessed September 3, 2009, http://winhttp.nsula.edu/creole/search.asp?surname=balthazar&givenname=&mother=&father=&birth=&death; 1900 U. S. census, Natchitoches Parish, Louisiana, population schedule, enumeration district (ED) 70, p. 6-B (stamped and penned), dwelling 116, family 127, Peter F. Balthazar [erroneously indexed as Peter F. Balthgar]]; digital image, *Ancestry.com,* accessed February 10, 2011, http://search.ancestry.com/iexec?htx=View&r=an&dbid=7602&iid=004120184_00564&fn=Peter+F&ln=Balthgar&st=r&ssrc=&pid=5962344; citing NARA microfilm publication M623, roll 569.

2. Mills, *Forgotten People*, 222, citing McGuire Diary, 19-17.

3. 1830 U. S. Census, Natchitoches Parish, Louisiana, p. 60 (penned), line 9, Louis Batthasar.

4. Mills, Gary B., "Patriotism Frustrated: The Native Guards of Confederate Natchitoches," Louisiana History 18 (Fall 1977): 440-41; Mills, E. S. *Isles of Canes*, "Lecomte Slave Roots," genealogical chart.

5. National Park Services, Civil War Soldiers and Sailors System, "African Americans/Slavery," *Civil War.com,* accessed November 27, 2010, http://www.civilwar.com/overview/abolition-and-slavery/148533-african-americans-slavery.html. paragraph, 3.

6. National Park Services, Civil War Soldiers and Sailors System, "The Emancipation Proclamation," a transcription*, Archives.gov,* accessed November 27, 2010, http://www.archives.gov/exhibits/featured_documents/emancipation_proclamation/transcript.html.

7. James G. Hollandsworth, Jr., *The Louisiana Native Guards* (Baton Rouge: Louisiana State University Press, 1998), 16-17.

8. Joseph T. Glatthaar, *Forged in Battle: The Civil War Alliance of Black Soldiers and White Officers* (New York: The Free Press, 1990), 124, citing David C. Edmonds, *The Guns of Port Hudson*, vol.2, 49.

9. Hollandsworth, Jr., *Louisiana Native Guards*, 70.

10. Compiled Service Record, Felicien Balthazar, (Pvt., Co. A 1st Regiment Infantry, Corps d'Afrique and Co. D 74th Regiment U. S. Colored Infantry, Civil War) Carded Records, Volunteer Organizations: Civil War; Records of the Adjutant General's Offices, Record Group 94; National Archives and Records Administration, Washington, DC.

11. Kranz, Rachel. "Pinchback, P. B. S." African-American Business Leaders and Entrepreneurs, A to Z of African Americans. New York: Facts On File, Inc., 2004. African-American History Online. Facts On File, Inc., accessed March 6, 2013, (http://www.fofweb.com/History/MainPrintPage.asp?iPin=AABLE0117&DataType=AFHC&WinType=Free:

12. Hollandsworth, Jr., *Louisiana Native Guards*, 71-73, 82

13. Ibid.

14. Compiled Service Record, Felicien Balthazar, Pvt., Co. A 1st Regiment Infantry, Corps d'Afrique; Carded Records, Volunteer Organizations, Civil War, Records of the Adjutant General 's Office, RG 94, NA-Washington.

15. Glatthaar, *Forged in Battle*, 79.

16. National Park Service, "*Civil War Soldiers and Sailors System*," database, *Civil War Soldiers & Sailors System*, entry for Felician [Felicien] Balthazar, accessed January 2, 2013, http://www.nps.gov/civilwar/search-regiments.

17. Glatthaar, *Forged in Battle*, 114.

18. Ibid., 169-70, 174-75.

19. National Park Service, "*Civil War Soldiers and Sailors System*," database, entry for Felician [Felicien] Balthazar, accessed October 10, 2009, http://www.itd.nps.gov/cwss/.

20. Felicien Baltasar- Marie Laura Christophe marriage, Marriage Book 3, 1866 to 1869, pp. 117-118, Natchitoches Clerk of Court Office, Natchitoches, LA.

21. 1870 U. S. census, Natchitoches Parish, Louisiana, population schedule, p. 4 (penned), dwelling 30, family 30, Felicien Baltazard [Balthazar], Laura Baltazard [Balthazar]; digital image, *Ancestry.com*, accessed March 21,2009, http://search.ancestry.com/iexec?htx=View&r=an&dbid=7163&iid=4269419_00280&fn=Felicien&ln=Baltazard&st=r&ssrc=pt_t3131577_p-107671181&pid=26100863; citing NARA microfilm publication M593, roll 518.

22. 1880 U. S. census, Natchitoches Parish, Louisiana, population schedule, enumeration district (ED) 29, p. 525-A (stamped), dwelling [illegible] family [illegible], Felicien Balthazar; digital image, *Ancestry.com*, accessed February 10, 2011, http://search.ancestry.com/iexec?htx=View&r=an&dbid=6742&iid=4241373-00294&fn=Felicien&ln=Balthazar&st=r&ssrc=&pid=9116762; citing NARA microfilm publication T9, roll 457.

23. 1900 U. S. census, Natchitoches Parish, Louisiana, population schedule, enumeration district (ED) 70, p. 6-B (stamped and penned), dwelling 116, family 127, Peter F. Balthazar [Erroneously indexed as Peter F. Balthgar]; digital image, *Ancestry.com*, accessed February 10, 2011, http://search.ancestry.com/iexec?htx=View&r=an&dbid=7602&iid=004120184_00564&fn=Peter+F&ln=Balthgar&st=r&ssrc=&pid=5962344; citing NARA microfilm publication M623, roll 569.

24. 1910 U. S. census, Natchitoches Parish, Louisiana, population schedule, enumeration district (ED) 92, p. 37-B (penned), dwelling 628, family 598, Laura Balthazar; digital image, *Ancestry.com*, accessed February 10, 2011, http://search.ancestry.com/iexec?htx=View&r=an&dbid=7884&iid=31111_4329981-00323&fn=Laura&ln=Balthazar&st=r&ssrc=&pid=167129910; citing NARA microfilm publication T624, roll 519.

25. "The American Cemetery," compiled by Nelda G. Liles, database, *rootsweb.ancestry.com*, accessed February 10, 2011, http://www.rootsweb.ancestry.com/~lanatchi/amera.htm, entry for Laura Balthazar.

26. Hollandsworth, Jr., *Louisiana Native Guards*, 109-112.

27. Heather Cox Richardson, *The Death of Reconstruction: Race, Labor, and Politics in the Post-Civil War North, 1865-1901* (Cambridge: Harvard University Press, 2001), 218.

Chapter 16

Marie Resida Balthazar
Gone too Soon

While searching for Bertha, I found her mother, Resida, the first born daughter of Félicien and Laura Balthazar. She was my first connection to my Cane River roots—roots entrenched in history. But try as I might to expose Resida's secrets, most of them, as you will discover, still remain her own.

Bertha's mother, Marie Resida Balthazar, born January 17, 1874,[1] was the oldest girl child of Félicien and Laura Balthazar. With three boys arriving before her, it must have been a welcoming sight for Laura to see her reflection in her first-born daughter. Did Laura know the course this child would take as she embraced her for the first time? Perhaps there was a hint in her innocent eyes that predicted she would lead a life of heartache similar to her infamous great-grandmother Rose Metoyer, the placée. As if to foreshadow her future, it was Resida's Aunt Marie Rose (the daughter of Rose Metoyer) who was chosen to be Resida's Godmother. She cradled Resida in her arms in the St. Augustine Church, on March 29, 1874, as the Reverend J. L. Galop performed her baptismal.[2]

Unlike her ancestors, the world Resida inherited did not see shades of gray. With the conclusion of the Civil War, race was seen primarily in black and white. The term free people of color was becoming passé. With the loss of the third caste system (free people of color), came a loss of privilege. As Gary Mills so eloquently stated, "The liberation of all men" shackled the people of Isle Brevelle with anonymity; the equality proclaimed by the Union lost for them their special prestige." They found themselves having two foes, the freed blacks and the "status conscious whites."[3]

Engaged in what appeared to be a concerted effort to cause disharmony among these foes was *The People's Vindicator*, a parish newspaper. It was said to be one of the most incendiary newspapers to exist during the post-Reconstruction era. Its owner was a veteran of the Confederate Army. Published under the motto "The Welfare of the People is the Supreme Law," by 1879 *The People's Vindicator* had declared itself the "Official Organ of the White Citizens of Red River, Sabine, Winn and Natchitoches

Parishes."⁴ Regardless of color, any voice, that would lend itself to pitting the races against one another, could find a platform in *The People's Vindicator*. Written in the paper, six months after the birth of Resida, on July 4, 1874, and almost ten years after the Civil War, the paper published an article entitled "Rumors of War." It stated, "On all sides we hear the cry and din of armed forces. This week 300 stands of arms had been seen passing through Cloutierville [a city near Natchitoches] for this city to equip the Negroes and protect them in their *rights* which are being *seriously menaced* by the *just demands* of the whites for their privileges."⁵

The following month, on August 1, 1874, a letter was sent to the paper by one of Resida's relatives, a free man of color, N. P. Metoyer. In the letter, entitled "Advice of a Colored Man to his Race," Metoyer espoused the following:

Dear friends and acquaintances, ye, formerly known as free men of color…I have deemed it my duty to tell you a few words in regard to your political status. Remember that we belong neither to the white nor the black race; that we occupy, therefore, a middle ground between too [two] shades of color, of which we are, as it were, composed. What ought we to do to get rid of this equivocal situation which will suffocate us, unless we can take care of ourselves? To whom ought we to appeal for relief? Ah! That is the question. Yet, we have to take a side, or remain neutral. But why should we remain neutral, when we have the same rights and privileges that those two races have, under the law? Are we not citizens as well as they? Yes! Only we do not belong to any race. It devolves upon us, therefore, to join the party who offer us more benefits; the party which is the wisest, the most enlighten, the more capable of protecting us; which party is that? I say without hesitation and in a loud voice, that if we wish to be men, as well as our children, in the future, we must, without hesitation, array ourselves on the side of the whites. If you want my reasons for so doing I can give you thousands." Metoyer proceeded to give several reasons to justify alignments with "the whites."⁶

Unlike N. P. Metoyer's call for free people of color to align with the white race, on September 19, 1874, an article entitled, "Is Our Government a Failure," also written in *The People's Vindicator*, stated its views on the participation of African Americans in government. It reported, "Negro equality means amalgamation and the downfall of the government, to be followed by alternate anarchy and despotism."⁷

These articles summarized the sentiments about the ending of the Civil War and the attempt at reconstruction. Hostilities had been created among the races. This was the up-side-down world for which Félicien fought, society created, and into which Resida was born, and it would be up to her to choose the path on which she would travel.

Resida's choice of paths was seldom filled with harmony. Very early in life, she was introduced to love, heartache, and tragedy. At the age of fourteen, she became a wife. Her groom of choice (fourteen years her senior) was Franklin Cross.[8] Franklin grew up as a farmer's son in Shreveport, Louisiana.[9] He was the oldest child of Levy and Nancy Cross. Before meeting Resida, Franklin worked as a farm laborer in Shreveport.[10] He may have been visiting his sister, Nancy Marie Morin, or his brother, John, on the Isle Brevelle, on Cane River, when he first laid eyes on his bride-to-be. In the state of Louisiana, he had to sign a $500.00 bond to marry Resida.[11] The purpose of the bond was to ensure that no marriage laws would be broken by the planned marriage. In the late nineteenth century, this was not a meager amount of money to lose if the bond was broken. It must have been an intense love that resulted in Franklin and his sister's husband, Eugene Morin, signing the bond in August of 1888. With bond signed, Franklin was free to marry Resida. On September 13, 1888, the 28-year-old Franklin and the 14-year-old Resida took their vows before the Catholic priest and became one.[12]

Though love may have been intense when it was new, the marriage did not survive. What happened during their brief time together was not recorded for eyes to read. There are no records of children born, and after less than two years of marriage, Resida was alone. Nothing has surfaced to tell what happened to Franklin. He may have had an unfortunate accident and died. This was not uncommon in the rural area in which he lived. Death from poisonous snakes and farming accidents were not unusual. He may have succumbed to some type of illness or disease. With few doctors to service the population, this is also feasible. Or he may have been a victim of the hostile environment of the time in which he lived. After the Civil War, and during the era of reconstruction, it was not unusual for a Black man to have an untimely demise. Abuse, intimidation, torture and even the killing of freed people were being committed by white gangs.

In 1889, the south witnessed a dramatic increase in the lynching of African Americans. According to a writer from the New York Times, southern lynch mobs assumed that "if anything goes wrong, it is always safe... to kill a Negro."[13] Could this have happened to Franklin? After scouring hundreds of newspapers, searching church and court records, and visiting numerous gravesites, the disappearance of Franklin from the annals of history is an enigma. The question still lingers. What happened to Franklin? But for the sixteen-year-old Resida, life continued. She soon found herself in love and marriage again. Her new husband of choice was twenty-six-year-old Arthur Lecour.

Unlike Franklin, Arthur had grown up in Natchitoches parish. He was the son of Bruno and Perrine Porter Coton-Maïs Lecour. Franklin's brother, John H. Cross, was married to Arthur's sister.[14] It is highly probable that holiday gatherings brought Arthur and Resida together. This close proximity undoubtedly caused a friendship to blossom. Resida's marriage in the Catholic Church, for a second time, gives high credence to the fact that Franklin must have met an untimely death. The Catholic Church is known to perform second marriages in the church in cases of a first annulment or the death of the first spouse. Whatever the case might have been, Arthur, like Franklin before him, signed a $500.00 bond to marry Resida. On May 6, 1890, the two stood before Reverend Francis Grosse and took their vows.[15]

Resida began having children within the first year of marriage. On January 23, 1891, the couple had their first born, Joseph Howard Lecour.[16] The following year, on October 15, 1892, Theresa made her way into the world.[17] With the arrival of Mary Agnes, on October 23, 1893, the Lecour household was complete.[18]

For a time, this couple, like most couples, immersed themselves in the day-to-day routine of being a family. But in late September of 1895, five years after their marriage, an unspeakable tragedy struck. *The Louisiana Populist,* a Natchitoches newspaper, reported that according to Mr. Jno. H. Henry of Henryville the following incident happened:

Arthur Lacour (colored) went down the railroad track, presumably to go home. He must have gone to sleep on the track, for several hours later, a man stumbled over his gun and portions of his body, scattered along the track. A search resulted in finding pieces of the unfortunate man for half a mile. He was literally ground to pieces, there being nothing by which he could be identified, except his gun and his clothing…As his killing was entirely accidental, the railroad company was exonerated.[19]

Because of the racial animosity at the time of Arthur's death, the assumption that he went to sleep on the railroad tracks appears dubious. Evidence of racial turbulence had been escalating since the Civil War ended. Between 1882 and 1903, two thousand sixty African Americans were lynched in America. The numbers of lynching perpetrated against African Americans were higher than among all other races combined. In 1892 and 1893, lynching of African Americans was at its highest. In 1892, one hundred fifty-six lynchings occurred, and in 1893 one hundred five occurred. In Louisiana between 1882 and 1903 two hundred thirty-two African Americans were lynched.[20] To say that Arthur's death was the result of him going to sleep on the railroad tracks seems highly improbable. But despite the circumstances, Resida found herself twice without a husband. At the age of twenty-one, she was now a widow with three young children under the age of five to provide for.

Resida, with a family to care for, made a third commitment. After the death of Arthur, Monroe Lawson came into her life. On February 19, 1897, Monroe (like Franklin and Arthur before him) signed a $500.00 bond to marry Resida. They were married on February 27, 1897.

Six months after the marriage of Resida and Monroe, on August 26, 1897 a rare glimpse into the lifestyle of Isle Brevelle, Resida's ancestral home, was published in *The Louisiana Populist*. Painted, in words, was a portrait of Resida's world at the time of her marriage to Monroe.

According to the article, the people of Isle Brevelle formed a "society and a world of their own." They were descendants of French, Indian, and Negroes combined with "a dash of Spanish." The women, as a rule, were virtuous. On Sundays, the Saint Augustine Catholic Church (built by Resida's ancestors), on the Isle Brevelle was crowded. When there were disputes, they were tried by the community patriarch who was viewed as sacred. Up until his death in 1856, Resida's great-great grandfather, Augustin Metoyer, was that community patriarch. The people lived in white-washed houses made of adobe, or mud walls. For entertainment, the people on the Isle would dance and play music. Huge pots of gumbo would be cooked on a fire and black coffee would be served to the guests. Nearly every Sunday, hundreds of people gathered to view horse racing at the 24-mile ferry. The people, the writer concluded, was honest, law-abiding, and devoted to one another.[21]

This was the world into which Resida had been born and to which she belonged— a simple world created by her ancestors and filled with honesty and love. This was not the world in which she found herself in 1900. She and Monroe decided not to live in the close knit community of Isle Brevelle, and instead made their home in the town of Natchitoches.

Although it was only a short distance away, unlike the Isle Brevelle, time in the town of Natchitoches had moved forward.

At some point, while married to Monroe, Resida had a brief interlude with Bertha's father, (my great-grandfather), Joseph Metoyer. With the many Josephs who existed in the vicinity of Cane River in the late nineteenth century, it has been impossible for me to identify Bertha's father. This mystery has yet to be unraveled

In spite of this brief interruption in the lives of Resida and Monroe caused by Resida's infidelity, the couple remained together. In 1900 they resided on Seventh Street in Natchitoches.[22] Monroe worked as a day laborer. Unlike a farm laborer, as a day laborer, he may have worked for the town of Natchitoches, or he may have worked odd jobs.[23] Like many African-American women in the early twentieth century and many of her female neighbors on Seventh Street, Resida worked as a laundress. This would have afforded her the time she needed to take care of her children and to contribute to the household income. Resida would typically have collected the laundry from her clientele on Monday. On the days that followed, the clothes would be boiled, scrubbed on a washboard, rinsed, and hung out, starched and ironed. On Saturday the clothes would be returned to the client. As a laundress her salary would have averaged a meager $3.39 per week.[24]

In an attempt to learn more about Resida's new husband, I browsed through hundreds of census records for a Monroe Lawson born about 1846 in Louisiana with parents born in Louisiana, as was recorded in the 1900 census. I searched the 1870, 1880, and the 1910 censuses. Only two men with the first name Monroe were found during this timeframe. They were both in the 1880 census. I found a Monroe Lawson classified by the census taker as black and born in 1835. I also found a Monroe Lawson born about 1848 living with his mother, wife, and two children, classified as white by the census taker.[25] The latter's birth date, though not exact, was only two years off; therefore, I inferred that he was the most likely candidate. This led me to two possible conclusions. Unlike Resida's previous two husbands, her last mate of choice was not a person of color, or he had been misidentified in the 1880 census because he or his first wife was visibly white. Either scenario was possible.

In her book, *Marginality and Identity*, Sister Jerome Woods wrote, "A marital union between a white person and the descendants of a Negro, regardless of how remote the Negro ancestry, was against the law. Before such a marriage could be legally performed, the white party was required to take an oath that he had Negro blood."[26] If this was the law when the couple met, was Monroe so in love with Resida that he took this oath? Or was it just a case of mistaken racial identity? Either conclusion can be drawn. But in 1900, Resida (now called Rose) and Monroe, along with the children, Howard, Agnes, and Bertha resided on Seventh Street as a Black family.[27] (There was no mention of Theresa, so I determined she probably died at a very young age). The couple must have been doing well financially, because, unlike many of their neighbors who lived on Seventh Street, they owned their home mortgage free. Rose had acquired some education because according to the 1900 census she was able to read and write. Her oldest child, Howard, was enrolled in school. Only the lovers know how long their relationship endured. I have found no records for the couple after 1900. The final chapter, on the lives of Resida and Monroe Lawson, remains to be written.

In 1910, Resida's children were living in separate homes. Bertha had returned to her mother's roots. She lived on Isle Brevelle with a couple, Cora and Joe Alex, who had lived next door to Resida and Monroe when they lived on Seventh Street in 1900,[28] and Agnes (now a young mother) lived in Natchitoches with a friend.[29] The whereabouts of Howard in 1910 is still a mystery. Having gathered this information about the separation of the children, chances are Resida died between 1900 and 1910.

In the Immaculate Conception Church records in Natchitoches there is a death of a Mary Rose Balthazar in 1901. She would have been about the same age as Resida.[30] There was no other Rosa Balthazar of that age known to relatives. I do not know with certainty if this is Bertha's grandmother, so for now, I will continue gathering evidence until hopefully I can definitively say she has been discovered.

After searching tirelessly and nearing the end of a wonderful journey, I came to the conclusion that Resida's ambition, and temperaments were similar to her great-grandmother, Marie Rose Metoyer. As I shadowed Resida's life's journey she appeared to follow in Rose's footsteps. Or, had Rose returned to give life a second chance just to relive her initial tragedy and heartache? With less than three decades of living and loving, the young, mystifying Resida appeared to evaporate without a trace, leaving her daughter, Bertha, to continue her bloodline in the forever revolving circle of life.

Searching For Bertha

Marie Resida Balthazar's Family

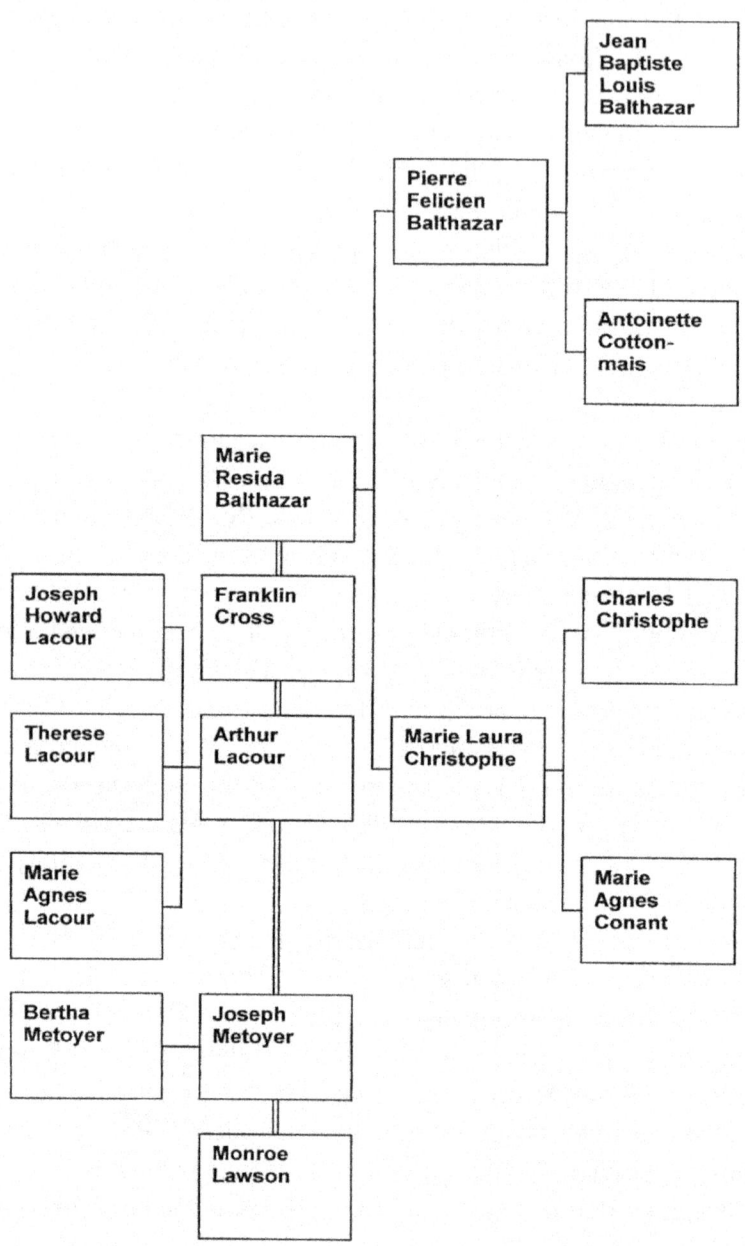

Linda S. Manuel

Marie Odalie Balthazar
Sister of Marie Resida Balthazar
Godmother of Bertha Metoyer

Courtesy of Renee Roque

Endnotes

1. Marie Resida Balthazar, baptismal certificate (1874 baptism); issued 2002, St. Augustine Catholic Church, Natchez, Louisiana; privately held by [Linda S. Manuel, Gahanna Ohio].

2. Ibid.

3. Mills, G., *Forgotten People*, xxix.

4. *Library of Congress, Chronicling America, The People's Vindicator,* "About the People's Vindicator. (Natchitoches, La.) 1874-1873," accessed February 10, 2013, http://chroniclingamerica.loc.gov/lccn/sn85038558/.

5. Jas. H. Cosgrove, et.al, Editor, "Rumors of War," *The People's Vindicator*, 4 July 1874, http://chroniclingamerica.loc.gov/lccn/sn85038558/1874-07-04/ed-1/seq-2/;words=Rumors+War?date1=1874&rows=20&searchType=basic&state=Louisiana&date2=1874&proxtext=rumors+of+war&y=15&x=15&dateFilterType=yearRange&index=1.

6. Cosgrove, editor, "Advice of a Colored Man to his Race," 1 August 1874, http://chroniclingamerica.loc.gov/lccn/sn85038558/1874-08-01/ed-1/seq-3/;words=Advice+Colored+Man?date1=1874&rows=20&searchType=basic&state=Louisiana&date2=1874&proxtext=advice+of+a+colored+man&y=10&x=13&dateFilterType=yearRange&index=0.

7. Cosgrove, editor, " Is Our Government a Failure," 19 September, 1874, (http://chroniclingamerica.loc.gov/lccn/sn85038558/1874-09-19/ed-1/seq-1/;words=our+Failure+Government?date1=1874&rows=20&searchType=basic&state=Louisiana&date2=1874&proxtext=Is+our+government+a+failure&y=10&x=17&dateFilterType=yearRange&index=0.

8. Natchitoches Parish, Louisiana, Marriage Book 10, p. 509, Franklin Cross-Marie Resida Balthazar, 1888, recorded bond and license (with original signatures) and return; Natchitoches Clerk's Office, Natchitoches, Louisiana.

9. 1870 U. S. census, Caddo Parish, Louisiana, population schedule, p. 387 (stamped), p. 47 (penned), dwelling 385, family 385, Frank Cross; digital image, Ances*try.com* accessed September 6, 2009 http://search.ancestry.com/iexec?htx=View&r=an&dbid=7163&iid=4269409_00187&fn=Frank&ln=Cross&st=r&ssrc=&pid=30578852; citing NARA microfilm publication M593, roll 508.

10. 1880 U. S. census, Caddo Parish, Louisiana, population schedule, Ward 6 Caddo, Enumeration District [ED] 16, p. 3 (penned), p. 247C (stamped), dwelling 23, family 26, Frank Cross; digital images, *Ancestry.com,* accessed October 6, 2010, http://search.ancestry.com/iexec?htx=View&r=an&dbid=6742&iid=4241286-00261&fn=Frank&ln=Cross&st=r&ssrc=&pid=5883051; citing NARA microfilm T9, roll 449.

11. Natchitoches Parish, Louisiana Marriage Book 10, p. 509 (1888), Franklin Cross-Marie Resida Balthazar.

12. Ibid.

13. Richardson, *Death of Reconstruction,* 17, 218-291.

14. Shirley Chevalier, Natchitoches, Louisiana (chevaliers@nsu.edula) to Linda Manuel (aceteach13@wideopenwest.com), 13 January 2010, "Descendants of

Bruno Lacour-Lecour-t," citing family chart. John H. Cross was married to Adelaide Lecour— sister of Arthur Lecour; 1870 U. S census, Caddo Parish, Louisiana, pop., sch., p. 47 (penned), dwelling 385, family 385, John Cross and Frank Cross; digital images, *Ancestry.com*, accessed October 6, 2010, http://search.ancestry.com/iexec?htx=View&r=an&dbid=7163&iid=4269409_00187&fn=John&ln=Cross&st=r&ssrc=pt_t3131577_p-19249690&pid=30578853; citing NARA microfilm M593, roll 508.

  15. Natchitoches Parish, Louisiana, Marriage Book no. 11, p. 372, Arthur Lecour-Resida Cross, 1890, recorded bond and license (with original signatures) and returns; Natchitoches Clerk's Office, Natchitoches, Louisiana.

  16. Joseph Howard Lecour, baptismal certificate (1891 baptism); issued 2009, St. Augustine Catholic Church, Natchez, Louisiana, privately held by Linda S. Manuel, Gahanna, Ohio.

  17. Theresa Lecour baptismal certificate (1892 baptism); issued 2009, St.Augustine Catholic Church, Natchez, Louisiana, privately held by Linda S. Manuel, Gahanna, Ohio.

  18. Mary Agnes Lecour baptismal certificate (1893 baptism); issued 2002, St. Augustine Catholic Church, Natchez, Louisiana, privately held by Linda S. Manuel, Gahanna, Ohio.

  19. Hardy L. Brian, editor, "Arthur Lacour's death," untitled article, *The Louisiana Populist*, 27 September 1895, 2013, http://chroniclingamerica.loc.gov/lccn/sn88071004/1895-09-27/ed-1/seq-3/;words=Lacour+Arthur?date1=1895&rows=20&searchType=basic&state=Louisiana&date2=1895&proxtext=arthur+lacour&y=5&x=10&dateFilterType=yearRange&index=0.

  20. William H. Glasson, *"*The Statistics of Lynching,*"* *South Atlantic Quarterly*, Volume 5, no. 4 (October 1906): 344-345.

  21. Brian, "Isle Brevelle," *Louisiana Populist*, 26 February 1897, http://chroniclingamerica.loc.gov/lccn/sn88071004/1897-02-26/ed-1/seq-2/;words=Brevelle+Isle?date1=1897&rows=20&searchType=basic&state=Louisiana&date2=1897&proxtext=Isle+brevelle&y=7&x=16&dateFilterType=yearRange&index=0.

  22. 1900 U. S. census, Natchitoches Parish, Louisiana, Ward 1, enumeration district 70, p.21-B (penned), dwelling/family [illegible], Monroe Lawson [erroneously indexed as Manny Lawson] household; digital image, *Ancestry.com* , accessed September 10, 2003, http://search.ancestry.com/iexec?htx=View&r=an&dbid=7602&iid=004120184_00594&fn=Manney&ln=Lawson&st=r&ssrc=&pid=5963812; citing NARA microfilm T623, roll 569.

  23. "1900 Census Instructions to Enumerators," article, Minneapolis: University of Minnesota, *Integrated Public Use Microdata Series: Version 5*(http://usa.ipums.org/usa/voliii/inst1900.shtml: accessed 28 February 2011), article 167.

  24. Rita G. Koman, "Servitude to Service: African-American Women as Wage Earners," article, Organization of American Historians Magazine of History, *Oxford Journals*, accessed February 28, 2011, http://maghis.oxfordjournals.org/content/11/2/42.full.pdf.

  25. 1880 U. S. census, Natchitoches Parish, Louisiana, population schedule, Ward 3 Natchitoches, Enumeration District [ED] 33, p. 21 (penned), p. 624A (stamped), dwelling [illegible], family [illegible], Monroe Lawson; digital images, *Ancestry.com*, accessed October 6, 2001, *http://search.ancestry.com/iexec?htx=View&r=an&dbid=6742&iid=4241373-00492&fn=Monroe&ln=Lawson&st=r&ssrc=&pid=6789383;* citing NARA microfilm T9, roll 457.

26. Woods, *Marginality and Identity*, 25.

27. 1900 U. S. census, Natchitoches Parish, Louisiana, Ward 1, enumeration district 70, p.21-B (penned), dwelling/family [illegible], Monroe Lawson [erroneously indexed as Manny Lawson] household; digital image, *Ancestry.com* accessed October 5, 2001, http://search.ancestry.com/iexec?htx=View&r=an&dbid=7602&iid=004120184_00594&fn=Manney&ln=Lawson&st=r&ssrc=&pid=5963812; citing NARA microfilm T623, roll 569.

28. 1910 U. S. census, Natchitoches Parish, Louisiana, Ward 9, enumeration district 91, p.13-A (penned), dwelling [illegible], family 5, Bertha Metoyer [erroneously indexed as Ruthy Metoyer]; digital image, *Ancestry.com* accessed October 5, 2004, http://search.ancestry.com/iexec?htx=View&r=an&dbid=7884&iid=31111_4329981-00221&fn=Rerthez&ln=Metoyer&st=r&ssrc=&pid=9246566; citing NARA microfilm T624, roll 519.

29. 1910 U. S. census, Natchitoches Parish, Louisiana, Ward1, enumeration district 80, p. 8-B (penned), dwelling 173, family 178, A. [Agnes] Jones; digital image, *Ancestry.com* accessed October 5, 2004, http://search.ancestry.com/iexec?htx=View&r=an&dbid=7884&iid=31111_4329980-01107&fn=A&ln=Jones&st=r&ssrc=&pid=9240148; citing NARA microfilm T624, roll 518.

30. Immaculate Conception Church, Natchitoches Parish, Louisiana, Church Registrar, p. 30, entry 5, death of Mary Rose Balthazar (1901) ; Natchitoches, Louisiana.

Chapter 17

Bertha
The Grandmother I Never Knew

Searching for Bertha transported me to times and places I never envisioned. I traced my French bloodline to the 17th century, from the parish of St. Denis de Reims to the parish of La Rochelle in France. In Natchitoches and New Orleans, Louisiana, I uncovered secrets of my ancestors dating back to the 18th century. Through the science of DNA, I was able to travel back to Bertha's maternal ancestor's (Agnes Poissot) African journey. Yet, Bertha, born in 1899, was a persistent enigma. She was as elusive as her mother. The one person I most desperately sought to discover would only release fragments of her existence, but finally she did release them, reluctantly, over long periods of time.

I started my journey to find Bertha in 1992, twenty-one years ago. With the surname Metoyer, the Christian name Bertha, and the city of Natchitoches, Louisiana, my expedition began. My initial stop, the Saint Augustine Church, on Cane River, in Natchitoches parish, directed me to the Immaculate Conception Church in the city of Natchitoches. It was there that I discovered that Bertha was born on July 22, 1899, and she was baptized on September 3rd of the same year.[1] To say I was overjoyed with this discovery is an understatement. It would not be long, I rationalized, before I would know all about my grandmother and the relatives she had left behind. Little did I know this feeling of euphoria would be short-lived. For several years after this initial unearthing, I wrote and called several places to learn more about Bertha, to no avail. I had the pleasure of corresponding with Sister Jerome Woods who unfortunately had merged the information for my grandmother, Bertha Metoyer, with another Bertha Metoyer's background. Sister Woods made available to me several of her genealogy charts she had prepared during her research on the inhabitants of Cane River during the writing of her book, *Marginality and Identity*. These records assisted me in identifying the Bertha she had intertwined with my grandmother. After Sister Wood's demise, a Sister, at the rectory in Texas where Sister Woods had resided, gave me further records that had been documented by the deceased nun. These assisted me in further identifying who my grandmother was not, but who she was remained an enigma. It was not until 2000, with the assistance of a distant cousin, Kathleen Balthazar, that I determined Bertha's mother's given name was Marie Resida Balthazar. I had finally discovered Bertha's beginning, and I was able to proceed on what would become a fascinating expedition.

My grandmother, Mary Bertha Metoyer, was the creation of what appears to be an illicit love affair. While married to her third husband, Monroe Lawson, Bertha's mother was intimately involved with Joseph Metoyer. Because of this indiscretion, Bertha was conceived. On July 22, 1899, she made her appearance into a household that consisted of two half-siblings, Howard and Agnes Lacour, and her stepfather, Monroe Lawson. Bertha was taken to the Immaculate Conception Catholic Church on September 3, 1899 and baptized. Present at her baptismal was her biological father, Joseph Metoyer, her mother, Resida Balthazar, along with her godparents, Louis Conant (Resida's cousin) and Odalie Balthazar (Resida's sister).[2]

One can only speculate about the dynamics between Resida and Monroe as a result of her infidelity, but for a brief period of time they did coexist as a couple. In 1900 they lived as a family in the town of Natchitoches on Seventh Street. Bertha was ten months old. Both Resida and Monroe were gainfully employed and home owners. As revealed, in the previous chapter, I discovered a Rosa Balthazar who died in 1901. Because of the intensive research I have done, I've come to believe that this is more than likely Bertha's mother. If this is correct, I have to conclude that Bertha never knew the essence of a mother's love. At the age of two, she was an orphan. What her life was like for the next eight years is unknown, but living without a mother's guidance and affection had to affect the emotional development of such a young child.

It was not until 1910 that I was able to locate Bertha again. She was living with Cora and Alex Joes, an elderly couple who had been neighbors of Rose and Monroe when they resided on Seventh Street.[3] At that instance, I felt great sorrow because this virtually solidified my intuition that Bertha had lost her mother at a very young age. There was some comfort in knowing she had returned to her mother's roots on Isle Brevelle. This would have given her access to her mother's numerous relatives. Perhaps this gave her the sense of family and belonging that every child needs during their formative years. But without a mother to help her navigate the nuances of the world, I would come to understand some of the decisions Bertha made later in life.

Bertha's first choice, on record, was her marriage to Jerry Pikes. Unlike the light-skinned, almost white, complexioned suitors her ancestors had selected as mates, Jerry was medium brown, medium height with black eyes and black hair.⁴ Bertha could not have known the chaos that Jerry would bring into her life. At the age of nineteen, on March 31, 1918, Jerry and Bertha became one. Unlike her mother, and numerous ancestors before her, Bertha was married, not by a Catholic priest, but by the Methodist minister, W. L. Dyas.⁵ Rev. Dyas was a well-known minister who served in Methodist churches throughout Louisiana. In 1907, Rev. Dyas guided the members in the Keithville Fairview Methodist Church in Keithville, Louisiana in building better church facilities. He served as a minister in Pineville, Louisiana at the Wesley United Methodist Church and in Mansfield, Louisiana at the Shady Grove Methodist Church. He would also have a presence in a community where Bertha would later reside.⁶ Could the choosing of Rev. Dyas to marry her have been Bertha's first attempt at rebelling against the Catholic faith and the moral values of her Cane River roots? Only she can answer that question, but what is definite is that once she left the comfort of her mother's Cane River roots, she never returned.

On February 3, 1920, two years after Bertha and Jerry married, they lived in Natchitoches on Front Street. Jerry worked as a farmer on his "own account." This meant that he was gainfully employed as an independent farmer and was not a waged or salary worker. Along with farmers like Jerry, their neighbors included contractors, teachers, mail carriers, cashiers, a druggist, a plumber, and a doctor. Bertha was a housewife.⁷ This caused me to conclude that Jerry and Bertha lived on a middle class street in Natchitoches, and they probably lived a middle class lifestyle. The fact that they lived on Front Street in 1920 seems highly unusual because the street was predominately white. According to the census that year, only five Black families and one mulatto family resided on Front.⁸ History does not say how they coexisted with their neighbors in 1920, but even as late as 1964 Front Street was considered off-limits to Blacks.⁹

After her marriage, Bertha did not reside long in the Natchitoches area. Her departure from the area was a departure initiated by fear. A year after the 1920 census recorded the couple residing on Front Street; Bertha was pregnant with their child, my mother, Willie V. Pikes. Shortly afterwards, disharmony touched the lives of the young couple. The exact date and time cannot be determined, but during the pregnancy, Jerry experienced a break from reality that caused Bertha to flee for her life.

According to accounts heard from relatives, Jerry threatened to end Bertha's life. He had gone as far as digging a grave underneath their house to bury her. Alone and pregnant, I can only imagine her fear. But one day, she decided she would leave. As a young child, I often wondered what happened to cause this turn in events after only three years of marriage. Years later, I gathered Jerry suffered a mental breakdown. Although the event that triggered Bertha's departure happened in 1921, it was not until 1925 that records indicate Jerry got professional support for his illness. He was admitted to the Central Louisiana State Mental Institution in Pineville, Louisiana on March 16, 1925. For twelve years of his life, he was a resident in the hospital. Finally, on February 23, 1937, his death from influenza released him from the institution and his mental anguish.[10] My heart aches for the lonely and tragic life my grandfather lived, but if it had not been for the decision Bertha made during her pregnancy with my mother, I may not be here to tell our story. Because she made the choice to survive, her legacy lives on.

Young, alone, and pregnant, Bertha must have been apprehensive about leaving the only life she had ever known to begin a new life in a town she may have never seen. With death as an option, she had no other choice. Like many inhabitants who left Natchitoches in the early 1920s, the city selected for relocation was Shreveport, Louisiana. Shreveport is a city about seventy-five miles northwest of Natchitoches. Unlike Natchitoches, it was a larger more developed city that offered jobs. Upon entering the city, Bertha probably marveled at the sight of the electric streetcars. During the period when she would have arrived, it was the golden age for the streetcar system in Shreveport.[11] Streetcars were a far cry from the horses and carts in Natchitoches. Despite having to leave her birthplace, Bertha must have been elated knowing there were Cane River relatives who had come to Shreveport before her.

Bertha's journey to her new home would have taken about five hours down a gravel/perhaps dirt road known today as Highway 1. Who took her down this road and when have never been revealed. Twice I made this trek in an attempt to recapture a glimpse of what she must have experienced on her journey. Modernized and far beyond the scope of what it was in the 1920s, I could not recapture her spirit. What I do know is that her life reignites in the city of Shreveport, in the St. Paul's Bottoms area—an area developed in the 1880s to accommodate Black residents leaving rural farm areas to find employment in warehouses on Shreveport's waterfront. During the nineteenth and early twentieth century the Bottoms area was a prime example of a Louisiana working class neighborhood. It was also once a part of Shreveport's infamous red light district.[12]

Shreveport's red light district, like Storyville (the red light district in New Orleans) was an area of ill repute. From 1902 to 1917, the district was where men could proposition a prostitute and no one could be held accountable for their actions. As history goes, the leaders of the city decided, in late 1902, to designate an area to serve as a "red light district for the habitation of women of immoral character." The area was named St. Paul's Bottoms for the Saint Paul African Methodist Church that was on Caddo Street. It was February of 1903 that the area was officially designated as the red light district. Though prostitution was not legalized, it was regulated. The women who worked in the area had to register with the police and make appointments with city physicians. After being designated the red light district, this predominately Black area of town attracted madams and women of "immoral character." At the height of the district's existence there was said to be about forty houses inhabited by the prostitutes. The larger Victorian Houses were run by white madams with white prostitutes who serviced only white men. Other smaller houses were operated by creoles of color and Black madams who serviced both white and black men. The average price of a "lady of the night" varied from one to three dollars. As World War II approached, with concern for the well-being of soldiers that would likely be housed in Shreveport, a decision was made to close down the district. A referendum was held in the fall of 1917 to decide on the fate of the district, and by a narrow margin, the decision was made to shut down Shreveport's infamous red light district. [13]

Though the red light district was officially gone in 1921 when Bertha arrived, remnants of the past remained, and stories were often told. Prostitution had somewhat diminished, but it was not entirely gone. Instead of being sanctioned, it was now underground and illegal. It was in this area of town that Bertha found herself pregnant and over seventy miles away from her roots. This was nothing like the small rural town that she once called home. To a small town girl this "big city" had to be a cultural shock. Yet this was the environment that would surround and influence Bertha for the next seven years of her life.

Having fled Natchitoches, Bertha found shelter with a stranger, Cora Carter, at 516 Dillingham in Saint Paul's Bottoms. On what may have been a crisp fall day or night, October 13, 1921, Bertha gave birth to her first child, my mother, Willie V. Pikes. With Cora, who came to be known to me as Mama Cora, Bertha found solace and comfort for two years.[14] But, in 1923, Bertha made a second attempt at marital bliss. Her second mate of choice, William Green, would prove to be almost as disastrous as her first.

William and Bertha continued their lives in the St. Paul's Bottom area. They rented a one story frame duplex at 500 Dillingham, not far from Mama Cora's residence. The neighborhood they lived in had unpaved roads and consisted of houses that would be found in a working class neighborhood—bungalows, shotgun houses, and cottages. For a period of time the couple managed to live respectable lives. William earned a living as a truck driver, and Bertha cared for my mother and the home. It probably came as no surprise when one spring day, April 24, 1924, a new life was presented to the family, another daughter, Lillian. For two years the couple lived, and perhaps loved, on Dillingham. Between 1926 and 1927, they would move twice; first to 1423 Calcote, not far from Dillingham, and finally to 1649 Hotchkiss, away from the Bottoms. It was on Hotchkiss, that Bertha gave birth to her final daughter, Addie—born three years later, but on the same day as Lillian, April 24, 1927.[15] At the time of Addie's birth, William operated a road grader for the city of Shreveport and Bertha had found employment as a domestic worker. Addie's birth would officially signify Bertha's last live appearance as a residence in the city of Shreveport. Driven from her first home in Natchitoches due to insanity, she would find herself driven from her Shreveport home due to cruelty.

My Aunt Addie's recollections of her father were of a very cruel man. She remembers him as a domineering person who viewed his family as his possessions. For these reasons, I feel, Bertha once again decided to flee. She originally left my mother, along with the other children, but she later came back to claim her. Addie and Lillian remained with their father and grandmother. Being the malicious person my aunt alleged her father was, I can only speculate, that the two girls were left behind because William would not allow Bertha to have *his* children. As reminisced by my Aunt Addie, "When mama came to get Willie V., she was combing my hair, and she didn't want to go. So, Willie V. took off running." Evidently she was a very fast runner, because according to my aunt, "Willie V. outran the horse." Eventually, my mother was caught, and she left with Bertha. When they departed, fearing William, no one was privy to their new location. It was not until 2000 that I came to know where they had gone.

With the official appearance of the 1930 census, I found Bertha again.[16] This was a joyous day for me. Seeing my mother, eight-years-old, and her mother together in the census brought tears to my eyes. I remember tracing my fingers over their names on the computer screen. It was a very surreal moment. I could picture the two of them together, mother and daughter, safe and content. At last I had found them. In April, 1930 their home was on Port Caddo Road in Marshall, Texas. Bertha had remarried again. Her husband was a farmer, and she worked as a laundress in a private home. No one could have known this would be Bertha's final year with my mother.

Bertha's last mate of choice was John H. Jackson. I later found on my grandmother's death certificate that the H stood for Henry.[17] Curiosity caused me to wonder about John Henry. I had to know who he was and from where he had come. As I had done with Monroe Lawson, Bertha's stepfather, I searched the records endlessly for a John Henry Jackson, or John H. Jackson, or Henry Jackson. I used the criteria given in the 1930 census for John when he was married to my grandmother. He was said to have been born in Texas, about 1890, with both parents born in Tennessee. I looked through thousands of census records from 1900 to 1930. After months of comparing census records, I was able to find only one John H. Jackson who fit all the criteria and none classified their race as Black. I found John H. Jackson in the 1900 census, and again in the 1910 census.[18] Both Johns found in 1900 and 1910 were the same, and they were recorded as white. I had to consider that like her mother, Resida, Bertha's last mate of choice may not have been a person of color. Or could this, too, be a case of mistaken racial identity. Like Resida's husband, Monroe, I reasoned, John Henry was recorded as white in the census in 1900 and 1910 while unmarried and living with parents. In 1930, married to Bertha, he was recorded as Black. Although his race is speculative based on my census research, until evidence points me in a different direction this is my belief. Bertha's life was a reflection of her mother's. Both women had been married three times and their last mates were possibly white. Despite only knowing her mother briefly as a small child, Bertha was repeating her mother's life patterns.

When I discovered Bertha in the 1930 census, I was able to secure a death record for her. I always knew she died when my mother was about ten (she was really nine), but I had been unable to locate a record of her death. Now I knew why. I had searched under the names of Metoyer, her maiden name, and her two known married names Pikes and Green. I now had another name—Jackson. I sent off for a death certificate and received it a short time later. The certificate stated what I had known: Bertha died from complications caused by surgery. Her surgery was for an intestinal obstruction, and she died postoperative. As she had done her entire life, she found herself in an unfamiliar and terrifying position and decided to flee. As communicated to me by my aunt, Bertha had awakened in a strange and unfamiliar place and began to run. This time her flight had caused her life. She started hemorrhaging from the surgery, and she died, three days after Christmas, on December

28, 1930. She was buried in Hopewell Cemetery in Shreveport, Louisiana—a short distance away from the life in the Saint Paul's Bottoms she had once fled.[19] Like her mother, Bertha died during the third decade of her life. Like her mother, she left small children behind.

In 2005, my brother and I went in search of the cemetery only to discover that it had been abandoned and was now an unkempt field. This saddened me because I would never know her exact resting place. But now I do know that she was given a proper burial. And as surreal as it may sound, while I searched the world for her, she had been buried not far from a place where *I had once stayed and played, laughed and cried, and exposed my wide, sometimes crooked grin to the world.*

The journey to find Bertha was a long and wondrous journey. I traced my maternal African ancestors as they were forced to leave Africa. I traced my French ancestors through the bourgeoisie streets of France. I waded through the chain of slave records that held my ancestors captives, and I watched the chains broken as my ancestors bought and fought for their freedom. I witnessed my ancestors rise from slaves to slave masters and from poverty to riches, and back again. I cheered as my ancestors fought for our country's freedom, and wept as the country they fought for betrayed their loyalty. I plodded through poverty, insanity, and infidelity, as I traced my family's roots. Through it all, I realized that my roots are human roots. By telling my story, I have told thousands of stories. The total sum is comprised of the good, the bad, and often the ugly. It tells a story of triumphs and tribulations filled with numerous peaks and valleys. I was urged to stop at the good, I was begged to omit the bad, and I was taunted for revealing the ugly, but it is the total sum of these parts that make us whole. Without them, my story would be a farce; therefore, I have bared my roots for all to examine and perhaps criticize. This was a journey I would gladly take again. Several times I stumbled and fell, ranted and raved, and stopped and started again. At times, tears of sadness drenched my face and told me to stop. Other times, tears of laughter bounced off my cheeks and urged me on. In the face of it all, I continued to make strides. The roads I traveled brought me family who became cherished friends. It gave me the roots I so desperately needed to make my psyche complete. Now I can validate who I am and from where I came. I know my roots. There is no greater gift than this.

Bertha Metoyer's Family

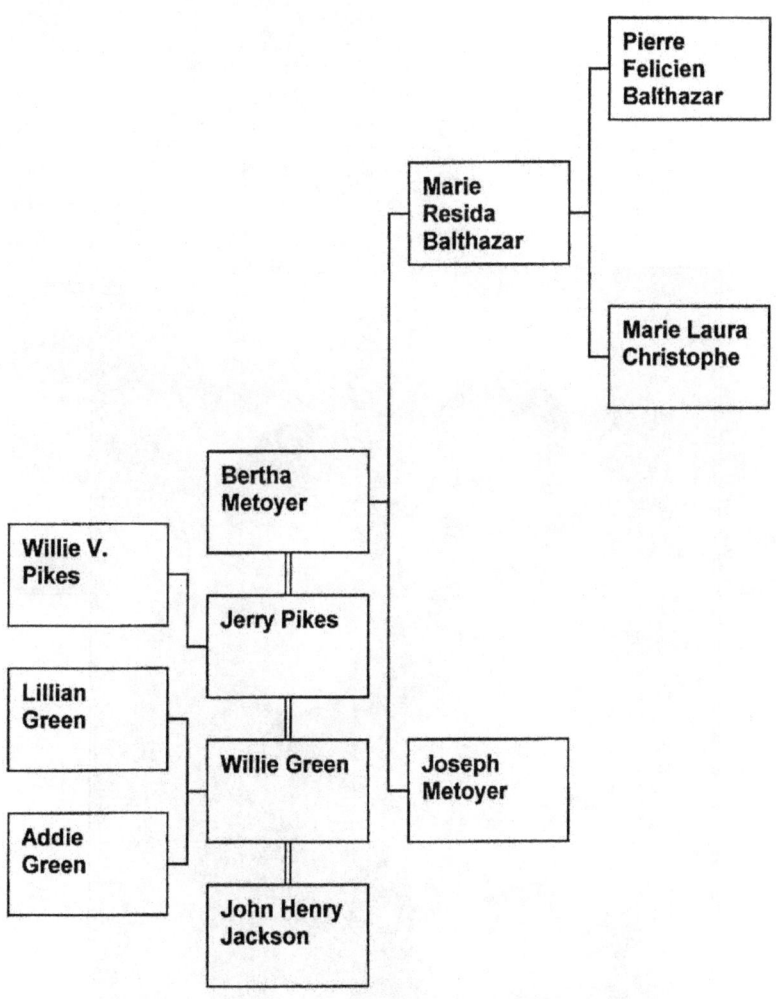

Willie V. Pikes-Smith (Linda Manuel's mother & Bertha's Daughter) with Fred Taylor

Linda Manuel and Aunt Addie Mae Green-Jackson (Bertha's Daughter)

Aunt Lillian Green (Bertha's Daughter) and Melvin Randall

Marie Agnes Lacour (Linda's Great Aunt) and Bennie Thomas

Endnotes

1. Bertha Metoyer baptismal certificate (1899), issued 2001.

2. Ibid.; 1900 U. S. census, Natchitoches Parish, Louisiana, Ward 1, enumeration district 70, p.21-B (penned), dwelling/family [illegible], Monroe Lawson [erroneously indexed as Manny Monroe]; digital image, Ancestry.com, accessed October 5, 2004, http://search.ancestry.com/iexec?htx=View&r=an&dbid=7602&iid=004120184_00594&fn=Manney&ln=Lawson&st=r&ssrc=&pid=5963812; citing NARA microfilm T623, roll 569.

3. 1910 U. S. census, Natchitoches Parish, Louisiana, Ward 9, enumeration district 91, p.13-A (penned), dwelling [illegible], family 5BerthaMetoyer [erroneously indexed as Ruthy Metoyer]; digital image, *Ancestry.com,* accessed October 5, 2004, http://search.ancestry.com/iexec?htx=View&r=an&dbid=7884&iid=31111_4329981-00221&fn=Rerthez&ln=Metoyer&st=r&ssrc=&pid=9246566; citing NARA microfilm T624, roll 519; 1900 U. S. census, Natchitoches Parish, Louisiana, Ward 1, enumeration district 70, p.21-B (penned), dwelling/family [illegible], Monroe Lawson [erroneously indexed as Manny Monroe]; digital image, *Ancestry.com,* accessed October 5, 2004,

http://search.ancestry.com/iexec?htx=View&r=an&dbid=7602&iid=004120184_00594&fn=Manney&ln=Lawson&st=r&ssrc=&pid=5963812; citing NARA microfilm T623, roll 569.

4. World War I Selective Service System Draft Registration Cards, 1917–1918, card for Jerry Pikes, National Archives microfilm publication M1509, imaged from Family History Library film roll 1684816, *Ancestry.com,* accessed February 2, 2013, http://search.ancestry.com/iexec?htx=View&r=an&dbid=6482&iid=LA-1684816-3298&fn=Jerry&ln=Pikes&st=r&ssrc=&pid=31767955.

5. Natchitoches Parish, Louisiana, marriage certificate no. 32, Jerry Pikes-Bertha Metoyer, 1918, recorded bond and license (with original signatures) and returns: Natchitoches Clerk's Office, Natchitoches, Louisiana.

6. Shady Grove, UMC, "Our History," accessed March 10, 2013, http://faithfulliving.org/index.php?id=history0; Jane Parker McManus, submitter, "United Methodist Church Cemetery," accessed March 10, 2013, http://files.usgwarchives.net/la/rapides/cemeteries/wesleymeth.txt; Methodist Episcopal Church, T. Mason and G. Lane, *Minutes of the annual conferences of the Methodist Episcopal Church: Spring Conferences 1913,*"(New York, 1913) digitized book, accessed March 10, 2013, http://archive.org/stream/minutesannualco05churgoog#page/n8/mode/2up.

7. 1920 U. S. census, Natchitoches Parish, Louisiana, enumeration district 38, p. 22-A (penned), dwelling 471, family 325, Bertha Pikes; digital image, *Ancestry.com,* accessed January 3, 2004, http://search.ancestry.com/iexec?htx=View&r=an&dbid=6061&iid=4300972_01092&fn=Bertha&ln=Pikes&st=r&ssrc=&pid=60363796; citing NARA microfilm publication T625, roll 617.

8 Ibid.

9. Addendum to: Front Street (Commercial Buildings), Cane River Heritage Area Commission, accessed February 27, 2013, http://lcweb2.loc.gov/pnp/habshaer/la/la0400/la0454/data/la0454data.pdf:

10. Barbara Brossette, RHIT, Health Information Director, Central Louisiana State Hospital, addressed to author, September 30, 2010.

11. Eric Brock, *Eric Brock's Shreveport* (Gretna, Louisiana: Pelican Press, 2001), 88.

12. City of Shreveport Historical Committee Report: April 2012, 77, accessed February 25, 2013, http://www.shreveporttimes.com/assets/pdf/D918902358.PDF.

13. Eric Brock, *Red Light, Shreveport's St. Paul's Bottoms Red Light District, An Experiment in Controlled Vice* (Shreveport, Louisiana : Ramble House, 2004), 14, 17, 19, 34, 36, 38.

Kip Lornell and Tracey E. W. Laird, ed., *Shreveport Sounds in Black and White*, (Jackson, Mississippi: University Press of Mississippi, 2008), 147-48.

14. Story related to author by author's aunt, Addie Jackson; Willie V. Smith, SS. No. 439-96-1069, 13 February 1970, Application for Account Number, (Form SS-5), Social Security Administration, Baltimore, Maryland; Shreveport, Louisiana, City Directory, 1921, Cora Carter, Ancestry.com. U.S. City Directories, 1821-1989 (Beta), digital image, *Ancestry.com, accessed February 28, 2013*, http://search.ancestry.com/iexec?htx=View&r=an&dbid=2469&iid=12760869&fn=Cora&ln=Carter&st=r&ssrc=&pid=747443406.

15. Shreveport Historical Committee Report, digital image, *Shreveporttimes.com*, accessed March 2, 2013, http://www.shreveporttimes.com/assets/pdf/D918902358.PDF;

Louisiana Bureau of Vital Statistics, birth certificate no.40772 (1925), Lillian Green; Office of Vital Statistics, Baton Rouge;

Shreveport, Louisiana, City Directory, 1923, Wm. Green (Bertha), Ancestry.com. U.S. City Directories, 1821-1989 (Beta), digital image, *Ancestry.com,* accessed February 28, 2013, http://ancestry.com; also subsequent years by the same title: 1924, 1925, 1926, 1927;

Louisiana Bureau of Vital Statistics, birth certificate no.445 (1927), Addie Green; Office of Vital Statistics, Baton Rouge.

16. 1930 U. S. census, Harrison County, Marshall, Texas, enumeration district 7, p. 19-B (penned), dwelling 397, family 420, Bertha Jackson; digital image, *Ancestry.com*, accessed May 11, 2005, http://search.ancestry.com/iexec?htx=View&r=an&dbid=6224&iid=4547977_00122&fn=Bertha&ln=Jackson&st=r&ssrc=&pid=63099453; citing NARA microfilm publication T626, roll 2354.

17. Louisiana State Board of Health, Bureau of Vital Statistics, death certificate no. 1662 Register no. 15400 (1930), Bertha Jackson; Bureau of Vital Statistics, Baton Rouge.

18. 1900 U. S. census, Dallas County, Dallas, Texas, enumeration district 133, p. 11-B (penned), dwelling196, family 199, John H. Jackson; digital image, *Ancestry.com* accessed May 21-23, 2005, http://search.ancestry.com/iexec?htx=View&r=an&dbid=7602&iid=004118455_00130&fn=John+H&ln=Jackson&st=r&ssrc=&pid=70524128; citing NARA microfilm publication T623, roll 1626;

1910 U. S. census, Dallas County, Grand Prairie, Texas, enumeration district 106, p. 4-A (penned) dwelling 61, family 62, John H. Jackson; digital image, *Ancestry.com,* accessed May 26-228, 2005, http://search.ancestry.com/iexec?htx=View&r=an&dbid=7884&iid=4449280_01141&fn=John+H&ln=Jackson&st=r&ssrc=&pid=126803440; citing NARA microfilm publication T624, roll 1544.

19. "Bertha Jackson's death certificate."

Linda S. Manuel

My Roots Revealed

Ancestors	Lifespan	Relationship
Pikes, Willie V.	1921-1980	Mother
Pikes, Jerry	1898-1937	Grandfather
Metoyer, Bertha	1899-1930	Grandmother
Pikes, Henry	c1850-1922	Great-grandfather
Pikes, Alice	c1855-Unknown	Great-grandmother
Metoyer, Joseph	Unknown	Great-grandfather
Balthazar, Marie Resida	1874- Unknown	Great-grandmother
Balthazar, Pierre Felicien	1845-1910	2nd great-grandfather
Christophe, Marie Laura	1847-1929	2nd great-grandmother
Balthazar, Jean Baptiste Louis	c1807-c1853	3rd great-grandfather
Coton-Maïs, Marie Antoinette	c1807-Unknown	3rd great-grandmother
Christophe, Charles	c1828-1866	3rd great-grandfather
Conant, Marie Agnes	1828-1875	3rd great-grandmother
Balthazar-Monet, Jean Baptiste	c1774-1812	4th great-grandfather
Metoyer, Marie Rose	1793-1856	4th great-grandmother
Coton-Maïs, Antoine	1775-1840	4th great-grandfather
Bellepeche, Marie Louise	c1790-Unknown	4th great-grandmother
Christophe, Firmin Capello Sr.	c1794-1890	4th great-grandfather
Mayeux, Marie Françoise	c1795-1872	4th great-grandmother
Conant, Florentin	1794-1858	4th great-grandfather
Metoyer, Marie Louise	1797-1847	4th great-grandmother
Dupré, Jean Baptiste	c1731-1781	5th great-grandfather
Catherine	Unknown	5th great-grandmother
Metoyer, Louis	c1770-1832	5th great-grandfather
Lecomte, Françoise	c1771- Unknown	5th great-grandmother
Conand/t, Joseph	c1763-1830	5th great-grandfather
Metoyer, Marie Susanne	1768-1838	5th great-grandmother
Metoyer, Nicolas Augustin	1768-1856	5th great-grandfather
Poissot, Marie Agnes	c1771-1839	5th great-grandmother
Dupré, Jacques	c1700-1736	6th great-grandfather
Philippe, Anne Marie	1709-1781	6th great-grandmother
Metoyer, Claude Thomas Pierre	1744-1815	6th great-grandfather
Coincoin, Marie Therese	c1742-1816	6th great-grandmother
Lecomte, Jean Baptiste	c1736-1784	6th great-grandfather

Searching For Bertha

Victoire Marguerite	Unknown	6th great-grandmother
Conand, Jacques François	c1740-1821	6th great-grandfather
Brillat, Marie Anne	Unknown	6th great-grandmother
Poissot, Athanase	1746-Unknown	6th great-grandfather
Françoise	c1760-Unknown	6th great-grandmother
Schup, Philipp Adam	c1672-Unknown	7th great-grandfather
Anna Martha	1676-Unknown	7th great-grandmother
Metoyer, Nicolas François	1715-1766	7th great-grandfather
Drapron, Marie Anne	c1714-1748	7th great-grandmother
François	c1715-1758	7th great-grandfather
Marie Françoise	c1715-1758	7th great-grandmother
Poissot, Remy	1706-1788	7th great-grandfather
Philippe, Anne Marie	1709-1781	7th great-grandmother
Metoyer, Jean	c1655-1729	8th great-grandfather
Galloteau, Françoise	1684-before 1743	8th great-grandmother
Drapron, François	c1690-before 1743	8th great-grandfather
Naudin, Anne	c1694-1733	8th great-grandmother
Poissot, Mamert	c1670-1737	8th great-grandfather
Pongey, Suzanne	c1680-Unknown	8th great-grandmother
Schup, Philipp Adam	c1672-Unknown	8th great-grandfather
Anna Marthe/a	c1676-Unknown	8th great-grandmother
Galloteau, Nicolas	1639-c1694	9th great-grandfather
Jobart, Marguerite	Unknown -c1695	9th great-grandmother
Galloteau, Claude	c1606-before 1672	10th great-grandfather
Lequex, Guillemette	c1620-Unknown	10th great-grandmother
Jobart, Claude	Unknown	10th great-grandfather
Contant, Françoise	Unknown	10th great-grandmother

    Lifespans have been taken from several sources: Birth and Death certificates from Louisiana Vital Records Bureau, in author's possession; Baptismal certificates and Death records from Saint Augustine Catholic Church, in author's possession; Baptismal certificate and Death records from Immaculate Conception Church, in author's possession; Census Records from *Ancestry.com*; Baptismal and Death records from *Archives Départementales of Charente-Maritime and de la Marne*, courtesy of Ms. Methvin; Mills, E. S., Natchitoches, 1729-1803; Mills, E. S., Natchitoches, 1800-1826; Mills, E. S., "The Natchitoches Genealogist," Vol. XXIV, April 1999. Mills, E. S. *Isle of Canes.*

Appendices

Louis Metoyer and Sylvestre Bossier Land Dispute Court Documents[1]

The following documents are from the court case between Sylvestre Bossier, et.al, and Louis Metoyer. Included are copies of land petitions submitted by Louis, testimony for the plaintiffs and the defendant, court summons, and rulings by the judge. Due to the age of the documents and the handwriting some of the words were barely legible. Despite this I have tried to adhere as closely to the original writing as possible adding some punctuation for clarity. Not all documents were legible; therefore, not all of the documents are included. But I have included as many as I could so that you could fully understand the significance of the case for our ancestor, Louis Metoyer.

Louis Metoyer, Pardo,[2] free resident in this district under your Majesty's charge, requests of you very humbly, that he wishes to cultivate and procure possession of uncultivated lands pertaining to the dominion of Your Majesty. These lands are located in the Isle Brevelle, bordering on the upper part with the Bayou Plat, and I might also add it has upwards and downwards boundaries with my brother Augustin and it extends from one side of the river, around twenty arpents to the front and from the other side around fifteen arpents. However, as Your Majesty is well informed, those lands lack depth; furthermore, I will have to construct half of a considerable bridge over the Dho Bayou Plat; from which, it is hoped, Your Majesty will be able to benefit of its service as will your Sir Governor-General of this Province, hoping that Your Worthy Excellency is able to grant me the land mentioned above they being of an absolute necessity for me to cultivate my crops; this is a grace that I request with the intercession of Your Majesty.

Natchitoches 20th of December, 1795
Marked with a cross, Pardo, X Luis Mettoyer
21 February 1795
My dear Sir and Commandant
Sir Governor-General
I have evidence that the petition of the interested applicant does

not present itself with any impediment, on the contrary, it will result in great benefit to the Public, the construction of a bridge over the Bayou Plat; Furthermore, there is in existence [something] similar on the Dho Bayuco that has already been granted, for which I request of Your Lordship, to grant him the grace he asks.

Natchitoches, 21st of December 1795
Luis De Blanc

New Orleans, May 18th of 1796

The Surveyor General of this Province or anyone in particular named by him for this purpose, will establish the boundaries of twenty arpents of land to the front of one side of the river, and fifteen arpents on the other side as is requested in the above petition made by the applicant. Regarding the lack of depth, other vacant plots of lands are not causing any inconvenience to neighboring properties and this petition is granted with a precise condition requiring him to build a road and to carry out regular clearing of the land within the term of one year. And if this condition is not achieved within one year the concession will be nullified. However, if three more [years] pass and these lands have not been properly established no power will be able to expropriate these lands from him. He will be granted an extension, but will need to pay again the surveying and demarcation fees, to myself, enabling me to provide the applicant with the correspondent form title.

[Signed] El Baron de Carondelet
Registrado

June 11, 1805

The undersigned, J. Bte Paillette, land surveyor of the district of Natchitoches, certify to whom it may concern that, by act of the 10th day of this month, we have, upon the request from Mister Silvestre Bossier, inhabitant who informed us of certificate of concession duly notarized, inspected and surveyed a plot ten arpents, extending beyond of and on either side of the Red River, located in the flat Bayou in Brevelle, for the purpose of establishing the deed for the concession granted to him by decree stated 18 April 1789, ordering same.

We certify further that, in accordance with the law, we were assisted by his immediate neighbors who voiced no objection to the recording of the common boundaries and who, along with ourselves, signed the minutes thereof; we did find on said plot an inhabitant named Louis Metoyer, a free mulatto, who declared believing that he is the landowner of this same surveyed plot.

Delivered this present document in lieu of the minutes and of the drawing of the plot pending the drafting of same, which we did draft and register, emergently and in accordance with the regulations, with Louisiana General Engineer, on 11 June 1805.

12th December 1816

I certify that the claim of Mr. Sylvestre Bossier for a tract of eight hundred arpents of land on the Bayou Plat in the Parish of Natchitoches has been reported by the Board of Commissioners among other claims for the Parish of Natchitoches and classed among those which in the opinion of the said Board ought to be confirmed. I further certify that by an act of Congress passed during the last session all claims reported by the said board of commissioners and recommended for confirmation have been confirmed with the exception only as to claims exceeding in extent [illegible] League Square---Given under my hand at the Land Office Opelousas 12th October 1816.

Levin Wailes
Register Land [Office]

---

28 April 1817

Mr. Louis Metoyer,

You are hereby summoned to comply with the [illegible] of the answered petitions and to file your answer hereto in writing with the clerk of the District Court for the 6th District in and for the Parish of Natchitoches at his office at Natchitoches within ten days after the service hereof and if you fail herein judgment will be given against you by default.

Witness Jos. S. Johnston, Judge of the said court this 28th day of April in the year of our Lord 1817

---

6 May 1817

Citation

S. C. Bossier
S. Bossier
I. Baldwin
   Vs.
Louis Metoyer

Served a copy of the within together with a copy of the answered petition to Louis Metoyer within named in person this 6th of May 1817.
   Jas. Loccard

---

28 October 1817

Sylvestre Caesar Bossier
S. Bossier Curator ad Bona   Court Seventh District
Isaac Baldwin Curator ad Litem   Parish of Natchitoches
Of Pamela Bossier
   Vs.
Louis Metoyer

Louis Metoyer Answers Complaints by the Plaintiffs

The answer of Louis Metoyer, the defendant in the above cause.

The defendant for answer saith a letter swear these allegations thus set forth in the petition of the said plaintiff are untrue and this he pray may be argued of by a jury. He prays also that he may be hence dismissed with his reasonable costs [illegible].

And for further answer he says that the land which he possesses and which the said plaintiff claims is his own by a just and legal title.

And for further answer he says that he has been in possession of the property claimed upward of ten years with a just title and that the said plaintiff and none under whom they claim are present had a claim.

And for further answer this defendant said that he had in possession of the land claimed by the said plaintiff by a just title and that consequently they cannot recover the said land without paying for the improvements made on said land are over the four thousand dollars and this he prays may be argued of by a jury he prays who hence dismisses over his costs.

      W. Murray
    [Attorney] in court for Defendant

  The defendant claims under an order of claim by date the 18 May 1796 and a commissioners certificate B no. 1953 in his own name and by undisturbed possession since that time to wit May 18, 1796.

---

6 November 1817
Isaac Baldwin, Esq.

Sir

You will please to take notice that on the 21st of November instanter between the hours of ten in the morning and four in the afternoon at the office of the Judge of the Parish of St. Martins the testimony of Louis DeBlanc will be taken to be disproved as evidence on the part of the defendant in a suit by you instituted in this district court seventh district parish of Natchitoches in which Sylvestre Caesar Bossier, Sylvestre Bossier Curator ad Bona and Isaac Baldwin Curator ad Litem are Plaintiffs of Louis Metoyer Defendant at which time and place you will attend if you think proper.

W. Murray
[Attorney] For Louis Metoyer
Rapides, Nov. 6, 1817

---

11 December 1817

Placide Bossier and J. J. Poillette You are hereby commanded to appear in the District Court for the Parish of Natchitoches to testify the truth according to your knowledge in a case pending therein wherein S. C. Bossier, S. Bossier, and I. Baldwin Plaintiffs and Louis Metoyer defendant in the part of plaintiff and herein you are not to fail under the penalty of Two hundred and Fifty dollars.

By the Court
Sam H. Sibley, Clerk

To Felix Trudeau,

You are hereby commanded to appear in the district Court for the Parish of Natchitoches instanter to testify the truth to your knowledge in a case pending therein, wherein C. Bossier and [illegible] is plaintiffs and Ls. [Louis] Metoyer defendant on the part of defendant and herein you are not to fail under penalty of Two hundred and Fifty Dollars.

By order of the Court
Sam H. Sibley, Clerk

---

17 June 1818

To P. D. Cailleau Lafontaine JSV
Judge of the Parish of Natchitoches

Know ye that [respecting] confidence in your integrity and [illegible] we do hereby authorize and direct you to take the deposition of Joseph Metoyer [regarding] the matters in controversy for and in the

District court of the Parish of Natchitoches wherein Sylvestre Bossier [illegible] are Plaintiffs and Louis Metoyer is the defendant, and the said deposition so that you will transmit under your hand and seal to the clerk of said court forthwith—

Witness the Hon. Jos. S. Johnston, Judge of the said Court 17th day of June 1818

Sam H., Clk.

---

17 June 1818

Sylvestre Bossier   In the District Court

Vs.   Seventh District

Louis Metoyer   Parish of Natchitoches

Sylvestre Bossier & Isaac Baldwin

Take Notice

That at five o'clock this evening I will proceed to take the testimony of Joseph Metoyer before the Honorable P. D. Cailleau Lafontaine Judge of the Parish of Natchitoches at the house of the said Joseph opposite the port of Natchitoches to be read in evidence in the above cause in consequences of this witness age and infirmity of the said Joseph Metoyer.

17 June 1818
W. Murray
Attorney for Defendant

---

20 July 1818

Bossier
Vs.
Metoyer

Mr. François [illegible] states that Metoyer has worked on the land for twenty or twenty one years - that he has lived on the land 14 0r 15 years- and that he cultivates on both sides of the river and within 10 arpents of the Bayou Plat, and that Metoyer assisted in clearing the river.

Mr. Tauzin states that he was on the land in the fall of 1788 and saw Bossier at work with three Negroes, that he was cutting cane on the land, but had no house and did not live on the land— that he has often passed there since and never saw him on the land after.

François Bossier brother of the plaintiff states that he, Sylvestre Bossier, worked on the land claimed in the fall of 1888 and had several Negroes and had cut several acres of cane. But he did not live on the land afterwards and that he opened the road in front.

Antoine Conde has known that the land has been occupied and cultivated for 15 or 16 years by Metoyer.

Mr. Pailette states that he was called on by Bossier to survey the land in question – that he made the survey and after he had done it saw Mr. Metoyer, who was living on the land and told him he surveyed it. Mr. Metoyer replied that the land was his, the Plat marked B in a court process held [illegible] of the survey and proceeding that there were about $(45)^3$ arpents on both sides of the River cleared.

Capt. Trudeau the former commandant of the Post for 8 years previous to the change of Government that he received the [illegible] on archives from Mr. DeBlanc- that he found among them a bundle entitled remise [illegible] that he asked Mr. DeBlanc what was this object for returning those titles– he said the inhabitants were in the habit sometimes of returning their titles not wishing to settle them or improve them– that he remembers distinctly the title of Mr. Bossier the Plaintiff was among them and remained among those until the archives man delivered [them] to Capt. Trudeau. That there were many others in the [illegible] or bundle –that while he was commandant, he delivered back one of those titles to the person who had returned it to the office– the Party having again solicited a new concession for the land, it not having been granted to any other person he returned the old title telling him it was as good as the new one– he further states that he delivered the title to Metoyer soon after it was made and that he went to live on the land soon afterwards and has cultivated the land ever since – that's the same year or the year after the defendant made the road through the land.

The defendant excepts to the [illegible] of all the Parol Evidence,

1 because Parol Evidence is inadmissible with regard to land
2nd the abandonment must be in writing and not by [illegible]

It is in proof that there are about ninety arpents of the land clear, a variety of testimony was taken to prove the [case?] of the improvement and the rent— But the parties agreed to submit that to judgment of the court.

The above two sheets contain all the witnesses in this case.

Jos. H. Johnston
Judge of District

---

20 July 1818
The Case of Bossier vs. Metoyer Natchitoches District Court Land Claim 1818

Parish of Natchitoches

S. C. Bossier
S. Bossier
J. Baldwin
Vs.
L. Metoyer

This suit is instituted for the recovery of a tract of land of ten arpents front on both sides of the Red River at the Bayou de Plat—on which the defendant now lives. The Plaintiff married Mary Jean Lambre in October 1787, by whom he has two children, who are now joined with him in this suit–The mother having died in the year 1794—The Plaintiff's title is a request the 2nd October 1788 and an order of survey the 18th of April 1789. Certificate of confirmation by the commissioners—the order of survey is upon the usual conditions. It appears that in the fall of 1788 he cut several acres of cane and opened the road in front that he never lived on the land, nor improved it afterwards—and that about this time, he gave up the idea of holding the land and surrendered his titles to the commandant as was usual at that time as the evidence of his abandonment —The title was filed away by the commandant in a bundle of papers called titles returned to the domain and remained there dead until after the change of government, from whence it has been taken in a manner not known or explained and entered in the commissioners office on which they issued the certificate—The land remained vacant until the Defendant petitioned for the land on the 20 December 1795 and an order of surveying issued the 18th May 1796. That he began soon after his improvement and has actually lived on and cultivated the land 14 or 15 or 16 years. It is clear therefore that all the rights of Silvestre Bossier have been lost by prescriptions, having suffered the defendant to remain more than ten years in the [public?] peaceable enjoyment of the land.

The rights of the two children have been preserved [illegible] their minority. The court is of opinion that the Plaintiffs had a legal title to the land, and that evidence of the surrender of his title and the abandonment of his land is not such, according to the decisions of the Supreme Court, as will divest his rights or destroy his property. The surrender was evidently made according to the known usage practice of Natchitoches. That they were considered as the strongest evidence, which could be given, that the party had abandoned and had no longer any title. This was a local custom and must in every case depend upon parol evidence[4], which has been uniformly held insufficient to invalidate a legal written title.

A stronger case than the present can never be presented in which the application of general rules of law necessary for the safety of all property will mark greater injury and injustice. The claim of the plaintiff, a mere naked legal right, offered under circumstances not altogether favorable or satisfactory, is strongly contrasted by the pain and honest and equitable claim of the defendant supported by twenty years possession of the land. Yet the court, can invoke no principle that will not contravene this current of authority, or violate the most essential rules of law.

It is ordered, adjudged, and decreed that the plaintiff Silvestre Bossier having lost his part of the land, by the lapse of time that he do not recover against the defendant but that the defendant be forever quieted in his possession of one half of the said land and that he recover against the said Silvestre Bossier one half of the costs up to this time in this case to be taxes. And it is further ordered, adjudged, and decreed that Sylvestre Cesar Bossier, Isaac Baldwin, curator ad litem, and Pamela Bossier and children representing the rights of Mrs. M. J. Lambre recover jointly of the defendant one equal half of the said tract of land of ten arpents front on both side of the Red River and the Bayou de Plat—and the judge of the Parish of Natchitoches proceed to divide and partition the same between the parties according to the law –dividing the same into lots if practicable—But if not to proceed by court on licitation—unless the parties consent to an amicable partition or to a sale at public auction.

Having executed this order that you make due return of your proceedings to this court for homologation—and the said plaintiffs will recover of the defendant the other half of the cost of the suit, except the cost of the partition, which will be equally paid to the Parish Judge by the respective parties. It is further ordered, adjudged, and decreed that said defendant Metoyer recover of the said plaintiffs for the balance of the improvements for the cleared land. To with for 45 arpents at the rate of twenty-five dollars per arpent—making eleven hundred twenty-five deducting two hundred-fifty dollars for the rent for the years 1817 and 1818 since this suit was brought. With that he recovers eight hundred and seventy five dollars from the two parties recovering the land. The Plaintiff claims rent for the land since Metoyer first settled on the land. But the court is of opinion that having settled on the land with a title and in good faith, that the occupying claimant is not bound to pay the rent, until the suit is brought by the accused party to recover the land.

Jos. S. Johnston
Judge 6th District
20 July 1818

---

24 July 1818

S. Bossier?? Vs. Louis Metoyer Appeal
Filed July 24th 1818

Know all men by them present that I Isaac Baldwin of the Parish of Rapides am held and firmly bound unto Louis Metoyer the sum of two hundred dollars and for this payment hereof I bind myself, my heirs and family by their presents. Sealed with my seal and dated this 24th day of July of this year 1818.

Whereas S. Bossier, S. C. Bossier, and I Baldwin curator ad litem of Pamela Bossier have filed their petitions of appeal for our final judgment rendered in parts against them from this District Court sitting in anNow that conditions of the above obligations is paid trusts of the said S. Bossier, I Baldwin and S. C. Bossier shall prosecute this appeal with officials and shall pay and perform any judgment that may be rendered [illegible] against them or if the execution that may issue on said judgment have been satisfied out of their proper goods, or chattels lands and [tenements?] here and in court [illegible] these above obligations to be void or [illegible] in full forever and [illegible]

Isaac Baldwin

---

27 July 1818

The Government of the state of Louisiana

To Louis Metoyer

Greeting

Whereas S. C. Bossier, S. Bossier and Isaac Baldwin curator ad litem of Parmela Bossier have this day filed in the office of the clerk of the District Court for the 6th district in and for the parish of Natchitoches, a Petition of appeal from a certain final judgment rendered against them in the said court which appeal is returnable in the Supreme Court for this Western District of the State of Louisiana on the 14th day of September next. You are therefore hereby cited to appear in person or by attorney in the said Court within day last foresaid to answer to this said appeal—Witness Jos. H. Johnston, Judge of the said Court this 27th day of July 1818.

Sam H. Sibley, Clk.

September 10, 1818

Supreme Court
Western District

The State of Louisiana to the Judge of the Sixth Judicial District, in and for the parish of Natchitoches.

Greetings:

Whereas the judgment rendered in the District Court in the case in which S. C. Bossier, S. Bossier and Isaac Baldwin were Plaintiffs and Louis Metoyer Defendant, from which the said S. C. Bossier, S.

Bossier and Isaac Baldwin took an appeal hath been annulled and reversed and in lieu thereof judgment hath been rendered in favor of the said Defendant, with costs of the said suit.

You are hereby commanded that you cause execution to issue against S. C. Bossier, S. Bossier and Isaac Baldwin the said Plaintiffs for the costs, of said suit both in the District Court and in this.

Witness the Hon. George Mathews Senior Judge of the said Supreme Court, at Alexandria in the Parish of Rapides this tenth day of September in the year of our Lord one thousand eight hundred and eighteen

Stephen E. Cuny,
Clerk of the Supreme Court for the Western District

---

14 September 1818

Bossier, S. Bossier,
 & Isaac Baldwin
   Vs
Louis Metoyer
Cost of the Appeal in the Supreme Court

To
Filing and registering record from inferior court	$ 2.00
Entering cause on the Docket	$ 1.00
Entering appearance of parties	$ 1.00
Recording motion in court	$ 1.00
Setting for Trial	0.50
Continuance	0.50
Entering final Decree and order to certify the same to the Court below	$ 2.50
Copy of Decree with certificate and seal	$ 3.50
Issuing a mandate	$ 3.00
Recording opinion of court 1025 words	$ 2.56 ¼

Tax fee	$11.00
Taxing costs with certificate and seal	$ 2.00

$30.56 ¼

I certify the above to be a true Bill of Costs in the Supreme Court.
        Stephen E. Cuny Clerk
        Of the Supreme Court
        For the Western District

---

14 September 1818

The Government of the State of Louisiana

To the Sheriff of the Parish of St. Landry

Greeting - We command you that you command from S. C. Bossier, S. Bossier, and Isaac Baldwin curator ad litem of Pamela Bossier the sum of eighty five dollars and 3/100 - costs which Louis Metoyer lately received by judgment of the District court of the Parish of Natchitoches and if they shall not pay the sum within three days after the demand that then you charge the same to be made of the personal estates of the said S. C. Bossier, S. Bossier and I. Baldwin except slaves in your parish if sufficient personal estates exclusive of slaves can be found therein. But if sufficient personal estates exclusive of slaves cannot be found therein, that then you cause the said sum to be made of the real estate and slaves of the said S. C. Bossier, S, Bossier, and I. Baldwin in your parish whereof they were owning on the 10th day of September 1818 into whose hands [illegible] the same may have come and that you have them [appearing] before our said court to render to the said Louis Metoyer for the judgment aforesaid within the time prescribed by [illegible] together within this writ.

Clk. District Court	32.35
Attorney	10.00
Clk. Supreme Court	30.50 1/3
Sheriff	12.12 ½

        85.00 3/4

Witness The Hon. H. A. Bullard
Judge of our Said Court this 7th day of April the year of our Lord 1819

---

4 May 1819

State of Louisiana
Parish of St. Landry
By virtue of the within terms [illegible] directed I have demanded the written sum of Eighty five dollars and 3½ /100 of the within named defendant which said sum of eighty five dollars 3 ½/100 I have received of them and have the same ready at the time and place within named to render to the within named Louis Metoyer as within I am commanded

          4th May 1819
          Theo Collins
          Sheriff Parish of St. Landry

Endnotes

 1. Sylvestre Ceazar Bossier, S. Bossie, curator ad bona, and Issac Baldwin, Curator ad litem of Pamela Bossie vs. Louis Metoyer, District Court suit 186, bundle 5 (Dec. Term 1817), Natchitoches Parish, Louisiana; Spanish translations, 215-17 by Translations Services, LTD, all other translations by author.

 2. Pardo is an indication that Louis was of mixed race. It denotes the brown skin color.

 3. Written above the 45 were the words forty or forty-five.

 4. A substantive common law rule prevents a party to a written contract from presenting extrinsic evidence that contradicts or adds to the written terms of the contract that appears to be whole.

Bibliography

Published

Arthur, Stanley Clisby. *Old New Orleans: A History of the Vieux Carré, Its Ancient and Historic Buildings*. 1936. Reprint, Westminster: Heritage Books, 2007.

Bittles, Alan H. *Consanguinity in Context*. Cambridge, UK: Cambridge University Press, 2012.

Brock, Eric. J. *Eric Brock's Shreveport*. Gretna, LA: Pelican Pub. Co., 2001.

Brock, Eric. J. *Red Light, Shreveport's St. Paul's Bottoms Red Light District: An Experiment in Controlled Vice*. Shreveport, LA: Ramble House, 2004.

Burton, H. Sophie, and F. Todd Smith. *Colonial Natchitoches a Creole Community on the Louisiana-Texas Frontier*. College Station: Texas A &M University Press, 2008.

Caughey, John Walton. *Bernardo de Galvez in Louisiana: 1776-1783*. 1934. Reprint, Louisiana: Pelican Publishing Company, 1999.

Chipman, Donald E., and Harriet Denise Joseph. *Notable Men and Women of Spanish Texas*. Austin: University of Texas Press, 1999.

Din, Gilbert C. "Father Jean Delvaux and the Natchitoches Revolt of 1795." *Louisiana History* 40 (Winter 1999): 5-33.

Foner, Laura. "The Free People of Color in Louisiana and St. Domingue: A Comparative Portrait of Two Three-Caste Slave Societies." *Journal of Social History*, 3 (Summer 1970): 422-23.

Giraud, Marcel. *A History of French Louisiana, Volume Five, The Company of the Indies, 1723-1731*. Translated by Brian Pearce. Baton Rouge: Louisiana State University Press, 1991.

Glasson, William H. "The Statistics of Lynching." *South Atlantic Quarterly*, no. 4 (October 1906): 344-45.

Glatthaar, Joseph T. *Forged in Battle: the Civil War Alliance of Black Soldiers and White Officers*. New York: The Free Press, 1990.

Hollandsworth, Jr., James G. *The Louisiana Native Guards The Black Military Experience During the Civil War*. Baton Rouge: Louisiana State University Press, 1998.

Lornell, Kip, and Tracey E. W. Laird. *Shreveport Sounds in Black and White*. Jackson: University Press of Mississippi, 2008.

Maduell, Charles R. *The Census Tables for the French Colony of Louisiana from 1699 through 1732*. Baltimore: Genealogical Pub. Co., 1972.

Martin, Joan M. "Plaçage and the Louisiana Gens de Couleur Libre: How Race and Sex Defined the Life of Free Women of Color." In *Creole, The History and Legacy of Louisiana's Free People of Color*, edited by Sybil Klein, 68. Baton Rouge: Louisiana State University, 2000.

McWilliams, Richebourg Gaillard, trans. and ed. *Fleur de Lys and Calumet: Being the Pénicaut Narrative of French Adventure in Louisiana*. Tuscaloosa, AL: The University of Alabama Press, 1988.

Mills, Elizabeth Shown. "Documenting a Slave's Birth, Parentage, and Origins (Marie Thérèse Coincoin, 1742-1816): A Test of "Oral History." *National Genealogical Society Quarterly* 96 (December 2008): 245-66

―――― *Isle of Canes*. Provo, UT: Ancestry Pub., 2004.

―――― "Marie Thérèse Coin Coin: Cane River Slave, Slave Owner, and Paradox. In *Louisiana Women: Their Lives and Times*," edited by Janet Allured, and Judith F. Gentry, 10-29. Athens, GA: University of Georgia Press, 2009.

―――― *Natchitoches, 1729-1803: Abstracts of the Catholic Church Registers of the French and Spanish Post of St Jean Baptiste des Natchitoches in Louisiana*. 1977. Reprint, Bowie, MD: Heritage Books, 2007

―――― *Natchitoches Church Marriages, 1818-1850: Translated Abstracts from the Registers of St. François des Natchitoches, Louisiana*. Tuscaloosa, Ala.: 1985.

Reprint, Bowie, MD: Heritage Books, 2007.

―――― *Natchitoches Colonials: Censuses, Military rolls, and Tax lists, 1722-1803*. Chicago: Adams Press, 1981.

―――― *Natchitoches, 1800-1826: Translated Abstracts of Register Number Five of the Catholic Church Parish of St. François des Natchitoches in Louisiana:* 1980. Reprint, Bowie, MD: Heritage Books, 2007.

―――― "Quintanilla's Crusade, 1775-1783: Moral Reform and Its Consequences on the Natchitoches Frontier." *Louisiana History* 42 (Summer 2001): 281.

Mills, Elizabeth Shown, and Gary B. Mills. "Slaves and Masters: The Louisiana Metoyers." *National Genealogical Society Quarterly* 70 (September 1982): 163-85.

Tales of Old Natchitoches. Tuscaloosa, AL: Mills Historical Press, 1994.

Mills, Gary B. "The Ancestry of Sieur Nicolas Augustin Metoyer, Fmc, Patriarch of Isle Brevelle." *The Natchitoches Genealogist* 8 (October 1984): 28.

―――― "Claude Thomas Pierre Metoyer." *Dictionary of Louisiana Biography; Ten-Year Supplement 1988-1998*, edited by Carl A. Brasseaux, and

James D. Wilson, Jr., 154-56. Lafayette, LA: Louisiana Historical Association, 1999.

———*The Forgotten People: Cane River's Creoles of Color.* Baton Rouge: Louisiana State University Press, 1977.

——— "Patriotism Frustrated: The Native Guards of Confederate Natchitoches." *Louisiana History*, 18 (Fall 1977): 440-41.

New Orleans City Directory. New Orleans: Pelican Gallery, Inc., (1805).

Phares, Ross. *Cavalier in the Wilderness; the Story of the Explorer and Trader Louis Juchereau de St. Denis.* Baton Rouge: Louisiana State University Press, 1952.

Richardson, Heather Cox. *The Death of Reconstruction: Race, Labor, and Politics in the Post-Civil War North, 1865-1901.* Cambridge, MA: Harvard University Press, 2001.

Robbins, Kevin C. *City on the Ocean Sea: La Rochelle, 1530-1650: Urban Society, Religion, and Politics on the French Atlantic Frontier.* Leiden: E. J. Brille, 1997.

Robichaux, Jr., Albert J. *Civil Registration of Orleans Parish Births, Marriages and Deaths, 1790-1833* Rayne, LA (P. O. Box 147, Rayne 70578): Hébert Publications, 2000.

Schweninger, Loren. "Antebellum Free Persons of Color in Postbellum Louisiana." *Louisiana History* 30 (Fall 1989): 345-64.

Seebold, Herman de Bachelle. *Old Louisiana Plantation Homes and Family Trees.* 1941. Reprinted, New Orleans: Pelican Publishing, 1971.

Traer, James. *Marriage and the Family in Eighteenth Century France.* Ithaca, NY: Cornell University Press, 1980.

Whittington, G. P. *Rapides Parish, Louisiana: A History; Published in One Volume as a Historic Activities Project of the Alexandria Committee of the National Society of the Colonial Dames in the State of Louisiana.* 1932. Reprint, Alexandria, LA: Red River Press, 1970.

Woods, Frances Jerome, Sister. *Marginality and Identity: A Colored Creole Family through Ten Generations.* Baton Rouge: Louisiana State University, 1972.

Manuscripts

African Ancestry (Washington, D. C.). Mitochondrial DNA (mtDNA) Sequence Report, Kit 1022762," prepared for Linda Manuel, Gahanna, OH, 3 May 2011. Privately held by Manuel, 2013.

Blake Collection. Bexar Archives. University of Texas. Austin, TX. .

DeBlieux Collection. Cammie G. Henry Research Center. Northwestern State University. Natchitoches, LA.

Department of Veteran's Affairs. War of 1812 Pension Application Files Index.

Family Tree DNA (Houston, TX). Mitochondrial DNA (mtDNA) Sequence Report, Kit N81988," prepared for Linda Manuel, Gahanna, OH 25 May 2010. Privately held by Manuel, 2013.

France. Châlons-en-Champagne. Reims. Saint-Denis. États-civil (Births, Adoptions, Baptisms, Divorce, Marriages and Deaths), 1792-1877. Archives Départementales de la Marne, Châlons-en-Champagne.

France. Châlons-en-Champagne. Reims. Saint-Symphorien. États-civil (Births, Adoptions, Baptisms, Divorce, Marriages and Deaths), 1792-1877. Archives Départementales de la Marne, Châlons-en-Champagne.

France. Charente-Maritime. La Rochelle. Saint-Sauveur. États-civil (Births, Adoptions, Baptisms, Divorce, Marriages and Deaths), 1792-1877. Archives Départementales de Charente-Maritime, La Rochelle.

France. Charente-Maritime. La Rochelle. Série E. Archives Départementales de Charente-Maritime, La Rochelle.

Immaculate Conception Church (Natchitoches, Louisiana). "A Death and Burial Register kept by A. [Andrius]." Parish Rectory. Natchitoches.

Lanoux, Pie. "Joseph Conand's Estate." Creole Heritage Center. Natchitoches, Louisiana.

Louisiana. Baton Rouge. Adams vs. Hurst, 1836. Natchitoches Parish Records. Louisiana State University Archives. Baton Rouge.

Louisiana. Baton Rouge. Louisiana State Board of Health. Bureau of Vital Statistics. Death Records.

Louisiana. Natchez. St. Augustine Catholic Church. (Birth, Baptism, Marriage, and Death Records). Natchez.

Louisiana. Natchitoches. Immaculate Conception Catholic Church. (Birth, Baptism, Marriage, and Death Records). Natchitoches.

Louisiana. Natchitoches. Marriage Records. Office of Clerk of Court, Natchitoches.

Louisiana. Natchitoches. Melrose Collection. Cammie Henry Research Center. Northwestern State University, Natchitoches.

Louisiana. Natchitoches. Natchitoches Colonial Archives. Office of Clerk of Court. Natchitoches.

Louisiana. Natchitoches. Parish Court Files, 1805-1850. Office of Clerk of Court, Natchitoches.

Louisiana. New Orleans. Notarial Archives. Acts of Leonardo Mazange.

Louisiana State Land Records. State Land Office. Baton Rouge.

Military, Compiled Service Records. Civil War. Carded Records, Volunteer Organizations. Records of the Adjutant General's Office, 1780s-1917, Record Group 94. National Archives, Washington, D. C.

Opelousas Notarial Archives. Archives and Records Service. Baton Rouge.

Social Security Administration. Applications for Account Numbers, Form SS-5. Social Security Administration, Baltimore, MD.

Electronic

Adam, Madame. "The Dowries of Women in France." *The North American Review* 152 (January 1891): 37. Accessed October 21, 2012. http://www.jstor.org/stable/25102113.

American State Papers. Public Land Claims 3:175. http://memory.loc.gov/cgi-bin/ampage?collId=llsp&fileName=030/llsp030.db&Page=175.

Ancestry.com. "Louisiana Slave Records 1719-1820." Accessed December 24, 2012, http://search.ancestry.com/search/db.aspx?dbid=7383.

Ancestry.com. "Marne, France Marriages 1529-1907." 2008. Accessed December 20, 2009, http://search.ancestry.com/search/db.aspx?dbid=1312.

Ancestry.com. "New Orleans, Louisiana, Death Records Index, 1804-1949." Accessed December 24, 2012., http://search.ancestry.com/search/db.aspx?dbid=6606.

Ancestry.com. "U. S. Federal Census Collection." http://search.ancestry.com/search/group/usfedcen.

Ancestry.com. "U. S. City Directories, 1821-1989 (Beta)." Accessed February, 2013. http://search.ancestry.com/search/db.aspx?dbid=2469.

Bartholomew, J. *Togo Land, the German Protectorate on the Slave Coast* [map]. 1885. Scale not given. "Perry-Castaneda Map Collection, Historical Maps of Africa." Digital image. University of Texas Libraries. Accessed July 2, 2010. http://www.lib.utexas.edu/maps/historical/togo_land_1885.jpg. .

Biographical and Historical Memoirs of Northwest Louisiana, Comprising a Large Fund of Biography of Actual Residents, and an interesting Historical Sketch of Thirteen Counties. Nashville: Southern Publishing Company, 1890. http://books.google.com/books/about/Biographical_and_Historical_Memoirs_of_N.html?id=ZucxAQAAMAAJ.

Brian, Hardy L., ed. "Arthur Lacour's Death." *The Louisiana Populist.* September 27, 1895. Accessed February 9, 2013.

    http://chroniclingamerica.loc.gov/lccn/sn88071004/1895-09-27/ed-1/seq-3/;words=Lacour+Arthur?date1=1895&rows=20&searchType=basic&state=Louisiana&date2=1895&proxtext=arthur+lacour&y=5&x=10&dateFilterType=yearRange&index=0.

———. "Isle Brevelle." *The Louisiana Populist.* February 20, 1897. Accessed February 11, 2013. (http://chroniclingamerica.loc.gov/lccn/sn88071004/1897-02-26/ed-1/seq-2/;words=Brevelle+Isle?date1=1897&rows=20&searchType=basic&state=Louisiana&date2=1897&proxtext=Isle+brevelle&y=7&x=16&dateFilterType=yearRange&index=0.

Bureau of Land Management. "Land Patent Search." Database and images. General Land Office Records. http://www.glorecords.blm.gov/PatentSearch: 2009.

"City of Shreveport Historical Committee Report: April 2012." Accessed February 25, 2013. http://www.shreveporttimes.com/assets/pdf/D918902358.PDF.

Currey, Thomas. *Reports of Cases Argued and Determined in the Supreme Court of the State of Louisiana: Volume IX.* New Orleans: Benjamin Levy, 1836. Accessed January 19, 2013. http://books.google.com/books?id=CiwtAQAAMAAJ&printsec=frontcover&source=gbs_ge_summary_r&cad=0#v=onepage&q&f=false.

Cosgrove, Jas. H., editor. "Rumors of War." *The People's Vindicator.* July 4, 1874. Accessed February 10, 2013. (http://chroniclingamerica.loc.gov/lccn/sn85038558/1874-07-04/ed-1/seq-2/;words=Rumors+War?date1=1874&rows=20&searchType=basic&state=Louisiana&date2=1874&proxtext=rumors+of+war&y=15&x=15&dateFilterType=yearRange&index=1.

———. "Advice of a Colored Man to his Race." *The People's Vindicator.* August 1, 1874, Accessed February 10, 1874.

    (http://chroniclingamerica.loc.gov/lccn/sn85038558/1874-08-01/ed-1/seq-3/;words=Advice+Colored+Man?date1=1874&rows=20&searchType=basic&state=Louisiana&date2=1874&proxtext=advice+of+a+colored+man&y=10&x=13&dateFilterType=yearRange&index=0.

———. "Is Our Government a Failure." *The People's Vindicator.* September 19, 1874. Accessed February 10, 2013.

    (http://chroniclingamerica.loc.gov/lccn/sn85038558/1874-09-19/ed-1/seq-1/;words=our+Failure+Government?date1=1874&rows=20&searchType=basic&state=Louisiana&date2=1874&proxtext=Is+our+government+a+failure&y=10&x=17&dateFilterType=yearRange&index=0: accessed 10 February 2013).

Dial, Susan, ed. "La Belle Shipwreck." Texas Beyond History. The University of Texas at Austin. (October 16, 2008). Accessed February 28, 2011. http://www.texasbeyondhistory.net/belle/. .

Durey, Jill. "The Church, Consanguinity and Trollope." Accessed January 12, 2013. http://www.docstoc.com/docs/74736776/The-Church_-Consanguinity-and-Trollope.

"The Genographic Project." Database and articles. National Geographic's Society. National Geographics. Accessed September 23, 2012. https://genographic.nationalgeographic.com/genographic/lan/en/journey.html.

Grewe, Bernd-Stefan. "Woodlands." *European History Online (EGO)*. Institute of European History. Accessed October 21, 2012. http://www.ieg-ego.eu/en/threads/backgrounds/nature-and-environment/bernd-stefan-grewe-woodlands.

Johnson, Penny. "Eulalie de Mandeville: An Ethnohistorical Investigation Challenging Notions of Plaçage in New Orleans as revealed through the Lived Experiences of a Free Woman of Color." Master's Thesis, University of New Orleans, 2010. Accessed December 17, 2012. http://scholarworks.uno.edu/td/1285.

Koman, Rita G. "Servitude to Service: African-American Women as Wage Earners." *Organization of American Historians Magazine of History,* 11, no. 2 (Winter 1997): 42-49. http://maghis.oxfordjournals.org/content/11/2/42.full.pdf.

Krantz, Rachel. "Pinchback, P. B. S." African-American Business Leaders and

Entrepreneurs, A to Z of African Americans. New York: Facts on File, Inc., 2004. African-American History Online. Facts on File, Inc. (2004). Accessed March 6, 2013. http:// www.fofweb.com/History/MainPrintPage.asp?iPin=AABLE0117&DataType=AFHC&WinType=Free.

Louisiana.gov. Division of Administration. Office of Land Sales. Accessed December 1, 2012. https://wwwslodms.doa.la.gov/WebForms/DocumentViewer.aspx?docId=510.00078&category=H#1.

Lowe, Frederick H. "Cameroon Plans Restoration of Notorious Slave Trade Port." *The NorthStar News and Analysis*, July 19, 2012. Accessed April 14, 2013. (http://www.thenorthstarnews.com/Story/Cameroon-Plans-Restoration-of-Notorious-Slave-Trade-Port).

Mason, T., and G. Lane. *Minutes of the Annual Conferences of the Methodist Episcopal Church: Spring Conferences 1913.* New York: The Methodist Book Concern, 1918. Accessed March 10, 2013. http://archive.org/stream/minutesannualco05churgoog#page/n8/mode/2up.

McManus, Jane Parker, submitter. "United Methodist Church Cemetery."

Accessed March 10, 2013. http://files.usgwarchives.net/la/rapides/cemeteries/wesleymeth.txt.

Merrick, Edwin T. *The Revised Civil Code of the State of Louisiana, with References and Acts of the Legislature Up to and Including the Session of 1912.*(1899; reprint, New Orleans: F. F. Hansell and Brothers, Ltd., 1913): 410. Accessed April 5, 2013. *Googlebooks.com.*

Mills, Elizabeth Shown. "Isle of Canes and Issues of Conscience: Master-slave Sexual Dynamics and Slaveholding by Free People of Color." Between Two Worlds: A Special Issue of The Southern Quarterly: A Journal of the Arts in the South 43 (Winter 2006): 158-75. Accessed December 4, 2012. *Historical Pathways.* http://www.historicpathways.com/download/isleofcanes.pdf.

Mims, Edwin, and Glasson, William, editors. "The Statistics of Lynching." *South Atlantic Quarterly*, January to October 1906. Accessed February 10, 2013. http://books.google.com/books?id=_3Z9AAAAMAAJ&pg=PA342&lpg=PA342&dq=south+Atlantic+Quarterly+statistics+of+lynching&source=bl&ots=apvNc_kCxn&sig=ZVRU2jCAYBSrsgPXdz1a2d2LZAU&hl=en&sa=X&ei=9FJQUcnDOeTB4AO3nYCADg&ved=0CDQQ6AEwAA#v=onepage&q=south%20Atlantic%20Quarterly%20statistics%20of%20lynching&f=false.

National Park Service's War Soldiers and Sailors System."African Americans/Slavery." Accessed November 27, 2010. http://www.civilwar.com/overview/abolition-and-slavery/148533-african-americans-slavery.html.

National Park Service. "Civil War Soldiers and Sailors System." Accessed October 10, 2009. http://www.itd.nps.gov/cwss/soldiers.cfm.

Northwestern State University of Louisiana. *Louisiana Creole Heritage Center.* Database and articles. Accessed February 10, 2011. http://winhttp.nsula.edu/creole/search.asp?surname=metoyer&givenname=rose&mother=&father=&birth=&death.

Officer, Lawrence H. and Williamson Samuel H. *MeasuringWorth.* Accessed 2010. http://www.measuringworth.com.

Ruggles, Stevens, Alexander, J. Trent, Genadek Katie, Goeken, Ronald, Schroeder, Matthew B., and Sobek, Matthew. "1900 Census: Instructions to Enumerators." Minneapolis: University of Minnesota. Accessed February 28, 2011. http://usa.ipuma.org/usa/voliii/in.

Shady Grove United Methodist Church. "Our History." Accessed on March 10, 2013. http://faithfulliving.org/index.php?id=history0.

Taylor, Quintard, Bullitt, Scott, and Bullitt, Dorothy. "Louisiana's Code Noir (1724)." B*lackpast.org.* Accessed February 2, 2010. http://www.blackpast.org/?q=primary/louisianas-code-noir-1724.

U. S. Bureau of the Census, Fourth through Fifteenth Censuses, State of

Louisiana, 1820-1930, Population and Slave schedules. Digital images. Ancestry.com. http://www.ancestry.com.

U. S. Bureau of the Census, Twelfth through Fifteenth Censuses, State of Texas, 1900-1930, Population schedules. Digital images. Ancestry.com. http://www.ancestry.com.

U. S. Department of Interior. National Park Service. Historic American Buildings Survey. Cane River National Heritage Area Commission. Addendum to Front Street (Commercial Buildings). Accessed February 27, 2013. http://lcweb2.loc.gov/pnp/habshaer/la/la0400/la0454/data/la0454data.pdf.

U. S. Department of Interior. Bureau of Land Development. General Land Records Division. Accessed May 1, 2008. http://www.glorecords.blm.gov/details/patent/default.aspx?accession=437269&docClass=SER&sid=o5f5fub1.u51.

U. S. National Archives and Records Administration. Featured Documents. "The Emancipation Proclamation." http://www.archives.gov/exhibits/featured_documents/emancipation_proclamation/transcript.html.

War of 1812 Pension Application Files Index, 1812-1815. Accessed February 23, 2013. http://search.ancestry.com/cgi-bin/sse.dll?rank=1&new=1&tid=3131577&tpid=-107459451&ssrc=pt_t3131577_p-107459451&MSAV=1&msT=1&gss=angs-c&gsfn=Firmin+C&gsln=Christophe&msbdy=1796&msbpn__ftp=Louisiana%2c+USA&msddy=1890&msrpn__ftp=Natchitoches%2c+Louisiana%2c+United+States&cpxt=0&uidh=bmr&msddd=1&msddm=9&cp=12&pcat=39&h=90244&recoff=5+6&db=Warof1812_Pension&indiv=1.

World War I Selective Draft Service System Draft Registration Cards, 1917-1918. Accessed February 25, 2013. http://search.ancestry.com/cgi-bin/sse.dll?rank=1&new=1&MSAV=1&msT=1&gss=angs-c&gsfn=jerry&gsln=Pikes&cpxt=0&uidh=bmr&cp=12&pcat=39&h=31767955&db=WW1draft&indiv=1.

Other

American Cemetery. Natchitoches Parish, Louisiana. Claude Thomas Metoyer.

Searching For Bertha